D1643495

PARSLER

# THE SOCIAL IMPACT OF OIL IN SCOTLAND

# The Social Impact of Oil in Scotland

**A Contribution to the Sociology of Oil**

*edited by*

RON PARSLER

*University of Stirling*

and

DAN SHAPIRO

*University of Lancaster*

Gower

British Library Cataloguing in Publication Data

The social impact of oil in Scotland
1   Scotland–Social conditions
2   Offshore oil industry–North Sea
I   Parsler, Ron       II Shapiro, Don
309.1'411'0857       HN398.S3



Published by
Gower Publishing Co., Ltd.,
Westmead, Farnborough, Hants, England



ISBN 0 566 00375 9
Printed in Great Britain by Biddles Ltd, Guildford, Surrey

# Contents

# Contributors

Anthony P. Cohen     Department of Social Anthropology,
University of Manchester

Judith Ennew     Department of Social Anthropology,
University of Cambridge

Margaret Grieco     Jesus College, University of Oxford

Isobel Grigor     Department of Social Administration,
University of Edinburgh

J. Douglas House     Head of Department of Sociology,
Memorial University, Newfoundland, Canada

Dierdre Hunt     Department of Business Management,
Robert Gordon's Institute of Technology, Aberdeen

Robert Moore     Professor, Department of Sociology,
University of Aberdeen

Andrew McBarnet     Department of Sociology,
Polytechnic of Central London

Ron Parsler     Department of Sociology,
University of Stirling

John J. Rodger     Department of Social Studies,
Paisley College of Technology

Dan S. Shapiro     Department of Sociology,
University of Lancaster

# Introduction

The discovery of offshore oil in Britain has had large and obvious economic advantages. Less obvious, but no less significant, are the social changes brought about by these discoveries. The social impact of oil in Scotland has been marked in environments as dissimilar as the urban area of Aberdeen and the crofting communities of Shetland. This social aspect of the situation and the process of social acceptance of a new, powerful and alien industry was the focus of an International Conference organised by Dan Shapiro, sponsored by the British Sociological Association, awarded finance by the SSRC North Sea Oil Panel and held in Aberdeen in March 1978. A selection of the papers from this Conference were subsequently published in *The Scottish Journal of Sociology Vol. 3, No. 1,* November 1978. It is these papers, together with three others that had previously been published in the same journal which form the substance of this book.

The problems generated by the development of the oil industry are similar in kind throughout the world but, naturally different in that they are worked out through different cultures and social contexts. This is the first book to bring together work on this topic in Scotland and although much of the research on which the papers are based is continuing it is regarded as a contribution to an important area of sociology. More work needs to be done on this topic and more comparative studies need to be made on the basis of work already accomplished so that communities in any part of the world where the oil industry develops may have the benefit of the experience gained.

Ron Parsler

# 1 The Industrial Relations of Oil

*Dan Shapiro*

One of the most straightforward consequences of oil-related activity in the Northern half of Scotland[1] has been the creation of jobs. In May 1977 – the peak month for that year – nearly 26,000 people were wholly employed in directly oil-related jobs in this area, which is close to 10% of the employed population. Of course this employment is not evenly distributed so that, for example, for the area of West Ross and the Western Isles at this time the percentage of the employed population was not 10 but 29. If those who are *partly* employed in oil (e.g. some engineering workers) or indirectly employed in consequence of oil (e.g. hotel and transport workers) are included then this general total rises to nearly 15% of the employed population. That the vast majority of these jobs appeared since 1970 – indeed, more than half of them since 1975 – demonstrates the pace and scale of what has happened.[2] The creation of these new jobs entails either a large inmigration of workers or a significant change from previous to new forms of work, or (obviously) a combination of both.

It was this basic aspect of 'oil' that informed the choice of migrant labour and occupational change as the subject of the research that Robert Moore and I have been doing but, rather than interpret this over literally, we have preferred to use it as a 'peg' on which to hang a variety of partially connected topics. My usual procedure in talking about this research is to enumerate these main topics and go on to give a sort of Cook's tour of those with which I have been primarily involved. The trouble is that as the project has grown so has the tour and in its latest version it reads for about 2¾ hours. Clearly this won't do for now, so instead I should like to talk about just one aspect of the research, the 'industrial relations' of working for oil. Indeed, as we shall see, I shall only discuss one particular aspect of the industrial relations of oil, but in order to explain my choice of topic I must start by relating it to the project in its broader context.

I have referred to oil-related *activity*, carefully avoiding the term in more common currency, oil-related *development*. This is, of course, because it is precisely the *status* of events in the North of Scotland as 'development' that is one of the more important questions for sociologists (and victims!). Robert Moore refers to this in his paper and I have also made some brief comments in my introduction to this collection. The exploitation of North Sea Oil is being undertaken by multinational corporations within a global context of alternatives, so it is hardly surprising that several researchers in seeking to analyse these events have tried to make use of current theories of 'dependency' (implying, at the simplest level, the shift to outside the 'area' of control over the presence, pace and nature of advanced production)[3] or of the 'development of underdevelopment' (implying the weakening, through externally controlled 'development', of such independent productuve capacity as the area previously enjoyed).[4]

But if a 'state of dependency' is to have explanatory value as a sort of 'umbrella' concept under which oil activities may be characterised then it must eventually manifest itself in changes in concrete social relations. To this extent, that is, that 'economic relations' is a euphemism or shorthand for particular forms of social relations, then a state of economic dependency must be mirrored in a variety of 'dependent' social relations. It ought, if this is so, to make sense to speak, for example, of dependent political relations or dependent industrial relations arising in a situation of dependent development. Indeed, as I have indicated, it would be hard to see just what 'dependent development' meant at all if it did not mean some of these sorts of things — and that has, perhaps, been the tenor of some of the criticisms of the generality and vagueness of dependency theories.[5] Again, we are not alone in trying to move in this direction. For example, in a recent paper under the title 'Dependent industrialisation, dependent proletariat'.[6] James Whickham discussed in this sort of way changing relations between labour, (foreign) capital and the state in the Irish car industry.

It is from this direction, then, that I wish to pursue the topic. It would be possible to approach the industrial relations of oil in a variety of ways and there is no shortage of themes in the literature that might fruitfully be taken up in this context. To do so would be to use the context of oil in the North of Scotland as a set of relatively arbitrary examples. But my intention in this paper will be to see how far we can get in giving more priority to the particular setting, in treating it as more than arbitrary — to see, that is, whether it does make sense to consider the industrial relations of oil as 'dependent'.

But just what might be meant by 'dependent industrial relations'? The term dependent has often been used very loosely just as a synonym for 'exploitative'. Thus usage is of dubious validity as the term exploitation can only be given precision as a relation between *classes*,[7] and it cannot, in any case, be satisfactory here. Dependency in industrial relations cannot rest simply on exploitation for this would imply that non-dependent ('advanced', 'metropolitan') industrial relations are not exploitative. Following Kay (and others) we would in fact be more justified in concluding the reverse.[8] Dependent industrial relations must then, if it means anything, refer to particular *forms* of exploitation distinct from, and perhaps interacting with, those inherent in the labour market, in the treatment of labour power as a commodity.

Put this way, the question clearly relates to another issue that has figured centrally both in discussions of dependency and specifically in relation to the North of Scotland: the delineation and inter-relation of capitalist and pre-capitalist modes of production. The orthodox approach and that which leads to the most straightforward theoretical scheme is to regard the capitalist mode as relying purely on market relations for the exploitation of labour; put another way, to achieve market, exchange relations between commodities, including labour, *is* to achieve the expropriation of surplus value from labour. Modes of production prior to capitalism, by contrast, rest on social relations of production which are not those of the market but rely on other, ascriptive relations and on non-market constraints. And it follows from this that where relations of production are not purely market relations the mode of production is not a purely capitalist one but incorporates at least some pre-capitalist elements.

One of the difficulties with this simple formulation is that it does less than justice to situations where relations of production are clearly pre-capitalist and yet whose very existence is intimately connected with capitalist developments and economic relations. How this is treated will depend on whether relations of exchange or relations of production are allowed primacy. Thus, for example, A. G. Frank's argument[9] that economic relations in Latin America have, since the Conquest, consisted of a chain of metropolis-satellite relations with the final metropole located in Europe; hence that Latin America has had a market economy from the beginning; and hence that Latin America has been capitalist from the beginning. And in his renowned reply Laclau[10] criticises Frank precisely for taking relations of exchange rather than relations of production as the basis of his analysis, insisting that the feudal regime of the haciendas has survived — indeed been strengthened by — the insertion of Latin America into the world market.

This general question finds a particular reflection in the North of Scotland. The persistence of a particular form of peasant agriculture — crofting — and particular forms of manufacture — e.g. the Harris Tweed industry[11] — has led to the characterisation of the Highlands as pre-capitalist, or partially capitalist, by many, including agencies of development such as the HIDB. But this 'dual economy' model of the Highlands has been decisively challenged by Carter[12], drawing explicitly on Frank, who shows that the capitalist market had penetrated every corner of the North of Scotland; and by Hunter[13] who shows how the crofting system of agriculture (or, more accurately, labour reserve economy[14]) was itself the product of this market penetration.

The analytical problem of the conjuncture of these elements remains, however. The traditional solution has been to regard the co-existence of capitalist market relations and pre-capitalist relations of production as transitional — a process of primitive accummulation necessarily encompassing the breakdown of feudal rela-

3

tions.    Indeed, this notion of transition can be made to transcend its sometimes rather lame, residual status.    Thus, to stay with a local example, Carter, in discussing the inter-penetration of capitalist and pre-capitalist agriculture in the North-East, gives real point and elegance to the notion of a complex and extended transition.[15]    But there are very many instances where the conjuncture is not to be explained away as transitional[16] and it is precisely around these that theories of dependency and their successors were born.    I will not attempt to pursue this question directly here[17], but it returns our attention to the problem raised earlier. For if the persistence of pre-capitalist forms is to be seen not just as a transitional anomaly but as the actual result of a world capitalist system operating normally, then it follows that non-market social relations and hence industrial relations — Miliband's 'polite euphemism'[18] — are as much a product of capitalism's normal working.

This is precisely the point made by Philip Corrigan in a recent article[19]·  Drawing on a very wide range of sources from over the last twenty years he calls on us to recognise that ascriptive constraint, non-wage coercion and the un-freedom of labour far from being feudal relics characteristic of the early stages of industrialisation are entirely compatible with the expansion of capitalism and indeed frequently *increase* with its penetration.    And once the point is put it seems immediately absurd to deny to capitalism the panoply, the full, rich variety of coercion and constraint of which it is capable — in whatever way we may subsequently decide to analyse it.    The principal examples that Corrigan uses are bonded service relations in Britain in the 18th, 19th and early 20th centuries; slavery, neo-slavery and debt-bondage; and labour migration.    In a very direct parallel with dependency theorists he critices the evolutionary paradigms of both conventional sociology and marxism which blind them to the continuity of coercion.[20]

Corrigan emphasises the centrality of un-freedom to the capitalist labour process in *all* its forms — indeed, of un-freedom as constituting the labour process, of ascription as *'the manner in which* [the] division and circulation [of labour] is accomplished'[21] — citing Aufhauser's demonstration of the structural analogy between slavery and Taylorism[22], and pointing to the extra-economic social and ideological coercion inherent in the fragmentation into different labour markets[23]. His main *illustrations* however remain either historical or 'marginal' from the (obviously) myopic viewpoint of Europ-centred development models.    By focussing, in this paper, on a peripheral region of the 'mother of capitalism' and on fully enfranchised, unionised labour, I hope to bring these points a little closer to home.

When we embarked on the research we conceived the study of migrant labour along similar lines to those which Corrigan urges, and Robert Moore's paper to the 1975 BSA conference spells out in detail the necessity for an approach to migrant

4

labour in terms of its international class dimensions. We thought it likely that we would be following the latest North European wanderings of a super-exploited sub-class of 'guest workers' whose subordinate position would be constituted by their political and civil disenfranchisement, expressed in such things as work permits tying them to particular employers and particular sites and the threat of expulsion for troublemakers, and by their exclusion from the protection of 'native' trade union organisations. In view of what has happened in, e.g. Norway this was not an unreasonable supposition. That is, we anticipated that there would be differential access of different groups of workers to rewards, conditions, security, etc. and that struggles would occur between oil employers and groups of workers over work-force composition for just this reason.

This turns out to be not so much wrong as incomplete. What we find is not just a simple labour market within which some groups of workers are more advantage-ously placed than others; rather, there is a variety of alternative 'labour markets', the specificities of which are contributed to by varieties of non-economic con-straint. Employers, though obviously subject to constraints of their own, still largely retain the initiative in these alternatives tactically in the industrial relations struggle. Thus — to put it a shade dramatically — in considering the differential access of different groups of workers it is not so much that there are 'winners' and 'losers' but, rather, that there is a variety of ways of losing.

What I would like to do, then, is to look at this delicate intertwining of forms of constraint using examples taken from 'the industrial relations of oil'. It will, un-fortunately, be necessary to describe these very cursorily and schematically and so to state badly interpretations that really require detailed substantiation: a fuller treatment will be offered elsewhere[24]. The examples I shall use are two particular strikes, one at the concrete production platform fabrication yard at Kishorn in Wester Ross in November 1976, and one at the steel platform yard at Nigg on the Cromarty Firth in March 1977; and some aspects of industrial relations on offshore exploration and production rigs.

One of the key issues in studying the industrial relations of oil has been the ex-tent of unionisation. Before oil, union activity was with few exceptions very narrowly confined to the Aberdeen area and at the start of the research it seemed a completely open question what the effect of oil activity would be. Clearly there would be contact between local and migrant workers and clearly some, at least, of the latter would be union members. But we also anticipated that a proportion of migrant workers would be foreign 'guest workers' and so particularly vulnerable, and even in the case of UK migrants it was already clear that their major occupa-tional origin was the construction industry with its very mixed history of union-isation. It might, then, have been possible for oil employers to recruit non-union

5

itinerant construction labour resulting in a fragmented workforce sharing many of the characteristics of a disadvantaged alien working class. Hence there might have been relatively little pressure towards unionisation even from migrant workers. The position of local workers was equally ambiguous, combining an historical legacy of intense and effective class-based organisation and action[25] and of migration to work, with the passive acceptance of small-scale paternalist work relations. Equally, there might have been a high degree of unionisation among highly skilled and specialised tradesmen — most of whom would be migrants — and very little elsewhere, resulting in strong craft unions and high differentials with a sub-class of migrant *and* local unskilled and semi-skilled labour; the ghost of the 'labour aristocracy' walking again.

In fact, there have been virtually no 'guest workers' in oil activities onshore (and I should point out that, perhaps contrary to popular belief, something like 78% of oil-related employment in the North of Scotland is on-shore). Unlike other oil sites in northern Europe, the supply of natives has been quite adequate. And, in terms of sheer numbers, the record on unionisation has been a triumphant one: there has been massive unionisation of oil activities onshore to the extent that there are hardly any major sites which are not *de facto* closed shops, meaning that there has been heavy recruitment among local as well as migrant workers. This is the case both at Kishorn and at Nigg.

Sadly, I have no space to describe the fascinating background to platform fabrication at Kishorn, indeed I can only give a grossly reduced account of the dispute itself. Work started in earnest at Kishorn — a fairly remote part of Wester Ross — in 1975 and by mid 1976 roughly 2,000 workers were employed there — though by no means all of them by the main contractor, Howard-Doris. During the first, dry-dock, phase of the construction, until September 1975, the workforce could be divided into three groups on the basis of home location: those living in the general vicinity of the yard (roughly 21%, in 1976); those who were 'local' in terms of Highland geography, i.e. including East Ross and the Inverness area (22%); and 'travelling men' from further afield (57%). Of these, the third group lived in a work camp on the site; of the second group some were also in the work camp but the majority commuted to work by company bus or train, involving journey-times for some of up to 4 - 5 hours per day. Though virtually all the employees had (or laid claim to) experience in construction, most of those regularly working in large-scale industrial construction were in the third group.

The achievement of this workforce, with respect to the terms on which they sold their labour, were very considerable. The site had been entirely unionised from the beginning, virtually all Howard-Doris employees belonging either to UCATT or the TGWU. Although work conditions were often very arduous and hours were long — 12 hour shifts 7 days per week — earnings regularly topped £300 per week for all grades of construction worker, leave was one week off for every three worked (unique, at the time, in the British construction industry), and the (free) board and accommodation were of a very high standard. In September 1976 the second phase of construction began when the platform was towed out from the dry-dock to its first 'wet site', an anchorage three miles away. For those working on the wet-site the working day now increased from 12 to 13 - 14 hours on account of the boat journey to and from the rig, but leave was now one week off for every two worked.

A strike of Howard-Doris workers began on Monday, 1st November which — to vastly oversimplify a complex skein of issues — was over a cut in the rate of bonus from around 90p per hour to 40p, imposed by the management without consultation. This was done due to technical and weather problems which had halted production, but the men claimed that as the lost production was not due to any failing on their part the level of bonus should be maintained, as had been done in a similar situation shortly before. The men reacted to this as a straightforward, unilateral cut in pay — I argue elsewhere that this is an entirely reasonable interpretation in the context of the civil engineering industry — and it is clearly a 'perishable dispute'[26] of the kind that is lost unless action is taken without delay. My purpose here, however, is not to legitimise the strike but to look at its consequences. It was not — as industrial disputes go — embarked on in a precipitate or ill-considered manner. The shop stewards had 8 meetings with management over this issue, reporting back to site meetings in between, but could not persuade the management to alter their position, and the subsequent site meeting voted to strike.

The strike began on Monday. On Wednesday dismissal notices were issued to all those on strike; on Thursday they were ordered off the site and out of the accommodation. No arrangements for alternative food or accommodation had been made, though the stewards did have the use of a caravan outside the site. Even the nearest pub is 8 miles away. There was nothing for the men to eat and nowhere for them to stay, so the stewards had no option but to send them home. No arrangements were made to involve any of the men in picket rotas, not even those living locally. Over these few days it was raining and sleeting, with bitter cold winds.

Full-time officials from UCATT and the TGWU arrived on Thursday afternoon. They met with senior management who were now adamant that they would not reinstate any of the men. All strikers had been sacked as being in breach of contract, and they were recruiting an entirely new workforce. Everyone dismissed would be entitled to reapply and each application would be considered on its merits — in other words there would be no protection against victimisation. The officials met management several more times but could not budge them from this stand. Finally, on Saturday morning, they allowed it to be understood that they would give all of the shop stewards their jobs back *but* they would *not* recognise them as shop stewards. They would be allowed back on the understanding that they did not seek re-election. Meanwhile, there had been sporadic, disheartened and ineffective picketing of the main gate. Saturday midday, the officials advised the stewards to lift the picket and fill in application forms for their jobs: the strike was over. 440 men had been dismissed for taking part in the strike. Of these, about 400 applied for their jobs back, and of these about 300 were taken back.

In discussing this dispute elsewhere I have focussed mainly on two issues: what we can learn from it of the ideologies of industrial relations being employed by workers, site unions and management: and the nature of relations between workers, shop stewards and the full-time union hierarchy. But the point here is to emphasise the contribution made by the specific environment to this crushing defeat. There can, I think, be little doubt that it was the credibility of the company's threat to 're-man' — recruit an entirely new workforce — which was the crucial factor in their victory. This was, of course, in part a result of prevailing unemployment in the construction industry (194,000, or 13.6% in *August* 1976; as compared with 5.4% general unemployment) but this would not have been sufficient were it not for the geographical setting. We have seen how the two largest sections of the workforce were completely dispersed at the outset of the strike, leaving behind an unorganised rump of workers from the immediate locality, themselves the most dependent on employment provided by the company. In this fragmented condition the workforce would find it difficult even to know about, let alone prevent, the Company's re-manning efforts.

Now, the ability to re-man is not, of course, a distortion of the 'market'. On the contrary, it is a triumph of the market which posits precisely this sort of fragmented relationship between employer and employee, mediated only by laws of supply and demand (and control). But it is also very unusual, indeed almost unthinkable in an urban environment, and this directs attention to one way in which solidarity regularly succeeds in defeating the market — by exercising some control over it in a strictly *local* context. We can hardly doubt the force of this achievement when we look at what happens in its absence, as at Kishorn — a major defeat on a fundamental issue of principle from which the workforce never fully recovered. But this defeat was inflicted, not by any hidden hand but by power directly wielded by the company. What happened at Kishorn, then, was that one particular 'distortion' of market forces — the organisation of labour — was countered by other forms of non-market constraints: company control over food, accommodation and transport and its ability to use these as weapons to disperse and fragment the workforce. The result looks very like the hegemony of market forces of early industrial captialism (to the extent that this hegemony is not itself largely mythical).

However, of equal interest (from the point of view of this paper) is what happened to workforce composition in the aftermath of the dispute. I have mentioned above the proportions in which the workforce was divided in terms of home location: 21% from the surrounding area, 22% more broadly 'local' and 57% 'travellers'. This can be contrasted with the Nigg steel platform fabrication yard of Highlands Fabricators at which, in September 1974, 68% of all employees were local,[27] and this within a very tight geographical definition of 'local'.[28] It used to be my habit to use this contrast to argue that workforce composition was determined for the companies once certain fundamental decisions were taken, and hence that it would be naive to regard the distribution of employment opportunities between migrant and local labour as being principally a matter of overt recruitment policy. Thus, both these platform fabricators, Howard-Doris at Kishorn and Highlands Fabricators at Nigg, have a 'policy' of preference for local labour. But, I used to argue, for the companies the problem of recruiting local labour is partly one of numbers available but is more importantly one of skills, and the intention to employ local labour means relatively little unless it is backed up by an affective training programme and facilities. At Nigg Highlands Fabricators established a training school at the beginning of their operations and many hundreds of men passed through, receiving full paper qualifications and union ticket after six weeks training in trades that are normally time-served. Howard-Doris at Kishorn, on the other hand, did not set up significant training facilities.

This is a fairly obvious determinant of the composition of the labour force[29] but it has further and less obvious corollaries. If a company here is not prepared to train men on any scale then it must rely on attracting skilled migrant labour — 'travelling men'. But if it is to do so successfully it must implement an appropriate working regime. Thus travelling men, who are working away from home and families, 'travel' precisely in order to maximise their earning. They work in the context of an effective grapevine and will move on to wherever the terms are best. This, in the construction industry, means abundant overtime and preferably a seven day week. The local man, on the other hand, may have religious objections to working on Sunday, or be subject to pressure from his own community not to do so, and may also need weekends and other days off for working his croft or other primary activities. Ordinary working hours in the new industry may offer far higher earnings than previously, and his loss of leisure time is a real one to him.

Thus the company must choose which group of workers it is going to please, and if it is reliant on travelling men than its choice is already made. Thus, as I've described, working hours at Kishorn rose from 12 to 14 per day, seven days per week.

Concessions on free time took the form not of shorter hours but longer leave periods — one week off for three worked, subsequently increased to one for two. At Nigg, by contrast, the yard started by working two ten-hour shifts a day, subsequently reduced to two (sometimes three) eight-hour shifts. Since then maximum hours per week have rarely risen above 48 and there have been many months when this was reduced to 40.

The group on which the burdens of the working regime at Kishorn fell heaviest was the second of the three, those living in the East Ross and Inverness area who might be counted as 'local' in terms of Highland geography but who might have to spend as much as 4 - 5 hours per day commuting to work. The labour records at Kishorn revealed a very high turnover rate for this (substantial) section of the workforce — a typical picture of 2 - 4 weeks work followed by increasing lateness and absenteeism ending either in voluntary termination or dismissal. The experience to which these figures bear witness is perhaps best illustrated in the following statement by one of the more endurant on why he left his job:

'I was employed at Kishorn as a concrete labourer and was told that I'd be in the camp within 2 - 3 weeks. I'd been there 11 weeks and no chance of accommodation. I was getting up in the morning at 5 a.m. and getting home at 9 p.m. It was telling on my health and family so much that there was so many arguments and trouble that I was forced to leave.'

Quite apart from its effect on the people involved, it is clear that this situation also constitutes a problem for the company, and I took it as substantiating my argument as to workforce composition and working regime and as illustrative of the constraints imposed upon company and workforce alike once the basic avenue of approach was decided.

As to these basic policies themselves, why was it necessary for extensive training facilities to be established at Nigg while it was possible to avoid this at Kishorn, despite the fact that, if anything, it was Nigg that required more highly skilled labour? These decisions appeared, in their turn, to be constrained by a variety of factors, important among which were existing planning, development and housing environments.[30] More fundamentally, though, the two projects date from quite differenc eras: pre- and post– October 1973. Before this date the development of North Sea oil was a long-term speculation: since, it has become an urgent necessity. With this has come heavy pressure from the state and a change in the need to accommodate to locally articulated demands. Indeed, one may observe a steady withdrawal on the part of Highlands Fabricators from their earlier commitments on work-force composition and security.

This again, I believe, turns out to be not so much wrong as incomplete: the area of strategic choice remaining open to the companies has been underestimated. For a dramatic change in the recruitment pattern at Kishorn occurred in the aftermath of the strike. Suddenly, the company started to recruit workers from the Isle of Skye. Skye lies off the mainland directly opposite Kishorn, which is just ten miles, measured in a straight line, from its main ferry terminal at Kyleakin. To the observer, this sudden switch was electrifying: it was as though Columbus had just discovered the place. One month stress was being laid on the necessity of recruiting only men skilled and experienced in continuous pouring of concrete in industrial construction, and on the problems associated with hiring local labour; the next, a special ferry had been laid on to transport workers from Skye directly to the platform (now three miles nearer at its 'wet-site' anchorage) who rapidly grew to form a significant proportion of the workforce. It was not long before an Employment Service Agency official was estimating that 1 in 10 of the employed population of Skye was working at Kishorn.

The recruitment of workers from Skye mitigated a number of problems for the company, including that of transporting workers in the 'second' category which had become well-nigh impossible with the introduction of a 14-hour day: it had previously been intended to cope with this by increasing work-camp accommodation. But the timing makes it difficult to avoid the view that it was the strike that prompted a reconsideration of the possibilities of workforce composition. There might be disadvantages associated with insufficiently experienced labour; but these might be judged to be outweighed by the advantages of a docile, local labour force with reliance on militant, organised 'travellers' reduced. The validity of these stereotypes is a different matter but it is an obvious avenue of ideological representation for management.

To the lessons of the defeat over the strike, therefore, may be added those of the company's strategy recruitment. The labour market can be seen not to be continuous but segmented and, although benefits and penalties attach to each, the company retains the initiative in being able to select from these and wield them to its own overall advantage.

What is it, though, that constitutes this segmentation? The obvious distinction, that of level of skill, is precisely the one the company had just dispensed with. Nor was there any evidence either at Kishorn or at Nigg of an association between skill and militancy. It is, rather, its very 'localness' that marks it out, in conjunction with the desparate shortage of local work. At one level this is a routine labour-market phenomenon, but it could not operate except in the context of an ascriptive attachment mediated through the locality. This attachment is an exploitable commodity, it can be exchanged for a price and forms part of the basis of a dialectic of deference.[31]

I turn now to the second of these 'cases', a strike in March 1977 at the Highlands Fabricators steel platform yard at Nigg in East Ross, some 45 miles by road North of Inverness. This dispute also concerned payments and involved a very intricate and complex argument as to the men's entitlement. However, it will not be necessary to explore this argument in detail — whether the position of the men or of the company was more formally 'correct' as an interpretation of the bonus agreement between them — and the fact that this is not necessary is one of the key points of this example. For the company and its allies succeeded in preventing this substantive issue from ever figuring centrally in the process of the dispute.

In barest outline, then, the point at issue was this. Work on the third platform to be built at Nigg — for the Chevron oil company's huge Ninian field off Shetland — started in September 1975 scheduled for completion on 17th March 1977. Following the very successful completion of the first two platforms (for BP) negotiations took place over wage rates for the Chevron platform, but this was at a period of tight wage control limiting the direct increases possible. However, an alternative acceptable to the Department of Employment was found in the form of a 'completion bonus'that would be payable to each man if the platform was completed on time. The full bonus would be a maximum of £1,560 for skilled grades, reducing rapidly if completion was delayed. The importance of this element of earnings can be seen in relation to a normal week's pay which, at around £60 even for skilled grades, compares very unfavourably with earnings at Kishorn. At the end of February the company announced that, on the basis of current calculations and the amount of work remaining, work would finish about one month late and the bonus eventually payable would only be about £1,200. Any further delay would result in an immediate drop to about £650. The reason that this was contentious — apart from the historical status of the 'completion bonus' as a way around incomes policy — was that since the original agreement a variety of design changes and technical problems had arisen which had caused delays in production through no fault of the men and which, they claimed, had not been adequately taken into account in adjusting the target completion date. Moreover, the previous December some 450 men had been laid off *by the company* due to the then satisfactory progress.

This also is a clear example of a 'perishable' dispute: the target completion date was fast approaching and if the issue had been allowed to run its course through the various stages of the grievance procedure it would probably be too late to take action — the platform would already be completed and the case lost by default. Site meetings of the various shifts voted to strike, and the strike began on Wednesday 2nd March.

The result was the immediate unleashing of a campaign against the workforce and shop stewards on the part not only of the company but of trade union delegates and officials, backed up by government officers. The three basic premises of this campaign were, firstly, the damage to the national interest involved in delaying the completion of oil installations; secondly, the threat to British participation in oil-related contracts, and hence the threat to employment in Scotland, posed by the 'trouble-proneness' of British oil workforce; and thirdly that the strike, if continued, could only have one outcome which would be the closure of the yard and the cessation of platform fabrication at Nigg with the loss of 2,500 jobs. Two features of these premises of the campaign for a return to work seem to me most significant. Firstly, their total independence of any consideration of the substantive grievance behind the strike: if the shop stewards ever succeeded in getting the very complex arguments considered in detail, no sign of this emerged in discussion or in reports to site meetings. Secondly, their wild implausibility — with the *possible* exception of the second, an unmeasurable quantity always subject to propagandist use. There was no question of the dispute delaying the completion of oil installations as the platform could not in any case be towed out until the mid-Summer 'weather-window'; the platform would, then, be completed considerably sooner than necessary. Indeed, it is for precisely this reason that the company was able to sit out a four-week strike with equanimity.

The third premise, the closure of the yard, was certainly the most effective and so deserves to be considered more fully. The sum immediately at issue for the company was around £350 per man for a workforce of 2,500 or £875,000 in all (deductable, of course, against taxed profits). In view of differing levels of bonus for different skill grades, deducations for absence, and fluctations in the workforce, the total would probably be less. To set this in perspective I have made some necessarily very rough estimates of other aspects of the company's costs. Thus the weekly labour bill, including NI contributions, etc. would be in the region of £200,000. Hence the total projected wage bill including bonus (if the platform were completed on the target date) would be of the order of £21.5 million, taking *no* account of any supplementations for design changes, etc., which would certainly have been made and charged to the client. The 'extra' the company would have to pay would not be the bonus, which was already budgeted, but the wage bill for the period of the delay — roughly £800,000 for the projected month. This constitutes some 3.7% of the total wage bill. The total value of the contract for this platform was around £45 million, of which the disputed payment would constitute some 1.8%. The total value of capital invested by Highlands Fabricators at Nigg is especially difficult to estimate as it is spread out over time, but probably exceeded £30 million. In this context, the suggestion that an otherwise profitable operation would be abandoned over this bonus payment must appear wildly unlikely. Even more unlikely is the idea that it would be abondoned without first attempting some negotiated compromise on the level of bonus payment. Yet this is precisely what was suggested, and indeed more than this. For agreement in principle had already been reached in February between Highlands Fabricators and its client, Chevron, for another platform to be fabricated at Nigg following the float-out of current one, and some materials for this platform, principally steel, had already been delivered. Thus the cancellation of this order would immediately involve both company and Client in specific costs which could easily exceed the value of the disputed bonus.

From the first day — indeed the first hour — of the dispute the hierarchy of trade union delegates and officials identified themselves unequivocally with the company's position and made very considerable exertions (largely funded by the company) to persuade the shop stewards and the men to abandon the strike and return to work. In the first week of the strike a mass meeting was addressed by the full-time officials covering the area of the principal unions involved — AUEW Engineering and Construction Sections, Boilermakers and EETPU — who urged a return to work, and large advertisements appeared in the local and national press and signed by nation union officials declaring the strike unofficial and instructing the men to return to work. Local officials participated with the company in calling a mass meeting for 8th March to consider a return to work — although properly only the shop stewards' committee was empowered to convene such a meeting — and Jimmy Milne, General Secretary of the STUC, was flown up by plane and helicopter to address this meeting. In the event this meeting was adjourned by the shop stewards' committee and Jimmy Milne, a much respected leader of the Scottish trade union movement and clearly embarrassed by the irregularity of the situation, did not attempt to speak at the meeting. Negotiations continued for all of that day between management, Milne, union officials and shop stewards' representatives. Towards evening these parties were conveyed to Inverness airport, some by helicopter and others by humbler means, and thence to Aberdeen for discussions with Chevron, the clients for the platform. Chevron dutifully reaffirmed that the terms of their contract with Highlands Fabricators were established and no more money would be forthcoming from them. Later on these negotiations moved to London, involving union national officials who attempted to persuade the shop stewards to recommend a return. In an interview on local television the full-time delegates for one of the principal unions involved, and himself a former convenor of shop stewards at Nigg, solemnly announced that if the men did not go back the yard would close.

It is hardly surprising that the shop stewards' committee had difficulty in resisting this concerted pressure. In the second week of the strike they voted to recommend a return, but their resolve was stiffened by mass meetings on 10th and 15th March which voted to continue the strike. Eventually a meeting on 24th March was addressed by John Baldwin, General Secretary of the AUEW Construction Section, again threatening closure unless the workforce return. There followed a confused vote and Baldwin's declaration of a majority for a return to work, after which he only managed to leave the site with police protection.

These events clearly constitute an ideological struggle, but one conducted at an astonishingly crude and explicit level, with the battle lines clearly drawn. And although the abandonment of workers by their trade union hierarchies is not a particularly unusual event there are features of this dispute that seem amenable, at least, to analysis in terms of dependency. One aspect of this is dependence on the state and the use made of 'reasons of state': the recovery of North Sea oil must not be allowed to falter and this demands sacrifices of trade unions and workforces to the exclusion, if necessary, of serious consideration of grievances. An example of this can be seen in a resolution passed in June 1978 by the Offshore Industry Liaison Committee chaired by Dr Dickson Mabon, Minister of State for Energy.

'The Committee has been considering the effects on the industry of claims for extra payment at the termination of offshore related fabrication contracts. It is concerned lest conceding such claims could reduce the number of orders coming to the UK and so affect continuity of employment at our sites.

'The Committee recommends that contractors, trade unions and clients should act jointly to ensure that claims for termination payments in violation of existing agreements are rejected.'

Dr Mabon reinforced these remarks in interviews for radio and the press and it is likely that Nigg was uppermost in the minds of the Committee. In defending the resolution Dr Mabon pointed out that trade union, TUC and STUC representatives comprise almost 40% of its membership!

Another aspect of dependency is discernible in the notion of oil-related production as *privilege*. That Britain should be participating in oil-related production, that associated employment in an advanced productive sector is located in a remote peripheral region with severe job and economic problems, that training is provided to enable some locals to participate in this employment — all these are vulnerable privileges dependent on 'good behaviour' and liable, indeed likely, to be withdrawn as a consequence of 'irresponsible action'. And 'responsibility', of course, means driving a poorer wage/effort bargain than you otherwise might. It would therefore seem reasonable to add a dimension of ideological dependency in industrial relations to the structural (though non-market) dimension discussed in relation to Kishorn.

The last example I should like to turn to — again, very briefly, is that of work offshore. I pointed out above that some 22% of directly oil-related employment in the North of Scotland in this period is accounted for by work offshore — installed production platforms, pipe-laying barges, supply boats, drillships, but particularly exploration rigs. It is here, though, that the 'ethos of oil' achieves its most marked expression: the glamour of the interface between man-and-technology and a hostile environment, the fabulous wage, the 'machismo' life-style and rugged individualism of those who work there. The most remarkable and enduring feature of work off-shore, however, is the extreme disjunction between this myth and the reality it con-ceals; dangerous and degrading working conditions, management skulduggery, very low pay, and drunkenness and homelessness ashore.

Roustabouts and roughnecks — those who do general duties around the rig and who man the drill floor — are referred to as 'slave labour' by the oil industry throughout the world — they are nearly always locally recruited — and Scotland has not been treated very differently. In October 1973 an executive of a drilling company admitted the obvious in stating that all the drilling companies (most of them US based) had agreed between them to fix the wages for local labour. In 1972 the agreed wage for roustabouts was about *30p per hour*. By the end of 1973, in response to 'severe labour shortages' the rate had been fixed at around 54p and great displeasure was voiced at the fact that a 'renegade' was paying as much as 58 - 60p. At this time crews would have been working three weeks on and one week off, 12 hours per day and seven days per week, with *no* pay during the week off. By 1977 the rate had risen to about £1.10 per hour which is roughly com-parable to average onshore but looks less favourable when one realises that there are no bonus or other fringe payments, as in construction. The contracts which the men had to sign absolved the employers from responsibility with regard to ill-ness and injury: no sick pay and no compensation, and instant dismissal in the event of injury. The notorious phrase which encapsulated this was, 'Fall off that derrick, son, and you're fired before you hit the deck.' Attempts at unionisation were, and mostly still are, ruthlessly suppressed, anyone suspected of joining or of recruiting for a trade union being instantly dismissed.

Meanwhile, a few miles away across the Median Line, employees in the Nor-wegian sector enjoyed much higher wages, a wide range of social and welfare pro-visions, trade union representation, much higher standards of safety, and a degree of job security; this by virtue of government-backed agreements established at the outset of exploration. This situation is reflected in the harrowing tales related by rig workers, and fully supported in our own studies of work and safety conditions on the rigs, and in the astonishing labour turnover figures, often as high as 600% per year. Very few British nationals have been promoted to 'contact' positions where the high earnings begin. These are reserved for those of the same nationality as the parent company and form part of its 'permanent' crew. A rig returning to drill in US coastal waters, for example, would be prevented by US legislation from employing any foreign nationals.

16

It is in the case of work offshore that we do find the situation we originally anticipated would be more general — the super-exploitative use of foreign labour. This applies especially to pipe-laying barges and a (reducing) proportion of supply boats. Figures for a particular barge show that rates of pay for Lebanese and Indian cooks and stewards, Spanish welders, British engineers, and US contract men were in the ratios 3:10:30:45. With regard to leave, Lebanese and Indians worked one year on one month off; Spanish worked six months on 15 days off; British and American 3 months on 1 month off. This also applies to the boats that supply pipe barges. One of the largest operators in this recruits seamen almost exclusively from Spain and Portugal. They are flown over direct for six-month tours of duty and paid from Rotterdam through a Channel Islands bank. All employment contracts are signed at sea outwith territorial waters — Masters have explicit instructions on this. Some operators of rig supply ships also only employ foreign crews. One case which received some publicity involved a company — Star Offshore Services — which the government, to its subsequent embarrassment, chose to supply fishing support vessels in the last Icelandic 'cod war'. This company only employed Portuguese seamen on several of its ships. Work offshore is also exceptional among oil-related activities in its resistance to unionisation — though just why is a complex matter which I have no space to consider here.[32]

The point is that the maintenance of this situation has very little to do with 'labour market' forces — except insofar as, with 1½ million unemployed, there are always more people prepared to travel to Aberdeen and embark on the, by now, ritual procession around the drilling company offices and to endure, at least for a few weeks, the conditions they encounter. Rather, its maintenance is only achieved by an unremitting struggle in which the companies have managed, sometimes narrowly, to keep the upper hand. By controlling a closed and tightly policed environment management has largely succeeded in selecting, excluding, confusing, indoctrinating, insulting, intimidating and — significantly — rotating workers in such a way as to prevent their combination and maintain their fragmented, isolated condition. This is little short — and sometimes not short at all — of physical repression. The 'ethos of oil' is the ideology that reflects this condition: the propagandist use of capitalism as pure theory involving the notions of free competition and enterprise, each person carving out his own destiny in accordance with his abilities and his guts. The underlying reality, of course, is one in which his rate has been 'fixed' and his promotion prospects are nil.

In the various instances cited by Corrigan — migrant labour, bonding, allotments, serfdom, slavery — coercive power is being used is order to pay the worker at, and often below, the cost of his reproduction and maintenance. In the case of oil-related employment wages offshore have in the past been not greatly above subsistence; and there is now plenty of evidence that employers, in their haste to secure orders and start production, underestimated the vulnerability of their workforces and have since recouped some of their earlier generosity. Nevertheless, it is clear from, for example, the level of earnings available at Kishorn that this is not the main focus of employers' power. What is being affected is the other side of the 'effort bargain' equally, historically, the object of struggle: the amount and duration of effort and control over the labour process. That is, it reinforces both the formal and real subordination of labour, only imperfectly achieved especially in the relatively primitive and craft-dominated construction industry. In this particular 'product market' the rewards of this are sufficiently high for the depression of money wages to be far less salient. And this in turn is supported by the very high capital requirement and hence monopolistic position of producers.

This is easily illustrated for the three examples I have cited. The defeat at Kishorn was followed by the rigid enforcement of a quite draconian policy on lateness and absence. If a man was absent without a medical certificate more than once, or late more than twice, in a five-week cycle — that is two consecutive 14 day tours of 14 hours per day with one week's leave inbetween — he was dismissed without further question. This treatment was facilitated by the fact that an employee cannot appeal to an industrial tribunal until he has been emplpyed for six months and the company took the stand that, as the men were not reinstated but reapplied for their jobs, their employment commenced after the strike. Following the defeat at Nigg a new productivity agreement was put into effect — drawn up in secret negotiations between management, client, union officials and shop stewards — which laid down a 40% increase in productivity and tighter discipline, for no specified return.[33] The company's previous undertaking on retaining the 'local' component of the workforce in employment between contracts was also relaxed. In the case of work offshore, a considerable proportion of the work done would either be impossible, or would be very much more expensive, or would involve protracted and hence extremely costly delays if management were not able to expose workers to danger and difficulty to a degree that would be considered completely intolerable onshore.[34] This seems to be a far more important component in management's determination to retain control in the North Sea and to resist unionisation than the relatively insignificant cost of higher wages.

I have tried to show that there is some value in approaching the industrial relations of oil in the North of Scotland via the notion of 'dependency'; that doing so highlighted specific features which they have in common and which are related to their particular environment and peripheral status. However, I think I have also shown that — in this context at least — there is no such thing as 'dependent industrial relations'. This is certainly the case if the notion of dependency is promoted as a rival dimension of dominance and subordination. For the elements out of which this dependency in industrial relations is composed are not analytically dis-

18

tinct from those of industrial relations elsewhere. These structural and ideological elements of ascriptively based power and non-market coercion occur — with greater or lesser effect — in all work situation. So, for example, the position of garment workers, particularly women and especially immigrant women, is not very different from that of workers offshore. The position of workers in inner cities may be much the same as that of workers at Kishorn — a point nicely illustrated by the fact that the Kishorn employer, John Howard Construction, had used the identical tactic of remanning to break a strike in Liverpool a few years previously. And the ideological pressures from state and union no doubt feel much the same to workers at Nigg and engine tuners at Cowley.

## Notes

1 For convenience we define the Northern half of Scotland as comprising the Grampian and Highland Regions and the Northern and Western Isles.

2 These figures are drawn from a variety of sources including Department of Employment data and the work of the North Sea Study team in the Department of Political Economy, Aberdeen University. I am grateful to the latter — and especially to Tony Mackay, now at the Institute for the Study of Sparsely Populated Areas, Aberdeen University — for permission to use them.

3 See, e.g. the formulations of Dos Santos in 'The crisis of Development theory and the problem of dependence in Latin America' in H. Bernstein, ed *Underdevelopment and Development*, Harmondsworth: Penguin, 1973.

4 See Robert Moore's paper in this collection.

5 See, e.g. P. J. O'Brien, 'A critique of Latin American theories of dependency' in I. Oxaal *et al.* (eds) *Beyond the Sociology of Development*, London: Routledge & Keegan Paul, 1975.

6 Unpublished seminar paper given at the Department of Sociology, University of Edinburgh, March 1978.

7 See Bettelheim, quoted and discussed in Harold Wolpe, 'The theory of internal colonialism' in Oxaal *et el., op. cit.* 240 *et seq.*

8 'Capital created underdevelopment, not because it exploited the underdeveloped world, but because it did not exploit it enough' (Geoffrey Kay, *Development and Underdevelopment: a Marxist Analysis*, London. 1975; discussed in Foster-Carter, see note 17 below; on this see also David Rosenberg, 'Underdeveloped sociology', *Sociology* X, 2, May 1976).

9 A. G. Frank, *Capitalism and Underdevelopment in Latin America*, New York: Monthly Review Press, 1967.

10 E. Laclau, 'Feudalism and capitalism in Latin America', *New Left Review* 67, May-June, 1971.

11 The status of which is discussed by Judith Ennew in this collection and elsewhere.

12 I. R. Carter, 'Economic models and the recent history of the Highlands', *Scottish Studies* XV, 1971, pp. 99 - 120.

- - - - - -. 'In the Beginning was the Board: thoughts on the ideology of regional planning', mimeo, Department of Sociology, Aberdeen University, 1972.

- - - - - -, 'The Highlands of Scotland as an underdeveloped region' in E. de Kadt & G. Williams (eds), *Sociology and Development*, London: Tavistock, 1974.

13 James Hunter, *The Making of the Crofting Community*, Edinburgh: John Donald, 1976.

14 See note 19.

15 I. R. Carter, *Farm Life in the North East of Scotland 1840 - 1914: the poor man's country*, Edinburgh: John Donald, 1978.

16 Not, at least, in anything like the same sense – but see, *inter alia*, E. Mandel, 'The nature of the Soviet State', *New Left Review*, 108 March - April 1978, on revising the time-scale of periods of transition.

17 For an introduction to this debate see Aidan Foster-Carter, 'The modes of production controversy, *New Left Review* 107, January - February 1978.

18 '- - - - - "industrial relations", consecrated euphemism for the permanent conflict, now acute, now subdued, between capital and labour.' (Ralph Miliband, *The State in Capitalist Society*, Quartet edition, London, 1973, p. 73.)

19 Philip Corrigan, 'Feudal relics or capitalist monuments?  Notes on the sociology of unfree labour', *Sociology*, XI, 3 September, 1977.

20 *ibid*, 436 - 7.

21 *ibid*, 449: original emphasis.

22 *ibid*, 450.

23 *ibid*, 451.

24 In a book currently in preparation to be published by Penguin.

25 On which see Hunter, *op cit*.

26 See the discussion of this in J. E. T. Eldridge and G. C. Cameron, 'Unofficial strikes', in J. E. T. Eldridge, *Industrial Disputes* London:  Routledge & Keegan Paul, 1968.

27 From a survey conducted by the North Sea Study team (see note 2 above).  More recent figures from a survey of our own will be available soon.

28 Comprising, essentially, the East Ross and Cromarty areas and excluding Inverness.

29 I do not suggest that it is the only significant factor: housing policy and corresponding availability is another and is described in detail, for East Ross, by Isobel Grigor in this collection.

30 On which see Isobel Grigor.

31 I confess to misgivings over this reliance on 'attachment'.  My doubts are not so much theoretical – for one must be extraordinarily dogmatic to refuse to see the attachment that people display – but rather that *contemporary* 'Highland' political economy, with its wealth of 'unofficial' tasks and occupations, remains largely uninvestigated.

32 I should make it clear that the full force of these remarks does not apply to the very few rigs owned and operated by the British and part-British oil companies, BP and Shell Expro, where conditions were much better, most workers were on contracts and labour turnover has been much lower.  Both have, however, tacitly participated in resistance to unionisation offshore.

33 I am grateful for this information to Gordon Philip of the Department of Sociology, Aberdeen University, who has been involved in the observation at Nigg.

34 This aspect of work offshore has also been researched by Kit Carson and Hilary Idzikowski of the Department of Criminology, University of Edinburgh.

# 2 Northern Notes Towards a Sociology of Oil

*Robert Moore*

The Copernican revolution in our thinking about development and underdevelopment has, obviously enough, been accompanied by commentaries upon the underdevelopment of sociology (Frank, 1971b).  This aspect of underdevelopment has a specific meaning in the north of Scotland and it is with a discussion of this that the paper begins.  It is important to note that we do not experience underdevelopment *and* the underdeveloped state of sociology; the former being the state of the real world and the latter an irritating feature of our discipline.  The underdevelopment of sociology is *part of* the underdevelopment that we seek to understand.  In simple terms, part of the problem of being underdeveloped is that it is difficult to understand what is happening.  The locations of decision-making are remote, the decision-makers unknown or inaccessible and the criteria upon which policies are based are seldom made explicit.  One result is that we are able to assent to statements that describe broad processes in a general way but we find it difficult to ground analysis in specific events and localities.[1]  The paper is not, therefore, 'a sociology' but notes intended to raise points which will need to be debated — amongst many others[2] — in developing a sociology.  That these are *northern* Notes may need explaining.  The north and north east contains 14% of the population of Scotland and 1.4% of the UK.  In the small towns bad unemployment is measured in hundreds.  This has to be compared with the chronic unemployment of thousands and the industrial dereliction of the populous midlands.  Therefore the tentative analysis offered could be seen as one-sided in looking only at the apparently ill-effects upon a small population whilst millions may be benefitting.  One altrustic Peterheadian suggested that events in his town were in the 'national interest' and that even a 'St Kilda solution' was acceptable if it saved the British economy.  Drastic as this may seem, given that Peterheadians are neither a rare nor migratory species, such a policy might be acceptable for the greater good in a programme of accelerated capitalist accumulation or socialist reconstruction.  But the people of the north east might wish to debate the issue.  We might also wish to question the notion that there is a national interest which serves 53m people as against the 14,700 of Peterhead.  But the fact remains that what happens in the north east is relatively unimportant to the Scottish or UK population — and this is part of the problem which sociologists need to analyse.

## The Regions

A settler arriving in Northern Scotland in 1970 would have recognised social features that would have reminded him of life in a colony or an ex-colony.  The

21

area was one of primary commodity export. The local diet seemed rather limited with root vegetables and sticky cakes featuring in a restricted cuisine, with a few shops offering the elite metropolitan luxuries. In the schools English history was taught and like many Malayans and Nigerians students knew more of England under the Tudors and Stuarts than of the home country at any period. The University was engaged either in the reproduction of the local legal, medical and clerical elite or in equipping the most able young people to move away. London dominated television production and local media projected a demeaning kilts-and-caber image of caledonian idiocy. Such first impressions are plainly faulty, though amplified by living within the university's expatriate community. When, therefore, the multi-nationals arrived in pursuit of oil, and property speculators in pursuit of instant profit, rapidly followed by American anthropologists – the surest sign of under-developed status – it was to be expected that sociologists would turn to the literature on development and underdevelopment in an attempt to understand the events that were taking place around them.

There are therefore a lot of unfinished and abandoned papers on the sociology of North Sea oil developments. It was not that the theory was at fault. The work of A. G. Frank, for example, is highly relevant: his analysis of the underdevelopment of Brazil demonstrates processes at work not unlike those in Scotland. But his analysis is concerned with a chain of satellite-metropolis relationships extending from the provinces of a highly dependent third-world nation to European capitals. Scotland is on the periphery of a powerful nation-state and its current relations with the 'metropolis' are thus in some ways very different from those described by Frank. Similarly, Galtung has analysed the roles of the trans-national corporation (TNC's) and then concentrated upon those countries where the TNC's have a dominant role. Some third-world countries are in a strong bargaining position and others align themselves entirely with the TNC's rather than being subordinate to them or dominating them. Sociology is relatively underdeveloped in its analysis of the peripheries of metropolitan powers and conditions in which TNC's and states are in bargaining roles.

In retrospect what was lacking from our analysis was any clear understanding of society in the north and north east of Scotland. The north is not simply a rural backwater dominated by apparently 'feudal relics' (Corrigan, 1977) in the form of lairds. The regions of the north and north east have quite distinct characteristics which were recognised in *cultural* terms from the beginning of research; in Aberdeen University we referred to the Scandanavian and Gaelic Highlands and Islands and to Buchan as areas with distinct histories and different land tenures and languages. These are significant differences that have to be taken into account, especially when investigating the social and cultural effects of the impact of oil, but they are not the most salient features when it comes to analysis of the events we are trying to understand. Major companies, employing large labour forces have moved into the north, they have both brought labour with them and recruited locally. The main points of analysis, therefore, concern the articulation of these employers with the local economy and polity and the articulation of their labour relations with the existing relations of production in the north and north east.

The rural north of Scotland is geographically peripheral to the UK, but its development has been an integral part of British capitalism (Carter, 1974; Hunter, 1976) The history of the Highlands is well documented, kelp needed men, but sheep and deer did not. The Highlands were laid waste by sheep so that the towns could be clothed and fed. The population that remained engaged in crofting, a form of subsistence farming that made occupational pluralism a necessity: crofters were forced to turn to fishing and other subsidiary industries, to work the boats of the fish curers and merchants (Mewett, 1976). Model towns were built by landowners to house the dispossessed peasantry and to enable them to engage in fishing and cottage industry. They migrated to harvest the capitalist farms of Buchan, the Mearns and further south; others worked seasonally in Glasgow or now in the tourist industry. And, of course, they worked on the landlord's land. Rent levels were adjusted to ensure that men had to work for others, but the provision of their own subsistence meant that the employers did not have to pay the cost of reproduction of labour and could recover wages through rent. Legislation secured the crofter's tenure in 1886, but changes to this were set in motion in 1975.

In the north east a peasantry persisted in to the 19th century largely due to the availability of virgin land. Thus, peasants cleared the land for a landlord, made it profitable for capitalist farming, and meanwhile their sons and daughters provided labour for the middle and large farmers (Carter, 1978). Unionisation was late and not entirely successful but the resistance of the farm servants was embodied in an underground tradition of secret society, oaths and the 'horseman's word'. The depeasantisation of the north east, the advent of wage labour and then the numerical decline of wage-labourers with the rise of large scale, capital intensive farming, reduced the basis of solidarity and attenuated the tradition of resistance.

Around the north east coast fishing flourished and with it the associated industries of cooperage, transport for fish and coal, icemaking, fish processing, boat-building and repairing, the work was seasonal and entailed substantial migrations of boats, transport and process workers. This enormous industry experienced a catastrophic collapse in numbers. Today the inshore industry is much reduced in size but highly profitable, with technical change boats become more expensive and large fishing combines are beginning to penetrate a family and share-fishing industry. The cold store has made processing less seasonal and therefore led to decasualisation. The industry remains vehemently anti-trade union. The deep sea fleet, entirely the province of the combines, faces diminishing areas of operation and an uncertain future.

The whole of the north and north east has been an area characterised by continual movements of population, not only in the sense of continued depopulation but in the in-migration of construction workers. The military road and defence building of the mid-eighteenth century was followed by the building of the Caledonian canal; extensively military building has also taken place in the 20th century and today the north east probably has one of the highest concentrations of military installations (and prime nuclear targets) in the UK. With airfields and radar stations go military encampments with their steady turn-over of population and steady return of ex-servicemen who married local girls whilst stationed in the region. Hydro-electric schemes similarly brought a more transient form of labour in the form of navvies who encamped in remote areas and pursued their craft with a 19th century pride. If a navvy did not like his employer he would, like a Buchan farm servant, move on rather than form a union (Sykes, 1969).

What we have been describing are social relations entailing a high degree of dependency and subordination. They are, perhaps more noticeably than any where in the UK, forms of personal dependency to the landlord. According to John McEwan, some tenant farmers may not even protect their crops from the depredations of his landlord's game birds, but in less extreme circumstances it remains the case in the large estates that nothing happens that the landlord does not want. He controls building on his land more firmly than any Planning Department and can say whether shops or street lighting will be provided in 'his' village. The landlord is, as his title suggests, a power in the land. The farm servant is dependent upon the farmer and lives in a tied cottage. His wife may be required to provide some labour service in or around the big house. Whilst these relations may be the most noticeable they are not necessarily typical. The landlord who lives by rent is being replaced by the capitalist farmer who lives by selling agricultural produce in the market. Over 50% of farmers in the north east are owner-occupiers and 25% in the Highlands. Near Peterhead we found one farmer owning 15 farms totalling over 2,000 acres and worked very efficiently with a handful of employers. But the 'laird as fuedal relic' does remain and some capitalist farmers present themselves as such — for example the farmer who lets a cottage to students on condition that they occasionally hand round the cocktails and canapes at parties in the big house.

Perhaps the most obviously dependent group of employers are military personnel whose dependency and subordination extends to their domestic lives.

For different reasons the fisherman stands in a relationship of dependency to his skipper, because it is upon the skipper's skill that the size of the catch and its

24

value at market depend. Skippers and hands are at the mercy of wind, weather and EEC regulations.

Characteristics of all these occupational groups is that there is little that they can do to improve their market position through the organised power of their labour. If the relationship between landlords, farmers and farm servants was simply a cash nexus organisation would be more feasible, but the latter stand in a relationship of dependent tenure upon the former. The dependency is reinforced by local political power and traditions of passivity. If fishermen were to organise they would find the sea and fish impervious to union demands. The organised voice of the industry is heard at the level of ownership where attempts to influence EEC policies are made collectively.

The small towns present a further picture of dependency. Government, at least until the 1975 reorganisation, was in the hands of local proprietors — small capitalists, managers and subsistence shopkeepers. Labour has largely failed to mobilise to resist this domination and thus in Peterhead, for example, a policy of low rates and high council house rents prevailed. Bealey and Sewel have shown that although there was no organised resistance the electorate distrusted the Council deeply. The Councillors had an explicit policy of not consulting the public on important issues (Bealey and Sewel, forthcoming).

In the city of Aberdeen we find a different recent history. There is a strong tradition of union organisation and working class political activism. Aberdeen is a geographical isolated city which has acted as an administrative and service centre for the North and the Islands. In the industrial manufacturing sector local capitalists have been predominant: engineering and shipbuilding being in local hands. Building, transport, food production and processing were in local hands and connected to UK capitalism by market alone. Two schools and the University reproduced most of the middle class and enabled it to remain relatively closed and impenetrable to the socially mobile. Changes may be noted, food processing has been penetrated by multi-nationals and some famous 'local' names are now part of international combines. None-the-less Aberdeen showed many characteristics of satellite capitalism whilst also generating the substantial 'invisible' earnings of a regional metropole and entrepot.

Within the city with its large concentration of labour, differentiation of employers and landlords and spatial separation of the working class from employers, unionisation and the development of Trade Councils and Labour Parties took place. A city party organisation enabled Labour to dominate the city (and now the District Council). Strong unions represent transport and engineering workers, the construction trades are organised and local authority workers. Food processing, retailing, hotel and catering are less well organised.   The organisation of labour was widely feared to be one possible consequence of the arrival onshore of the oil industry, but in fact labour organisation had spread outside Aberdeen at least amongst skilled workers, to include engineering plants established by TNC's in, for example, Fraserburgh and Peterhead.   A degree of unionisation is also to be found in the Cromarty Firth where a navel base and later an industrial distillery and a smelter created significent concentrations of industrial labour.   This is the only area outside Aberdeen city where the trades unions have been a local political force, having actively campaigned for development projects for some years and been a relatively effective lobby (Varwell, 1975).   The dock labour force in Shetland is also organised, but outside Aberdeen unions exist largely in locations isolated from one another and situated in branch plants of major national and international undertakings.

These then, in rough outline, are the main features of class relations in the north and north east of Scotland.   We should not be surprised by the apparent modification of pure market relationships (in the Weberian sense) by relations of dependency.   As Corrigan has noted in a recent article such relations have persisted throughout the development of capitalism and are in no way incompatible with it (Corrigan, 1977).   And in making this assertion Corrigan is drawing on a substantial body of sociological literature including work of my own, all of which points to a substantial modification of simple market relations by other social factors.


*The Incoming Companies*

There is no one industry that one may call 'the oil industry' in the north.   Most of the activity onshore is undertaken by contractors in the construction industry who will build installations or bury pipes for any client.   There are firms engaged in the technically complex construction of large offshore installations.   There are firms providing supplies and services to contractors offshore.   There are companies which supply highly specialised scientific and technical manpower and others which simply supply manpower or womanpower.   There are also firms who offer management services in bringing all the foregoing together for a client.

Construction activity is not new to Scotland and at St Fergus, Sullom Voe and Flotta we are seeing the continuation of a construction tradition in the sparsely populated regions.   The construction industry has not been studied by sociologists since Skye's modest participation observation in the 1950's.   The labour is, as Skye's discovered 'free labour' in that a workman who does not like his work conditions may move to another site.   But not all the workers are itinerant or 'travelling men' and for locally recruited non-travellers especially the labour camp creates conditions of un-freedom.   The extreme isolation of Kishorn, Nigg and Sullom

26

Voe, for example, means that men have no alternative accommodation to the camp. Their 'service tenancy' does not necessarily create conditions of super-exploitation because the employers pay subsistence, but it does reduce the political independence of labour. As the men at Kishorn learned they are powerless if the management closes the canteen and camp. Like any evicted tenant they can choose only between starving on a bare hillside or migrating. Conversely the organisation of catering labour makes possible the closing of a site by the shutting of a camp. But as we have already noted catering labour is notoriously ill organised.

Labour recruitment policy varies between companies and many depend heavily upon a traditional workforce drawn from a particular geographical locality. Thus, one firm of mechanical engineers may recruit its labour amongst Glaswegians and another civil engineering firm may recruit in Northern Ireland. Each one has one or two 'old hands' who recruit from specific villages or kin groups. But recruiting also takes place from amongst different local groups; from the pool of unemployed from farm workers leaving the land as capital intensive farming expands, in crofting areas construction sites offer employment for the occupational pluralists, and for the small towns high wages may attract employed men from local firms to the sites.

Personal recruitment through intermediaries ensures a dependant workforce for the employer and the factor of remoteness gives a degree of political control not through the employer's monopoly of accommodation, but by common vetting of the candidate before they are dispatched northwards. The employers do not have to be content with the hands that await them at the site gate but may select on the basis of personal ties and selection procedures facilitated by public and private employment agencies. Perhaps one of the most effective social controls at the workplace is provided by the uncongenial geographical isolation which makes the pursuit of overtime and big bonuses a major objective on construction sites. It has been suggested that platform sites were located in remote districts in preference to the Clyde area because of the degree of control such locations afforded and because the Clyde was known to have a strong trade union tradition.

The pursuit of 'big money' also attracts locals to the site but their local ties to a croft or a family and community create demands which may be incompatible with shift, overtime and week-end working. (See Shapiro in this volume, on the problems of Kishorn work site in this respect). In many locations we have found a high turnover of locally recruited people. For those engaged in crofting the decision to stay on a site as full-time construction workers may result in hay standing uncut, the loss of crops, and the eventual reversion of the holding to rough pasture. The recruitment of local industrial employees may result in the previous employer poaching from a smaller employer with an eventual net loss to small firms who may go out of business. In these two cases we see active underdevelopment whereby local capitalists and small traditional businesses, upon which the locality will depend after the construction activity, are destroyed or weakened by oil.  It would be premature to say this was a general trend in the rural areas.

The attitude of incoming firms towards unions has been especially illuminating and Dan Shapiro is currently writing this up in a systematic way.  What has happened at Nigg and Kishorn is that the employers' initial expectations seem to have been of robust trade unionism in the construction industry (perhaps like the American hardhats).  They were prepared to adapt to this.  They found however, that the unions were poorly organised and that on remote camp sites with a variety of trades, subcontractors, local and travelling men, it was possible to defeat the unions — and that the national officers of the TU's could be expected to side with management, for reasons that we will see below.  With union power defeated the management have been able to impose their own terms upon the men.

On less remote sites, like St Fergus, there has been almost universal unionisation and industrial disputes of an inconclusive kind.  The main problems faced by management are the large numbers of subcontractors, the great diversity of skills and the diversity of tasks.  One major impression gained at St Fergus was that management were 'making it up as we go along' in terms of embodying new or altered plans into the construction task.  Foundations were being laid before the machinery to stand upon them had been designed.  Craftsmen complained to us that they were not allowed to do their work properly and that they were constantly changed from job to job.  The relative fragmentation of management therefore inhibited their chances of reducing union power had they wanted to do so.  One impression was that they passed the cost on to the client.  We also encountered attempts by contractors to provoke industrial action so as to avoid payment under the penalty clauses of their contracts; as this usually happened towards the end of a contract the workforce tenaciously resisted such attempts in order to preserve their bonuses.

The picture we have of the construction industry is not therefore a simple one: a strong union tradition is being attenuated by isolation, and — after the honeymoon period — by the assaults of the management.  On the other hand in less remote areas we find the same unions remaining relatively strong and encountering fragmented managements.

The offshore supply bases recruit locally and in some cases provide extensive training courses for locally recruited employees.  They also provide employment for women and thus offer completely different opportunities for women in a town like Peterhead.  The manual work entails mainly crane and forklift truck driving and slinging; there is a high proportion of clerical and administrative tasks and only 'good management' can make a firm efficient and profitable.  The bases have therefore taken some hundreds of workers from local employment into a new industry. The employment is likely to be as long-term as the offshore oil fields and to be located mainly in Aberdeen, Peterhead and Lerwick, but also in Montrose. The bases are also likely to attract related services around them, especially repairs, planned maintenance, technical and domestic supplies and warehousing. It should be noted that all these activities create jobs but that they are not defined as 'development' by the state even though development is largely equated with the provision of jobs. The significance of this will be discussed below.

The connection between the base and the offshore installation is maintained by helicopter and supply boat. These constitute the potentially weakest link in the industry because industrial action by helicopter or boat crews could be used as an industrial sanction in blacking or boycotting the installations and bringing them to a standstill. Recalcitrant workers can be flown off, but without supplies or relief crews work must cease. Boats could be brought from foreign ports but helicopters have a shorter endurance. Labour policy in this part of the industry is therefore especially interesting. The boats are largely manned by foreign crews on contract from third-world or Mediterranean seaboard countries. The major helicopter company successfully fought a bitter struggle against union recognition and another used management labour to keep helicopters flying (somewhat unsafely) during a maintenance engineers' strike. The former dispute was presented to the oil industry as a 'who controls the North Sea oil?' dispute and thus one of critical importance. The relative lack of alternative employment for pilots and the high proportion of ex-servicemen amongst them does not make it easy to form an effective union. But even more striking was the level of aggression by the owner against a white-collar 'professional' group who sought to form a union. The state oil corporation has a contract with this firm.


*Capital and the State*

But what of the oil industry itself? It only chose to locate itself in the North Sea (and therefore Scotland) because it was profitable to do so. Technical considerations alone make it the last place to choose because the North Sea offers one of the most hostile environments in the world and the cost of extracting oil and gas is therefore high. One benefit of the North Sea is that techniques developed there are likely to be effective anywhere in the world, and it is therefore a major source of technical innovation and knowledge.[3] The oil companies are there because there are profitably exploitable reserves of oil and gas. The profitability of oil and gas depends upon many factors including the size of the reserves, the geographical difficulties of extraction, the capital costs of doing so and transporting the products to the shore, but it also depends upon the world demand for and price of oil and the taxation regime under which the oil is extracted. It is not my intention to discuss work offshore, where capital can be seen red in tooth and claw and where technical problems and frontiersman ideology create a physically hazardous and politically subordinate working environment. Offshore, according to Mr Heath, we can see the acceptable face of capitalism. This must await detailed analysis in its own right.

The role of the state and especially of the state vis-a-vis the oil companies is immediately relevant to our anaylsis. The UK government has defined its major goals as the solution of national economic problems. Revenue from oil is seen as a solution to these problems and as a basis for the regeneration of industry and commerce. These goals entail the most rapid and profitable extraction of oil from the North Sea. In this the state's interests are at one with the oil companies. But the state has to generate revenue by taxation without destroying profitability and ensuring that taxation is not avoided by any of the many strategies open to transnational corporations. Questions of Petroleum Revenue Tax, royalties, terms of licensing and government participation have therefore been subject to negotiation and bargaining and in the game of bluff and counter-bluff the oil industry has achieved relatively favourable terms for its activities. None-the-less a taxation 'ring fence' has been placed around North Sea oil and steps taken to ensure that the oil is valued at its world market price and not sold cheaply to subsidiaries or collaborators. In this the state has shown its quite considerable power to control the oil industry.[4]

In order to ensure the rapid development of offshore resources the state also intervened to provide onshore fabrication yards for offshore installations and facilities for additional service bases at Peterhead. But it intervened still further in order to ensure a British stake in the North Sea through the establishment of BNOC. The state, has as it were, established its own oil company in order to expand its control over and profit from North Sea oil and to ensure a place for the development of British scientific, technical and managerial skills. This 'national' interest not only ensures a British share in oil, it thoroughly identifies the interests of the state with the oil companies which are amongst the most powerful capitalist institutions in the world.

The taxation regime brings many benefits to the oil industry. For example; the costs of finding and producing oil in a field may be set against Petroleum Revenue Tax and some of the costs may attract about a 75% 'uplift' which raises the amount which may be set against tax, abortive searches for oil may be offset against PRT in another field and an upper limit is placed on the level of PRT for all producers. Other aspects of oil operations may be offset against Corporation Tax — plant and machinery 100% in the first year, oil wells 40% in the first year and then 5% subsequently, building 50% and 4%. The state therefore provides fiscal incentives in the form of substantial tax benefits for the oil industry.

This taxation policy articulates rather poorly with regional development policies which are designed to encourage industry to underdeveloped or declining areas of the country. The whole of Scotland is a development area and this status long pre-dates the discovery of offshore oil. They are policies designed to redress regional imbalance by the promotion of 'development'. The development that the state wishes to promote is based upon a model of the process of industrialisation — and in many declining industrial regions a policy of *re*industrialisation has a logic. Because declining areas characteristically experience prolonged periods of unemployment one major objective of regional development policy is the creation of jobs.

The demand from regional authorities and the trades unions is for investments that create jobs and this has always been a prominent feature of the aspirations expressed in, for example, the Cromarty Firth and the Grampian Region. An equation something like this seems to be involved:

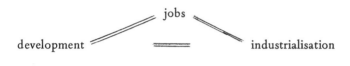

But because the model is basically a 19th century one a further element is included in the equation of industrialisation with the growth of manufacturing. Thus:

This view of development is reflected directly in the policies designed to aid industrial development. Regional Development Grant (20% cost of buildings and new plant), Removal Grant, Interest Relief Grant, Transferred Workers Removal Assistance, Tax Allowances are all paid for projects in manufacturing and processing (Interest Relief Grant and Removal Grant may be paid for mining and construction industries which increase, safeguard or maintain employment). Service industries receive very much more limited benefits and only if they have 'a genuine choice of location' (NESDA, 1977).

There is a clear equation of manufacturing with jobs (and presumably 'multiplier effects') and a view of services as non-productive. In the north and north east the only undertakings to gain the full benefit of these provisions are capital intensive activities such as refining, the manufacture of Ammonia or the separation of

Natural Gas Liquids.    As it happens none of these is likely to take place in the north and the north east, but only (subject to planning approval) on the fringe of a traditionally industrial area, namely Fife.    None of these processes create many jobs and, given the skill levels required, not all of these can go to locals.

The developments that will create long term employment — offshore servicing, maintenance, and repairs, special technical services and transport — attract little or no development aid.    This situation also favours the large corporations who are more likely to be engaged in petro-chemical processing, than the small firms engaged in servicing activity or activity classified as servicing by virtue of being non-manufacturing.

No attempts have been made by the Scottish Office to alter its development aid policies in order to allow the north and north east to maximise the benefits from oil.    It could be argued that servicing activity will come anyhow — it indeed has no genuine choice of location.    This policy too favours incoming companies and does not make cash available for very small firms or for local entrepreneurs who may not be able to enter the field at all unless they form joint ventures with incoming firms or become heavily dependent upon banks.

The stress on 'development' also goes some way towards explaining the attitudes of union administrators to shop-floor labour organisation in oil.    We cannot of course, ignore the logic of the argument started by Michels about  the oligarchic tendencies of democratic organisations nor the discussion of the reasons for rules and bureaucratic procedures becoming more important than the goals of the organisation.    But these are features of all union organisations.    In Scotland the unions have pursued the objective of 'jobs' since the first world war, they have seen the oil industry, downstream processors and construction companies not simply as the saviours of the UK economy but as the bringers of sought after jobs to deprived regions.    The idleness of the fabrication yards, the international nature of the offshore oil industry and the intense international competition for orders (and jobs) predisposes the union leadership to an alignment with capital and the state.    Therefore industrial action at, say, Nigg not only threatens the unions' and STUC's stable relations with employers, but is seen as a threat to subsequent contracts — an impression that management are not unwilling to promote.    Thus we have STUC officials arriving by company plane to tell the men to return to work on the employer's terms.    This undermines the bargaining power and ultimately the credibility of the local union, especially amongst locally hired men with little industrial or trade union experience.

The social consequences of oil developments onshore are left for the local authorities to cope with  in the public expenditure cuts.    The rating system has a redistribution element built into it so that unless there are substantial population increases the additional rateable values generated by onshore installations result in a *pro rota* reduction of the needs element in the Rate Support Grants. Again the taxation system operates to prevent the north and north east being able to benefit from the opportunities, by spreading the benefits very thinly throughout Scotland. The local authorities meanwhile have to provide extra housing and sewerage, more road repairs and more school places for the children of incoming families. The authorities are willing to provide these facilities because they represent a contribution to the provision of more jobs, but they are relatively unable to meet the extra costs. In fact, some authorities would probably be able to make increased claims for Rate Support Grant (needs element) on the basis of population increases, but the cancellations of the 1976 inter-decennial census in the interests of public economy have prevented accurate new population estimates.

The additional infrastructure provided by the local authorities is plainly of benefit to the local population especially when industries over-estimated their needs for housing and thus persuaded the District Councils to build houses which will eventually be used to meet the demands of the local waiting list. But much of the provision may turn out to be for relatively transitory needs. The one case when a local authority has ensured that developers meet infrastructural costs — Shetland — was cited by Harold Wilson as not being a precedent.

The costs of infrastructures have been raised by the activities of land speculators. One particular group of companies forced up land prices in Shetland, the Cromarty Firth and the Buchan area before being taken over by the parent company. Thus local authorities whether buying land for roads or houses, or compulsorily acquiring land for development have been forced to pay inflated prices. Land prices in Peterhead were sufficiently inflated for the SSHA to consider withdrawing from its undertaking to build houses there. The profits were considerable, speculators (or 'developers' as they prefer to be known) acquired large tracts of land knowing that a sale of only a small portion of it could make a 'killing' sufficient to offset the total acquisition costs.

There was also a political battle between 'developers' and local authorities because the developers produced grandiose schemes for industrial development, housing and commerce that came into conflict with County and (later) Regional plans. The developers were, in fact, making decisions of a kind and on a scale more appropriate to a local authority. The local authorities asserted their control — an assertion made easier by the failure of the petro-chemical developments upon which the developers' profits depended. But nothing could prevent the rise in the price of land that local authorities purchased. The Community Land Act — not enacted with oil developments in mind — might have gone some way to meeting this problem had it been passed earlier.

Local landowners — some of whom had themselves purchased speculatively — made considerable profits. Amongst the speculators were some with no knowledge of farming but who, in order to avoid Capital Gains Tax, purchased further land. This has resulted in a marked local degradation of agricultural land through mis-managements.

What this section has tried to show is that regional development policies are designed to attract manufacturing to deprived areas in order to take advantage of labour reserves. It is not geared to coping with industry imposed upon an area as a result of, perhaps, geological accidents. Secondly, the rating policies and planned legislation are not adequate to cope with the problems generated. Fiscal policies and regional incentives in the present context favour the large incoming corporations and the infrastructural costs are met locally. Finally, the local social impact of oil is so peripheral to the state's interest that it has not seen it as politically necessary to take any steps to empower the local authorities to deal more effectively with the problems they encounter. The state, therefore, has not played a neutral ring master's role in evening out the costs and benefits of oil, but rather has allowed conditions to continue in which resources are taken from the North of Scotland, but relatively little put back into the region.

## Concluding Discussion

The Scottish periphery is being used for the extraction of primary resources from the sea. The north and the north east is no stranger to primary extraction. The development (or underdevelopment) of the north and north east took place according to a *national* territorial division of labour: the north provided kelp, beef, wool, mutton, labour, sport, to sustain urban industrial growth in England and Scotland, and to contribute to a style of life for the propertied classes. The relative desolation of the Highlands is not simply the product of terrain and climate but of a system of social and economic relations. The current exploitation of oil is taking place according to an *international* division of labour; the capital needed could not be supplied by the UK alone, the technical knowledge is found in TNC's and concentrated in the USA and the Netherlands. Processing is carried out in various parts of the world according to markets and the location of plant.

The north and north east of Scotland was not chosen for development through oil; oil had to be developed at the most convenient landfall, the north of Scotland. The rural areas are providing the location for offshore fabrication and the trans-shipment of oil and gas, it is an obvious location for servicing offshore activity. All these activities demand labour and in the mainly rural locations the labour is to a degree unfree labour, and insofar as it is recruited locally drawn from areas with a long history of unfreedom and dependency. The isolation of the rural sites, the close management control of recruitment, the collusion of union officials with employers and the state in pursuit of national economic salvation, all combine to weaken the bargaining strength of labour. The issues are not, however, uncontested because the construction industry includes well-organised and militant trades. Again, the international nature of the oil industry contributes to weakening labour because yards can be manned by seaborne foreign workers or rigs manned and serviced from foreign ports.

The arrival of TNC's in the north and north east may lead to active underdevelopment if their labour demands lead to the closure of small local enterprises or the withdrawal of existing branch-plants of national and international firms in the area. The loss of fishing harbours could prove a major factor in underdevelopment, but it has not happened yet. (see Moore, forthcoming, for the extraordinary story of Peterhead harbour). The industrial work pattern on the remote sites could lead locally recruited men to abandon their rural-based occupational pluralism to become integrated into a high-wage, mobile construction industry or eventually into the urban working class. Speculation and planning blight might lead to further agricultural decline. Many factors have to be set against this, not least in the north east, the outcome of EEC agricultural and fisheries policies.

The exception to this seems to be the city of Aberdeen and possibly the town of Peterhead. Here there is every possibility of self-sustained economic growth based upon and around the oil industry. This growth will include industrial growth, but it will not be the manufacturing which is normally equated with development, and it will not necessarily be the growth of local companies. As Hunt's work has shown the proportion of incomer-owned manufacturing in the city is increasing. Growth in Aberdeen will in itself create a considerable number of complex labour-supply problems for employers.

The state defines the oil question in national terms and the effect on the north and north east are peripheral to these policies. The state identifies its interests with those of capital in the kind of economic and technical support it gives to the oil majors. This identification is cemented by the direct intervention of the state through its own oil corporation. The 'national' interest is represented by a share of the produce of the North Sea and tax revenues, the latter are to be used for economic regeneration in the areas of industrial decline. The main benefit to the north and north east of Scotland may be confined to the reduction of unemployment.

The north and north east remains an exporting region in the national and international division of labour. Its economic and political status may be characterised as peripheral and dependent. Whether we shall see the redevelopment of under-development is a question of time scale: we may soon see a progressive collapse of the construction industry in the area with consequential unemployment and emi-gration with surplus housing left behind — or even greater general dependency with the unemployment and their families living in new council houses or SSHA housing in areas where there is little work and little likelihood of work. Local capitalists will adapt to changes or go under. The oil industry and its onshore support is here for some time, but in the long run, like the black cattle and the sheep, it will go. But the circumstances of this long-run change is something upon which it is not possible even to speculate.

## NOTES

1 Further underlining the unreality of the theoretical demands made by research funding bodies (Moore, 1978).
2 For example, the world-wide strategies of oil majors are not discussed and nor is work off the Scottish shore.
3 Making the North Sea a potentially valuable training-ground for foreign skilled and pro-fessional personnel.
4 Legislation to extend taxation offshore was passed with considerable speed unlike the mea-sures to extend the Health and Safety at Work Act.

# REFERENCES

Bealey, F and Sewel, J.  A study of the politics of Peterhead.
(forthcoming)

Carter, Ian, 1974.  'The Highlands of Scotland as an Under-developed Region' in de Kadt and Williams. *Sociology of Development.*

Carter, Ian, 1976.  'The Peasantry of N.E. Scotland' *Journal of Peasant Studies.*  Vol. 3, No. 2 pp. 151 - 191.

Corrigan, P., 1977.  'Feudal Relics or Capitalist Monuments', *Sociology,*  Vol. 11, No. 3, pp. 435 - 463.

Frank, A. G., 1971a.  *Capitalism and Underdevelopment in Latin America.*

Frank, A. G., 1971b.  *Sociology of Development and the Underdevelopment of Sociology.*

Galtung, J., 1973.  *The European Community: A superpower in the Making.*  Universitets-forlaget.

Hunter, J., 1976.  *The making of a Crofting Community.*  J. Donald, Edinburgh.

MacEwen, J., 1977.  *Who owns Scotland?*

Mewett, P., 1977.  'Occupational Pluralism in Crofting', *Scottish Journal of Sociology,*  Vol. 2, No. 1, pp. 31 - 49.

Moore, R, 1978.  'Sociologists Not At Work' in *Power and the State* (ed) G. Littlejohn *et al,* Croom Helm pp. 267 - 302.

NESDA, 1977.  *Aid for Industrial Development.*

Sykes, 1969.  'Navvies' Work Attitudes', *Sociology,* Vol. 3, No. 1, pp. 21 - 35.

Sykes, 1969.  'Navvies, Their Social Relations', *Sociology,* Vol. 3, No. 2, pp. 157 - 172.

Varwell, A., 1975.  'The Social Impact of Large Industry', SSRC/Aberdeen Department of Sociology.

# 3 The North Sea Oil Story: Government, The Oil Industry, and The Press

*Andrew McBarnet*

At the end of 1974 the Department of Energy director of information wrote a lengthy and by all accounts vociferous memo to his Secretary of State. He complained that the oil industry was using the media, and particularly the press, to wreak havoc with the Labour Governments' newly announced policy intentions for offshore oil taxation and State participation in commercial North Sea oil discoveries. In a sense the gesture was an unwittingly generous recognition of the success of big business in its handling of a capitalist press. Certainly the director of information's frustration becomes easy to understand from a careful reading of the national press then and in subsequent years as the proposed measures were eventually acted upon. The firm impression you get from the news columns (as opposed to more explicit editorial comment on the leader page) is of a Socialist Government recklessly jeopardising the oil birthright of the nation by pursuing a doctrinaire oil-for-the-people policy bound to drive any reasonable profit oriented oil company off to some (usually unidentified) offshore prospect elsewhere in the world where things are done more equitably. During the period, the constantly quoted refrain from the North Sea operators is that they can only serve Britain's interests in getting the oil ashore if the Government water down their taxation and nationalisation plans. It is now a matter of record that the Government did in fact dilute all the policies laid out in the July 1974 White Paper.

Unfortunately, it is extremely difficult to assess systematically how far the Government was affected by a consistently negative if not downright hostile coverage of its North Sea oil policies. So, that potential blind alley will not be followed here. In passing, however, it should be noted that Ministers routinely receive a detailed rundown of what the papers have said on oil along with reports on articles raising issues affecting the Department. The line of questioning taken by key journalists (e.g. Financial Times, The Times) at private briefings in the Department is also analysed and circulated for the information of officials. The concern of this discussion is to identify the determinants of the North Sea oil 'story' as newspapers told it, in an attempt to explain how the emphasis of coverage took a predictable shape in 1974 and continues to be largely predictable today. The contention is that the reporting of North Sea oil provides a very striking case study in the structure of news, made more poignant by the fact that the whole offshore saga had all the makings of a bonanza for the press. If ever there was a bonanza in the coverage of North Sea oil, it is over now, dispatched to the business pages of the quality press whence it came. What should interest us is the implication of a national press able to turn on and off an ongoing 'story. such as 'North Sea oil' which if anything has grown in preceived national importance as the promised riches become a cashable reality. Conventional media research would normally look for explanation by concentrating on news values, the operations of the newsroom, on the profession of journalism, and above all on the well documented constraints both formal and informal which affect reporting.[1]    These include press ownership and control issues, the whims of a news editor, the journalist's need to keep a favoured contact sweet as well as the formal restrictions brought about by the laws of libel and other legal hazards.   So, it is possible to explain how the North Sea oil 'story' took off in the directions it did and then how it collapsed in terms of such considerations. However, the purpose of this paper is to introduce an overlooked aspect in the analysis of news coverage which, in the case of North Sea oil at least, has crucial consequences for any study of what makes news and why certain events, views, etc., are recorded in the press.

It is arguable that the raw material in the 'manufacture' of news — the source of stories and articles — has not been accorded sufficient attention.   Looking at the North Sea oil case, one is left with a strong suspicion that when dealing with large multinational companies or, for that matter, Government bureaucracies, much information for the press and thus eventually for the public becomes a matter of news management.   The information made available has been subject to careful planning and mediation before the press ever gets to process it.   The press's own role in the mediation of material may therefore not be as important as we perhaps imagine.   Outside the unpredictable happenings like the Ekofisk blow out or the recent trapped mini-sub, North Sea oil news is very much what someone other than the newspaper wants you to read.

Now to substantiate this sort of claim, one needs first to look briefly at the newsmaking process in the UK press in order to establish the importance of the role played by the sources of news stories.   Every paper yearns for the really unpredictable to fill the news columns, the big story that tells readers of something genuinely new.   The first oil fields to be found in the North Sea were just such news and were played for a time.   The, interest began to pall as yet another find was announced. More salient, papers couldn't rely on a new discovery every day however loudly they welcomed each new one.   In practice, therefore, leaving news to chance would come apart very quickly on an uneventful day.   The paper would panic about how to fill all the space so generously left by the advertisers.   The Glasgow Herald is not alone in holding immense picture blocks able to cover a page at a moment's notice in case of last minute mishaps.   But it can also be at a year's notice.   When Christmas comes around, old ladies write in to thank the paper for the lovely big photos of scenes from Scottish lochs to be found filling entine news pages.   But insiders know the pictures are there to cover up the total lack of printable news during the Festive season.

It is evident that newspapers need a regular supply of raw material. What's more, it needs to arise at a convenient time of day to meet print deadlines. It must also be in a manageable form for easy process. In order to accommodate these requirements they look for pre-ordained events to which they can 'send a man along' with a good chance of a story coming out of it. Indeed, if such a valuable asset as a staff reporter is sent out to an event, the news editor can be very sure of a story at the end of the day — unless of course such occupational hazards as refreshments for hard worked members of the press have been over generously laid on. The serious point is that a vicious circle has established itself whereby many organisations realise the newspapers' hunger for cheap to produce news and lay on press releases, meetings, briefings, facility trips and conferences all geared to feeding journalists with stories quick and easy to print.

The institutionalisation of so much newsmaking enables the newspaper to keep staff members down to a minimum so that it becomes even less able to produce original researched material of its own and has to depend still further on pre-ordained events. The familiar cry from news editors that they haven't got anyone to spare to cover something that has cropped up quite often means that too many reporters have been committed to events anticipated in advance.

In formal terms, the newspaper's home news arises from a number of main sources. There is the Diary which is basically a list of events scheduled to take place that day — Parliament, court proceedings, council meetings, important speeches, official visits and so on. Home news also relies heavily on the output of the Press Association and other wire services which can prompt newspapers into their own inquiries but as often as not provides comprehensive coverage of British news from which the paper can choose relevant items. Then there is the avalanche of press material aimed at attracting the attention of the press which lands on news desks every day. The deluge to be sifted emanates from every conceivable sector of the community, from Government departments and big companies to local community pressure groups and even individuals. But, as might be expected, the most abundant suppliers of press material are the large institutions. The Department of Energy, for example, puts out some 400 releases a year, British Petroleum issue 100 or so. Energy and oil as topics for inclusion on the day's news schedule have to vie with hand-outs and other packaged materials from every other Government department and virtually any important institution in the country which at some time wants to unburden itself of some 'news'. Obviously a release does not guarantee coverage, nor necessarily is it intended to. But what it does mean is that journalists' time is tied up sifting through the printed material for stories or possibly story leads to follow up. Not for nothing, therefore, does the trainee journalist have to sit as part of qualification a test in how to rewrite a press hand-out.

The next important source of stories available to a news editor come from 'contacts' of individual reporters and correspondents. A journalist is often judged by how good his 'contacts' are, referring to his ability to get well informed stories. This may involve no more than the simple device of phoning up the contact and simply asking how things are, or dining the contact on expenses. This can lead to a 'good story' or provide background for future use. However, the mythology of contacts, which specialist correspondents in particular have a vested interest in cultivating, obscures the fact that these contacts are at best well placed individuals within an organisation willing to talk to journalists off the record without a PR filter but no less loyal to the organisation because of that. (In British society it is extraordinary how loyal people are to their employers when speaking to the press compared, say, with the United States.) More usually, therefore, the contacts that journalists perennially use are simply favoured 'spokesmen' within press offices of large organisations. The idea of a whole army of Deep Throats lurking around multi-storey car parks itching to spill the beans to the press is — unfortunately — an amusing fantasy.

News comes from other places too. It can even be a genuine happening although the tendency of official sources to take over even the unexpected event should be noted. For example, the Department of Energy rehearses with the help of local authorities and the oil industry how it would handle the media in the event of a full scale North Sea emergency.

The significance of the source material for news mentioned here is that it fills the bulk of any day's news coverage in a daily paper. What might be termed the predictable and routine dominate. The implications are enormous because, if newspapers are prepared to accept such a construction of news, then they lay themselves open to considerable manipulation. Thus, if we take the example of the press conference, this may once have been a convenient way of apprising a lot of journalists of the same information. But now it is the subject of extremely careful planning on the part of any organisation to ensure that it is presented in the best possible light and that no embarrassing material is released. In other words, every attempt is made to set the agenda for that item of news and to frame the issues, the very roles that the press has always had claimed for it whether benevolently or malevolently. In this situation the options open to even the most conscientious reporter are limited. Only key and properly briefed personnel from the organisation are likely to attend a press conference so that skilful questioning is not going to elicit much which the organisation doesn't want people to know (roughly the definition of news espoused by Randolph Hearst). The larger and therefore normally more important the organisation, be it a Government department, company or other formal body, the more difficult it is for the journalist to penetrate. To return to the North Sea example, you can't ask the doorman at BP's Britannic House headquarters in London for the lowdown on what is really going on out in the Forties Field. But Sir David Steel, BP's chairman, or Jack Birks, the company's top executive in charge of North Sea operations, won't tell the journalist more than they want to — which invariably is very little. In these circumstances, an impromptu remark can be made into a better story than the hand-out speeches routinely distributed at press conferences (as much as anything to ensure that busy bar-propping journalists at least get the quotes right). But there would be no story at all from the off-the-cuff remarks — themselves often contrived — if the press conference had not been called to make top people available to the media.

What this amounts to is that newspapers use a great number of sources which have come to understand the structure of news gathering and presentation and therefore speak to journalists on their own terms and frequently at the time of their choosing. Thus, another important aspect of sources has to be borne in mind, which is that a good story for the newspaper is the one that has been authenticated by a believable source. A hierarchy of credibility is set up whereby the immediate and trained response of a journalist to any lead is to check it with the most authoritative source possible. This will enable him or her to sell the story to the news editor, the first of a number of gatekeepers dedicated to safety, safety for themselves from the wrath of superiors for allowing the irresponsible, contrary to policy, embarrassing or libellous item into the paper and safety for the organisation which in some way has to pick up the tab for indiscretions, whether by way of a libel action, complaint to the Press Council, the dropping of advertising by a prized client, or simply the rarely carried out threat to cancel a subscription.

Given this pressure for authority in stories it is inevitable that authenticating sources are in the main going to officials and special personnel hired and trained to deal with press inquiries. Both categories are expert in toeing official lines. The journalist's inquiries to some degree become the subject of expert management. This is not to say that good stories revealing hitherto unknown and potentially awkward information never emerge, more that a great deal of possible news material becomes a matter of negotiation in which the journalists needn't come out top.

Two further points should be added. First, the structured way in which journalists go about newsgathering reinforces or gives rise to what may be called formual news writing. At its simplest this means that a first paragraph, with the story summarised or the main point, will be followed by more detail and quotes, preferably conflicting, from people involved or affected by the story. The fact/quote approach raises again the newspaper's dependence on professional sources to make a story stand up, to use the reporter's expression. Any story without heavy enough support is played down or rejected. An oilrig worker's account of a fatal accident would weigh lightly against a different but official version from the oil company involved. Journalists tend to find themselves phoning endless spokesmen for authority knowing full well that the information then imparted is carefully textured. Yet, most journalists settle for formula writing. Among other things, it is hard work rooting out alternative information convincing enough to get printed — and why bother when news editors and their bosses will settle for less? The best way to enliven a boring press release, therefore, is to think of someone who will dislike or challenge the announcement contained in it and to phone for a reaction. The story can then read 'Local MP Hamish McTaggart attacked yesterday's decision by X oil company to buy Japanese equipment for its new offshore installation.' Second paragraph begins: 'This whole deal stinks,' said an angry MP for Yshire. Not until the third paragraph do we get the information which prompted the story — 'An X company spokesman said last night that the Japanese contract was only signed after consultation with the Government etc, etc . . .' The moral from this is that the journalist may manipulate things to get a story, but the information has already been pre-packaged. Again there would be no story at all without the company announcement and even the alternative sources for quotes or counter information are often well rehearsed.

The second point is in the form of a question. What is the alternative to this admittedly crude characterisation of routine reporting activity? The answer is usually said to lie in some form of genuinely investigative journalism. But, from the newspaper's point of view, such investigation is expensive, time consuming and, in crude production terms, not all that fruitful since the amount of material unearthed may not warrant the cost and effort expended when the main imperative is simply to fill the paper. In any case, the investigative story will often border too close to libel for the original research to be worth printing at all, especially when less spicy or controversial news apparently sells papers. The economic interest of newspapers in cheap raw material constitutes an important reason for most of the press — and the broadcast media even more so — to be in the passive state of being ready to react to events, of sending a man along when something happens rather than initiating stories and seeking out news.

We therefore have to ask ourselves just what controls the basic content and timing of much of our daily news fodder. The North Sea oil example provides some valuable insights which have an inescapable bearing for anyone who suspects that the press plays an important part a) in giving the general public some understanding of what North Sea oil is all about and b) in providing an atmosphere or climate of opinion within which national policy has to be worked out.[2]

Evidence presented here is based on ongoing research focused primarily on one aspect of North Sea oil press coverage — the Labour Government's offshore oil policy from 1974 onwards.[3] It aims to show that the period witnessed a sharp political and ideological struggle between a newly elected Labour Government and the oil industry along with its contractors (chorus provided by Tory and SNP voices for their own different reasons). Preliminary findings appear to confirm that the nature of the conflict was such that available public information would inevitably be structured to favour the interests of the oil industry. This is seen as particularly relevant given that the outcome of two issues — taxation of North Sea oil and the policy of State participation in commercial oil fields — was certainly regarded by all sides to be crucial to the future economic and political stability of the UK. Under consideration, therefore, is the press's participation in a very naked power struggle. Before breaking down some of the structural factors affecting the press's role, it is necessary to characterise — at least sketchily — the press's performance.

The search for oil in the 1960's and its discovery in 1969 was generally regarded by the press in news stories as something rather extraordinary, even unbelievable so that 'UK Ministers turn Oil Sheikh' was the sort of approach. Unimagined wealth could not be made much of a story, and indeed the Government's generous early licensing rounds reflected this incredulity. For the conspiratorily minded, there may well have been a deliberate underplaying of the North Sea's potential by the oil industry in its contact with the press. Meanwhile the natural gas exploration and production in the southern North Sea which has led to 98 per cent or more of the country's supply coming from this source was underplayed. This was partly because the oil industry's investment was comparatively modest and the return was good despite supplying to a monopoly buyer, the British Gas Corporation. Also the UK didn't seem to need natural gas when oil was so cheap. Thus the companies did not have much to beef about, nor did they have great bargaining power since Algerian liquid natural gas was being offered as a possibly cheaper alternative. However, the pages of the Financial Times, the only paper to take gas coverage at all seriously, carried a long running saga concerning the oil companies' threats to halt investment unless the right price for gas was offered. Shades of things to come . . . .

At the end of the 1960's when the first oil fields were discovered the picture changed. Ministers, the oil industry and the press united in a euphoria about what this could mean for the country. A huge and ludicrously cheap licensing round by the Tory Government was welcomed in the press as late as 1971-72 when major fields such as Brant, Forties, and Ekofisk were already announced and the real value of North Sea resources must have been evident. What was noticeable even then was the oil companies' warning about the immense cost of oil production in an untried hostile offshore environment such as the North Sea. The Energy Crisis in October 1973 and the quadrupling of oil prices should have swept away any lingering doubts on the profitability of the North Sea (particularly in a politically stable part of the world). Oil stories at this time still tended to concentrate on the latest find with reports on latest drilling positions reflecting a general optimism.

Labour's return to office changed thing dramatically. It was perhaps bad luck that the big oil companies were on the verge of taking decisions about oil production from the North Sea. Not only did that predispose the oil companies to be anxious about Labour's Manifesto promises to tax oil properly and to nationalise the North Sea assets, but a whole range of other interests were likely to be affected by Government policy. British industry wanted the business, local authorities and local people faced sudden, spectacular and not necessarily beneficial economic activity from platform building and the supply of offshore services, and the SNP demanded the oil for Scotland and the onshore work related to its exploitation to be undertaken in Scotland.

The new Government was faced with three key issues to settle 1) a taxation regime less full of loopholes 2) the State participation commitment and the setting up of the British National Oil Corporation 3) onshore development strategy.

On taxation the Government's announcement of measures to ensure a system less full of manifest loopholes set off a spate of headline stories suggesting that the oil companies could not survive in the North Sea and that only the larger fields would ever be developed. And, in any case, the public must not overestimate how much oil was there. In short, Britain's prosperity was basically being put in jeopardy by irresponsible Labour Ministers. Companies such as Conoco let it be known that their smaller fields could not go ahead if the Government's intention to introduce a high rate of Petroleum Revenue Tax was carried out. Occidental (with conspicuous help from Thomson newspapers, partners of theirs in the North Sea) expressed reservation about the Claymore field. Amoco lunched selected journalists to tell them that its southern North Sea gas operations were being reconsidered in the light of the possible consequences of PRT. Having got full value from the stories obligingly written after the lunch, the company took out full page adverts in a number of papers to reinforce its argument. And so on. It was difficult to get oil companies at this time to talk about anything other than penal taxation, the high risk investment of the North See, and the recklessness of Labour. The outcome? The final PRT measures were considerably diluted, special concessions were made for small fields. Amoco's case was conceded completely. For journalists at the time the refusal by oil companies to comment on the Government's final Bill was a measure of their approval. They had been eager to attack the proposed legislation but apparently had no views on the eventual tax. The 'We're still assessing the effects' comments never hardened into diatribes about Labour's legislation. Indeed, hints of oil companies paying little or no tax in the North Sea are just beginning to surface now — with difficulty because the oil companies hide behind commercial confidentiality and won't comment. Today, three years on,

BP expects to recoup its £850m investment in the Forties field by the end of this year (1978). The field has a life expectancy of 25 years and at peak will supply the equivalent of a quarter of the UK's oil requirements. BP has also recently upped its estimates for the rate of oil production from Forties. Occidental has upgraded Claymore's reserves having developed the field in a faster time than any other so far in the North Sea. Instead of headline treatment, these new facts appeared largely on the City pages. The political battle won, the focus has returned to its normal audience of investors, to the business news and optimism.

Coverage of participation has followed much the same pattern. Reports insisted that uncertainty about a Government stake in North Sea oil finds was causing companies to think again about putting money into UK offshore development. Financiers were holding off. Esso — joint owner with Shell of the largest chunk of commercial North Sea — bluntly announced that it would not be volunteering for participation as the Government had asked. Even when the Government told companies that they would be no worse off and no better off as a result of participation, the statement was not believed in public by the oil industry nor by journalists who chose to point to the lack of new North Sea oil developments. (Two years elapsed when no major platform was ordered for the UK sector, but there were plenty of reasons for this unrelated to participation.) The outcome? All the companies have agreed to participation in principle at least. In essence, the State through BNOC has a right to buy 51 per cent of the oil in all fields — at market price. No mention is now made of the equity stake clearly implied in the initial 1974 North Sea oil policy statement. Meantime press coverage in this area now includes inspired sniping at the growth strength of BNOC and its likely effect on efficient production and distribution of North Sea oil supported by quotes from the oil industry.

On onshore development, the situation was rather more complex. The outstanding difference in coverage by the press can be ascribed chiefly to the availability of sufficient counter-information to at least raise — albeit unsuccessfully in most cases — questions about the operations of big business. Journalists could actually visit some construction sites and report on local opposition, although McDermotts at Ardersier and MacAlpines at Ardyne Point made it a point of principle never to allow access except under very special supervision or for official press facility trips which give little idea of real work conditions, safety precautions and so on.

So, during the period, there were regular stories — mainly in the Scottish press — about the disruption by new facilities serving the oil industry, about the treatment of workforces, about the pressure on local infrastructure and the malaise of local government trying to handle the rapid build up of a new and unpredictable industry. Yet, it would be ingenuous to suggest that investigative reporting dominated the North Sea oil story onshore. The Drambuie planning application and subsequent public inquiry in 1973-74 got its fair share of coverage as did the presence of two old, now scrapped, Greek liners at Nigg Bay used as accommodation for Highlands Fabricators' workers. Because they were more difficult to track down and substantiate, land speculation stories emerged infrequently. In any case, the press was ambivalent. On the one hand, it salivered over the job prospects (always a good story). The popular papers went for the new big wages and how they were spent bringing out the human interest angle. Hence such tired old cliches as Aberdeen 'Sin City' and the Black Gold Rush. On the other hand, the environmental and social upheaval in remote and scenic areas of Scotland provided a story really good for the middle class readers of the quality press.

On the policy level, the press's ambilavence allowed big business a soft ride. Thus new work was consistently welcomed regardless of the impact on local communities. Companies helped this along by hedging announcements with grand statements of intent about contributing to, not to say ameliorating, local life. The fact is that every construction company which set up platform construction sites on the Scottish coast persistently breached specific planning conditions and undertakings. In the case of Howard Doris, conditions laid down by the Secretary of State for Scotland as a sine qua non of permission to build platforms at Kishorn were blatantly flouted. All this received much less emphasis in the press than the original big stories greeting 'Hundreds of jobs in new multi-million pound project'.

From its point of view, the Government faced the traumatic problem of satisfying the competing demands of numerous contractors seeking the use of coastal sites in environmentally sensitive areas of Scotland. In general, press coverage was not sympathetic. It quoted oil companies on the actual and threatened loss of platform orders to overseas competitors and oil companies and contractors on the much cited national interest in rapid planning procedures to meet exceptional circumstances. In this atmosphere the Government did act — too late and mistakenly. The policy of limited construction sites came after the first big rush of platform orders. But more seriously, the Government believed the oil industry's estimates of future platform demand and ordered the development of £25m worth of sites at Portadavie and Hunterston which have never been used and remain impressive disfiguring excavations on the coastline of Argyll and Ayrshire respectively. Having joined in the chorus for more sites, the press now helpfully remind the Government of its gaffe at periodic intervals. It's hardly a story that needs digging for!

The foregoing outline of press reporting on North Sea Oil policy matters is clearly only a summary based on preliminary research assessment and on personal experience as a contributor to the coverage, but it does point to predictable patterns in press behaviour. It calls for the shading in of the structure of North Sea reporting in the light of the earlier description of how press stories are constructed.

It is important first to notice where the North Sea oil story has been written. And the answer is of course that policy particularly, but coverage in general too, has been confined principally to the quality press. If we take 1976 coverage as an example (by which time North Sea oil press reporting was properly in its stride), only 14 items receiving anything like comprehensive coverage in the UK quality and popular national papers. These were: £40m to Burmah for Ninian, Briginshaw to BNOC, diver death, Gulf Conoco participation agreement, Deep Sea driller wrecked, BP participation deal, Nigg refinery approved by Scottish office, Shell to export 16m dollars worth of liquified natural gas, rescue from Forties field platform, Benn to lead participation negotiations, Burmah to get £87m for Thistle Field interest, Beryl field on stream, BP upgrade Forties and two deaths on Ocean Voyager rig.

The most striking point about these news column items is that they are all stories which depend on oil industry or Government sources making announcements to the press. The press has investigated nothing. In a whole year, less than 30 stories were even covered by all four quality papers, and of those reports it is difficult to find one which was not prompted by a formal announcement, press conference, or some other pre-arranged highly formal, controlled event with the source of newsmaking literally in command of the facts.

The tendency is underlined by looking at the totality of news of North Sea oil in 1976. By far the most mentioned category of press coverage concerns discoveries and appraisal results. The source of such stories is invariably an official statement (governed partly by the legal obligation of US companies to make public their results) which journalists will mould into a news storey sometimes with the help of further information from a 'contact'. The next most mentioned items are stories associated with the economy and the finance and business of North Sea oil. Information about contracts, commercial deals and other company news is of course routinely supplied to newspapers. The companies want the advertisement of their activities to inform or attract investors. The press wants the news product. Again, reporters may inject their own comment or assessment into such news but the information is rarely based on their own research beyond asking questions on the story initiated by the company. The same is true of economic news from the Treasury or other Government departments. The stories are packaged for the press. It is routine practice for Ministers to sit down with their advisors before a press conference and outguess the press so that all questions are foreseen and answered in advance. In an engagingly frank moment, Energy Secretary Tony Benn once drew the press's attention to something on his brief which by the end of the meeting reporters present had failed to ask about.

Basically because of the necessity for companies to report accidents, the press gets to hear of such news and therefore seems to pay a great deal of attention to offshore safety in a news content analysis. But, the story is not theirs and is supplied virtually in toto by company or official sources such as the Police or relevant Government body.

Given the dominance of particular sources, it is no surprise to find little news reporting in the UK national press of – in no special order – onshore impact in Scotland, planning issues in Scotland and onshore/offshore workforce conditions.

There is a good deal of coverage of policy (although in terms of volume not in the same league as the categories discussed already). However, policy stories follow the same trait of being prompted by official announcements, speeches, etc. The result is that on key issues such as taxation and participation there is a very distinct flavour to the information in the press precisely because the structures of newsmaking allowed sources within the oil companies to take an unusually high profile. There is a study in itself of the different ways companies chose to impart material to the press. Some went for the lunch and chat approach, others the formal announcement. The net effect was that speeches, with reporters present, attacked Government policy or expressed doubts about the oil bonanza. Reporters approaching oil company contacts were given juicy titbits – instantly news because it was different to a press release announcement – about the likely consequences of Government action. Following the story of taxation and participation was to witness the oil industry making use of reporters to push across its point of view, commenting much more freely than usual with good quotable material.

An interesting aspect of this was what amounts to a mistake by the Government in inviting consultations and discussions with oil operators before making any decision. The oil industry took full advantage by willingly talking about the state of proposed policy – for example, they claimed marginal fields would not be exploited unless Petroleum Revenue Tax was less than what the Government had outlined to them in strict confidence. The Government trapped itself into a defensive position because it felt unable to discuss details of a policy still being worked out confidentially with the companies. Luckless Department of Energy spokespersons were for ever in the situation of having to say that the companies' threats to pull out of the North Sea or to review their investment were based on speculation. Thus the oil industry got the headlines while the Department of Energy had to settle for rather feeble, down the story denials.

The consistency with which the oil companies got the better of the Government obviously raises questions about the role of the journalist. There is no need to rehearse the well established organisational constraints within the newsroom, nor to spell out the possible difficulties for North Sea oil correspondents when their own papers have investments offshore ... Even accepting these curbs on journalistic activity, there is also the practical question of how a reporter challenges official sources successfully on a regular basis given the lack of access and the reluctance of newspapers to embark on costly and possibly fruitless investigations. The oil story is virtually dead in the late 1970's because the oil industry has no major axe to grind (although its skirmishes with BNOC continue) and therefore does not want any publicity other than the company news directed primarily at the business pages of the quality press. There is little the reporter can do about this. An example to illustrate the point concerns the amount of oil supposed to be in the North Sea. This has always been a crucial issue for the debate on the policy to be adopted by the Government. Tough taxations, if plenty of oil was recoverable.

Against the industry's cautious estimates, journalists have only ever been able to find one alternative authoritative source willing to take issue with the companies. That source, Professor Peter Odell of Erasmus University, Rotterdam, has frequently been quoted arguing that the oil companies base their estimates of oil reserves, not on total exploitable quantities, but on what is profitable for them to produce — a rather different matter. By subtle insinuation, and in the case of BP, by a press release denial on one occasion, the oil companies have moved to isolate and effectively discredit Odell. In reporting terms, there is a limit to how many times the one man's voice versus the oil industry story can be told. It is perhaps salutory to note that Professor Odell has been taken on as a Government consultant in the Department of Energy.

The North Sea oil story, therefore, can be seen very much in relation to a structure of news reporting in which the role of management of information by sources has been left all too unconsidered. What we are talking about is the ability of multi-national companies to give themselves a good write-up in a capitalist press.

# NOTES

1   For a full review of the literature see: D. McQuail: Review of the Sociological Writing on the Press (Working Paper No. 2: Royal Commission on the Press) London HMSO, 1976.
Gatekeeper Theory and other determinants of press news values are usefully summarised in: B. Roscho: Newsmaking, ch. 7.   University of Chicago Press 1975.   J. Turnstall: Journalists at Work, chs. 2 - 3.   Constable 1971.

2   Useful studies on the UK press's role in agenda setting, defining issues and affecting the climate of opinion can be found in:   C. Seymour-Ure:   The Press, Politics and the Public, Methuen 1968.   The Political Impact of the Mass Media, Constable 1974.
P. Hartmann and C. Husband:   Racism and the Mass Media, Davis Poynter 1974.   J. D. Halloran, P. Elliot and G. Murdoch:   Demonstrations and Communication.   Penguin 1980. S. Cohen and J. Young:   Manufacture of News, Constable 1973.

3   Research funded by the North Sea Oil Panel of the Social Science Research Council is still very much ongoing so that all evidence and conclusions should be regarded as strictly tentative.   The author is a former energy correspondent of the Glasgow Herald.

# 4   Gaelic as the Language of Industrial Relations

*Judith Ennew*

The arrival of large-scale oil-related industry on a remote Hebridean island might seem to indicate the need for a sociological inquiry into the impact of modern industry on the 'crofting way of life', and the Gaelic heritage.   As will be seen below, this was the opinion of both the local authority and the Scottish Office when planning permission was sought for an oil-related industry on the island of Lewis. Although neither of the reports which ensued was sociological, the implications of both were that the situation was one in which capitalist relations would be introduced into the pre-industrial society of the island for the first time.   The argument of this article will be that such a suggestion is erroneous.   It will be suggested that the 'crofting way of life' is a transitional phase, and that capitalist relations are not new to the island.

Lewis is the most northerly and politically and economically the most powerful of the chain of islands known as the Outer Hebrides or Western Isles.   This has been since 1975 a single political unit, the only political unit in the United Kingdom which is simultaneously a Parliamentary constituency and a local authority. The island of Lewis itself has poor natural resources.   There is little arable land, and it is usually claimed that it has always been necessary for the inhabitants to find additional modes of subsistence to supplement agriculture.   Fishing has been a traditional source of both food and wages.   The townships occur largely on a mile-wide strip between the moorland and the sea.   A distinction can be made between the West coast settlements, where the fertile *machair* and open beaches favour farmer-fishermen;   and the East coast, where sheltered harbours and scant soil led to a way of life in which, originally at least fishing predominated over farming. From at least the early nineteenth century until the middle of the twentieth, Lewis men and women were also employed as fishermen and gutters by fishing enterprises from the mainland.   Wage labour has thus been a feature of the Lewis economy for some time.   Since the 1920's the Harris Tweed industry has provided a further element in the economical pluralism which is characteristic of crofting areas. (P. Mewett, 1977).

Almost one-quarter of the inhabitants of Lewis live in Stornoway, the only town in the Outer Hebrides.   Stornoway owes its position partly to the existence of a sandstone belt which provides good farmlands.   This is combined with its position facing the mainland of Scotland at a deep coastal indentation, which provides an excellent protected harbour.   This harbour has proved a centre for both local and mainland fishing operations.   The town was already a thriving sophisticated community in the nineteenth century.   During the Second World War it had certain strategic importance, and a NATO base is now situated at the nearby airport. It is a busy town, small in scale, but a vast cosmopolitan centre when compared to the townships of rural Lewis. It is thus not surprising that the 1973 Report *North Sea Oil and the Environment* should designate Stornoway as a High Priority Development Zone. Such Zones were seen as more suitable than other areas for oil developments 'in terms of their capacity to absorb developments, their labour supply and their pre-existing infra-structure support' (HMSO, 1973 p. 17). The Report suggested that smaller supply and servicing yards, in which steel jackets and modules are constructed, would fit more easily into the existing economic pattern of Highland life than huge platform construction yards (ibid p. 15). The onshore fabricators of smaller steel structures for the oil industry have employed two contradictory strategies when chosing sites for these production yards. Either they have selected areas where there is a requisite supply of skilled labour, or they have chosen to locate in an area where there is a large section of unskilled labour which can be trained to the firm's requirements (Manpower Services Commission 1975, p. 54).

With Stornoway designated a Priority Zone and some fabricating firms looking for areas of high unemployment as sites for yards, local newspapers were soon printing headlines such as STORNOWAY GETS THE SHEIKS (WHFP 28.9.73). Clearly any interested sheiks would be those whose plans included the training of unemployed, unskilled workers. The employment structure of Lewis in 1971, just before oil-related interest in the island, showed a characteristic rural pattern with 52.5% of the unemployed population in service industries. The total workforce was only 5,538, out of a population of about 20,000. Unemployment was running at an official 24%, a figure which gives no indication of under-development (Russel, 1973, 71). However both unemployment and underemployment were tempered by the economic pluralism of crofting. The actual number of registered unemployed was around 1,000. It is unwise however to compare Lewis unemployment figures with those of mainland urban areas, where, as one official somewhat dramatically pointed out 'such figures mean soup kitchens.'

In April 1973, representatives of Fred Olsen (UK) Ltd, a subsidiary of a Norwegian shipping group, visited the Arnish area south of Stornoway, and met with the landlords, a communal body known as the Stornoway Trust. The Trust unanimously agreed that a feasibility study for oil-related development should be carried out, 'without prejudice to any decision' (WHFP 5.10.73). The HIDB commissioned this survey. It reported that the south part of Stornoway harbour, at Arnish point, possessed the most suitable site in the Hebrides for an oil servicing base (HIDB, 1973 p. 16). Olsen had already commissioned a preliminary survey of Arnish point from a consultancy firm. Their report gave a history of the sponsor company, Olsen, which was founded in 1846 and has since expanded into a group with diversified activities. The group retains its original interests in ship-owning but was described as being 'heavily involved in activities such as oil service bases, oil exploration, real estate and freight and forwarding activities'. Fred Olsen himself, who is the Chairman of the Board, has a majority interest in the Aker Group of thirty or so Norwegian companies. This is one of Norway's largest business enterprises, with about 10,000 employees. Aker Group activities include ship building, oil rig construction, machine production and maritime technology. The Report stated that both Fred Olsen (UK) Ltd. and the Aker Group as a whole, intended to co-operate in the Lewis development. Moreover Aker's existing involvement with the North Sea oil industry is emphasised (Shipping Research Services Report 21.9.73; and Janes, 1977, D. 176).

The survey suggested that the project at Arnish should progress through several stages. It was categorically stated that future size and growth depended upon the availability of labour and its ability to acquire the necessary skills. The suggestion was that recruitment should be mainly from the island, but that it would be necessary to import technical expertise at an early stage. The first stage of a large plating shop was planned to provide opportunities for training, and provide Olsens with a notion of the availability and skills of labour. Further production was projected to include steel structures and the fabrication of decks for rigs. The report also stated that Aker would act as industrial and marketing consultants as well as customers 'at least in the initial phases'. In estimates of possible employment build-up the figure of 1,100 jobs by 1982 was given. This can be regarded as symbolically important in the phase leading up to the signing of the lease, for it corresponds almost exactly to the number of unemployed. Despite the fact that the long-term unemployed of Lewis are mostly unskilled, over 45, and regarded as largely unemployable, it was often suggested or implied that the Olsen development would solve the unemployment problem by mopping up this pool of labour.

In the following year, an Impact Survey commissioned by the Stornoway Trust was carried out by the County Planning Officer for Ross and Cromarty, as Lewis was part of this County area at the time. This report was an interesting document as it took into consideration both economic and social aspects of the proposed development. The former aspect was concerned with the provision of jobs. This is characteristic of most economic surveys of the area. But in this case the primary consideration was not the depressing unemployment figures but optimistic 'labour availability'. The most noticeable feature of oil-related impact studies is usually the concern expressed about the affects of new large-scale industrial enterprises on existing industries, and the effects of possible misgrant labour. In the case of the Olsen development unemployment and labour availability were merged because of the high unemployment rate. It was stated in the report that at least 60% of those to be employed would be Lewismen, with an optimistic estimate of

90%. It was stated that immigrant labour would only be necessary in the construction phase. The impact on local industries was regarded as negligible. The Harris Tweed industry was described as 'overmanned'. It was suggested that at present rates of production the industry could be maintained with a loss of one-third of the factory labour force and 50% of weavers. The enterprise was also not expected to be detrimental to either fishing or tourism (C. Pease, 1974).

One crucial feature of the report was a concern to show the economic prospects of the island *without* the project. This element was important for later relationships between island agencies and Olsens. The Tweed industry was described as being 'in recession', fishing as occupying only a small proportion of the workforce, tourism as only seasonal, and prospects of the existing economy alleviating present conditions almost nil. It was also stated that there were no prospects to other projects besides Olsen's in the area. In an Appendix to the Report the Lewis Development Officer commented that without Olsen 'existing industry and industry at present cannot hope to retain over the years a properly balanced community' (ibid Appendix 3, p xvii).

The social life of this 'properly balanced community' was clearly visualised throughout the Report as being based on the occupational pluralism of crofting, even though estimates of available labour did not specifically mention crofting as a category. It should perhaps be emphasised that crofting is implicitly always a category in any consideration of the island's economy, even if only conceptually. As the base line for occupational pluralism that status of crofter retains a paramount importance in the rural life of the island.

It can be claimed that crofts are becoming important more as sites for homes than for their agricultural value (J. Ennew, 1977), and it might be inferred that the activity of crofting is therefore relatively unimportant for the other employment activities of the crofter. Yet those crofts which are not worked are usually inhabited by older people, who would not in any case be available for employment. In many instances the agricultural land of these crofts is sublet to younger crofters who would have been potential Olsen employees. Although full-time employment means that crofters tend to leave previously ploughed land as grazing, and to prefer less demanding sheep to cattle as livestock, there is a whole range of necessary tasks on a croft which demands the presence of the crofter. Communal village activities such as fank days when sheep are moved from infield to outfield or dipped, are pressing obligations which tend to override employer/employee contracts. During the summer months peat cutting for winter fuel assumes a paramount importance, even for many Stornowegians, who may have rights in village peat banks. Similarly, participation in other village or kinship activities such as communions or funerals, have previously been given priority, and disrupt regular working hours in all forms of employment.

55

Most of the crofters who are also in full-time employment commute daily to Stornoway. It has been claimed, perhaps because of the way in which rural life disrupts business activities, that the basic living patterns of the town 'are those of the countryside from which it sprang' (Thompson, 1968, p. 158). Yet Stornoway represents a very distinct area of Lewis despite the fact that quite important officials may be absent from the office, leaving only a secretary who cheerfully states 'he's away at the peats'. There is undoubtedly an antagonism between Stornowegians and rural dwellers. Stornoway is the centre of employment, entertainment, business, government and administration. The difference is summed up in the language distinction. Many Stornowegians do not speak Gaelic, and until recently those who *were* fluent in the language would not always admit the fact, for fear of being labelled a country-dweller. The rural areas, on the other hand, become increasingly dominated by Gaelic speech as one moves further away from the town. For many of those who both live and work in the landward areas of Lewis, even the clipped and nasal accent of Stornowegians speaking English is the subject of comment and imitation, showing a distrust of town-dwellers.

Despite this distinction between town and country, and the obvious fact that some Stornowegians would be available for employment at the Olsen development, all those involved in the Impact Survey of 1974 turned the question of the social effect on Lewis life into a problem of the social effect on crofting. The Report stated that when the occupational pluralism of crofting is successfully managed it provides a traditional pattern of flexibility, which could be maintained under the scheme of shifts which Olsens proposed (op. cit. para. 4.1). The opposition between traditional way of life and modern industry could thus be conveniently mediated. Yet as Hunter has shown crofting far from a static tradition is merely a transitional form (J. Hunter, 1976). The image of the 'crofting way of life' far from being based on an atemporal system, is based on the oral testimony of the generation which came to maturity in the wake of the 1886 Crofting Act. This 'crofting way of life' no longer exists except as a memory, and as a symbol to which the equally symbolic 'oil industry' is opposed. Fundamental changes both legislative and social affected the 'crofting way of life' for 70 years before the arrival of the oil industry.

It is more relevant to the unique cultural aspects of Lewis to consider the issue of Sunday working. This was of more immediate consequence than the 'crofting way of life' and its attendant Gaelic heritage. Sabbath observance is regarded as a sacred trust by the strong pressure group of islanders, who see the island as the last outpost of true Christianity. Thus one Free Church minister, describing the state of religion in Lewis, stated his fear of the superficiality of religion on the mainland. 'Once that comes in it is not religion, it is lost', was his opinion. The Church of Scotland on the mainland, he claimed, does not do much about Sabbath observance unless it is pressured into action by the Free Church or the Free Presbyterian Church. The country as a whole has reached a 'post-Christian stage', with Lewis as the 'last bastion'. He asserted that attack on the ideals of Christianity is made through money and the notion of double-pay for Sunday work. 'That is what they'll seek to do here. There is so much unemployment here, and the temptations are so great. The industrialists are bound to look for profit. It is as if they had seven fields, and could only use six. The blame lies with the love of money and the profit motive. Human nature is the problem, and money is the root of all evil.'

Argument over the issue of Sunday working at the Olsen development was inevitable. The Impact Survey's bland statement that newcomers should not cause abrupt change (op. cit. para. 4.2) was a mere reassurance. The main battle over Sunday working had been fought and won even before the Stornoway Trust commissioned the Survey. Indeed, it was a precondition for the Survey to be carried out. Public disquiet had been partially allayed at a public meeting called by Olsen in 1973, when Michael Thompson, representing the company, stated that the company would try not to give in to commercial pressures entailing seven-day working. Yet it was not until after November 1973 when an assurance was given that there would be no Sunday working except essential maintenance, that the Trust agreed to enter into negotiations for the lease of the land at Arnish.

A major consideration for the Stornoway Trust in its negotiations with Olsen, was the provision of jobs. This reflected the islanders' primary concern at the time. In the public meeting questions like 'How many jobs?' and 'For how long?' were only overridden by the social imperative of Sabbath observance. There was public discussion not only of quantity of employment but also of its conditions. A local socialist on the Lewis Planning Committee stated in 1973 that the Olsen development was:

'a matter of great importance not just to Lewis but to the whole of the Western Isles. I do not think it should be left entirely to the Stornoway Trustees to take the decision. It is a matter of great importance to the new Western Isles Authority to get industry in. We know there is a lot of opposition from commercial and business interests in Stornoway. They are afraid that wages will rise. For too long the workers of Lewis have been on slave wages' (HPS 23.10.73).

The issue of disparity in wage levels between Lewis and the mainland was to rise again in union negotiations with Olsen. The history of this issue reaches back to a report made to the proprietor of Lewis in 1800, which stated categorically that the island potentially provided a supply of cheap labour (J. Headrick, 1800 pp. 24 and 37). It has, to a certain extent, been fostered by island agencies themselves. Advertising material designed to attract industrialists to the island tends to imply that the large pool of unemployed labour means both a low level of acceptable wages and a quiescent workforce. Yet as stated above, this same pool of labour contains many who are regarded as largely unemployable. Indeed, the island population structure is such that it is not only that industrialists need to be lured to Lewis, but young skilled workers who have already migrated to the mainland need to be lured back. The population of Lewis fell from 28,378 in 1921 to 20,739 in 1971, dropping by 5% in the decade between 1961 and 1971 (Comhairle nan Eilean para. 2.1.2). In addition to this net outward migration, there is a tendency towards seasonal or temporary migration. In the summer, men work on the Clyde steamers, and women in mainland hotels, many young men working away from home for up to 20 years before returning to inherit the family croft. Certain members of any one family may therefore be regarded as structurally present but physically absent. One thing which is clearly obvious from census figures and observations is that the island population is an ageing one (ibid, para. 2.1.5). Thus in one remote rural community, sheep husbandry for the entire village has to be carried out by the two or three men who are still active; cattle which require more care, are no longer kept; and both sheep and pasture are deteriorating as a result. In other villages the old and infirm may have to pay for their peats to be cut, because there are not enough young people in the village to perform tasks of community aid. Other elderly people have their visiting son from Edinburgh or Glasgow cut their peats while on annual holiday. In the meantime, the Home Help Service for old people stretches the island's Social Service budget to the limit and leaves little in the way of resources in time or money for other essential services (Comhairle nan Eilean. Social Work Committee 1976, p. 5).

This is the situation referred to by the Development Officer when he stated that the present economic conditions on the island could not maintain a 'properly balanced community'. This was also to the fore in HIDB policy over the Olsen development. The HIDB Oil Project Officer stated to me in 1974 that without Olsen the economic prospects of the island were 'very poor'. When the Stornoway Trust commenced negotiation, they therefore had this factor in mind. As one member of the Trust later stated, the prospect of Olsen in 1973 - 74 was one which allayed the depression caused by redundancies in the Tweed mills, adding that, 'Olsens are important here because they represent jobs not oil. They are a large international company with a good reputation here, and they could be making igloos for all the people cared'. Discussing later the depression of the community he commented that 'the next firm that comes here will not be able to pick and choose, there will be no begging. Luckily the decision to admit Olsens was not a public decision. We never admitted to a begging position. A referendum would have given so sweeping a 'yes' that this would have been shown as a desparate community.

In May 1974 at a Press Conference in Stornoway, it was confirmed that a deal had been concluded between Fred Olsen (UK) Ltd. and the Trust, for the lease of 93 acres of land at Arnish Point for 60 years, with a ten year revision clause.

58

When the Trust finally released a statement concerning the financial terms of the lease 2 years later, it was clear that they had not pressed a hard bargain. But this had never been their primary concern. When Michael Thompson referred at the 1974 press conference to the negotiations, he said 'If we came here with any ideas of an easy ride these were soon dispelled' (WHFP 24.5.74). This could have been merely an empty compliment to the islanders, or might have referred to the conditions of the lease laid down by the Trust which reflect social rather than economic concerns. Many of these conditions were set out when planning permission for the development was given in March 1974. Some of the most important clauses for the islanders related to Sunday working, others were concerned with such matters as rehabilitation of the land, and the use of landscaping and non-reflective colours on the site to reduce visual impact. But the most vital clause was that Lewis men were to be given priority in employment.

Just as it is possible to make different forecasts for the wealth to be derived by the United Kingdom from North Sea Oil, so it was difficult to prophecy the long term effects of the Olsen development on Lewis. An official report made in 1976, stressed the 'branch factory' nature of the development. The report stated that it would be likely to close if there were a contradiction in the Norwegian ship building industry (J. Hunter, 1976). Some islanders admitted this to be the case, realising that the Olsen development, registered as Lewis Offshore, was 'just a wee company on a bit of paper'. Others state that 'the building of tankers in Norway can have little or no bearing on the products of Arnish'. Certainly there was a subtle change in attitude on the island towards the development. This was probably in part a reflection of the disappointment in Scotland as a whole that 'oil' has not led immediately to enormous wealth for all, as production yards, hastily built, now stand idle, or have empty order books for the future. This has happened despite the fact that there has been an increase in overall activity in the country, particularly in high-technology industry. There seems to have been a lack of objectivity in expectations. 'Oil' has been a powerful symbol.

Excitement on the island in the early stages was high. The general manager of Lewis Offshore had 400 enquiries about employment prospects a year before production started, and before any posts had been advertised. Yet on the surface the company settled in very quietly and this may have been the result of the stated policy of 'keeping a low profile' and integrating into community life, on the model established in Norwegian rural areas.

Once Lewis Offshore reached the production phase of its development it became clear that the enterprise was neither controlled nor managed from inside Lewis. But the first general manager has been the only Norwegian in the entire workforce, and local staff were employed to deal with local operatives. Although the Board of Directors regularly visited Stornoway for meetings, it appeared from both press and labour informants that most decisions beyond regular day-to-day occurrences had to be referred to Head Office in London. As anticipated in the Shipping Research Services Report, two of the first three orders were 'internal' ones from the Aker Group, and the plans for these came direct from Norway. Although the buildup of the workforce was steady, by Autumn 1977 it was far short of the total of 1,000. By May 1977 there was a total of 234 employees. Of these about one-third were Stornoway based, showing that the proportion of rural to urban workers reflected the population distribution of the island as a whole. Of the rural dwellers approximately one third were crofters, a factor which might have had important effects on rural life in time, although the absolute numbers in any one rural area were not great. Yet many informants who were combining crofting with oil-related employment seemed to regard their work at Arnish as essentially a part of economic pluralism. Sometimes it was explicitly stated that they had returned to crofting because of a long-felt desire to return, in which Lewis Offshore had been the enabling factor. Others while admitting that their employment at Arnish curtailed time spent in crofting, seemed to regard their wages as an opportunity for capital investment in equipment to make time spent in agricultural activity more efficient.

Even during the most active productive phase in 1977 the enterprise did not seem to be fulfilling the implicit promise of a total solution to the unemployment problem. Only 39% of the workforce had been previously unemployed, and a total of 57 employees had entered or re-entered the Lewis workforce from elsewhere. A further 45 were in their first employment.

Once the initial excitement, with its public meetings and press conferences, had subsided, those Lewis people who were not directly involved in the project, ceased almost entirely to comment either in public or private about the situation. Nor did they seem to treat Lewis Offshore workers with any unusual interest. Even the phrase with which they referred to a Lewis Offshore worker had changed. In 1975 they might tend to say 'he's away at the oil'; in 1976 it would be 'he's away at Arnish'. As the workforce was fairly evenly distributed throughout the island, and the development some way out of town, one seldom saw a group of Lewis Offshore workers together. A van labelled 'Lewis Offshore' visited the town daily to collect the post, but it was not visually obtrusive. A group of operatives drinking in working clothes in one of the Stornoway bars similarly did not attract much attention. Lewismen crofters, fishermen and weavers in working dress wear a uniform navy-blue nylon boiler suit. Arnish working garb was a similar, heavy cotton garment, with the words 'Lewis Offshore' embroidered in small white letters above the pocket. The main distrinction was in the material used, and the absence of the woollen hat which crofters and fishermen tend to wear for outdoor work.

In 1976 and 1977 the minimum of news about Lewis Offshore appeared in local newspapers, and the subjects tended to be 'good news'. Reports would appear of the prospect of new orders for instance, or of a company social event. One strike was in fact covered more extensively in the *Financial Times*, than in either the *Stornoway Gazette* or the *West Highland Free Press*. One press man trying to gain information about an earlier strike, reported being told by the general manager, 'Did I realise the danger I could do to the community at large, because if people knew there was trouble in Lewis, they would be struck off the tenderer's list.' When the company imported 50 highly-paid Norwegian workers in the winter of 1976 - 77, the local press did not make an issue of the fact that this was contrary in principle to the terms of the lease under which local labour should be employed wherever possible. The reason given for this sudden, if temporary, recourse to foreign labour, was that it was needed to complete the first order for a pontoon barge, which was already well behind schedule. However the barge was not launched until well after the Norwegians had returned home after finishing the task, and it was later returned to Arnish because it lacked contracts.

Although the newspapers did not make an issue of the influx of foreign labour it was the subject of local gossip. The huge salaries earned, and the amount spent at local hotels, were apparently common knowledge. It was also frequently noted, with typical Lewis self-deprecation, that the Norwegians had commented on the poor quality of island workmanship. The company claim that it was in need of highly skilled, specially trained operatives had one unusual aspect. The training programme on the site, which was a feature of its early promise to the island, had at that time been suspended for many months. The local press discovered this only by accident, and received no answer to its request for a reason. Indeed, on a visit to the site, I was given the impression that the training programme was still in operation.

If disappointment was felt, it is seldom voiced. The HIDB Oil Projects Officer still expected 800 workers to be employed by 1981 'as in the original plan', and said that the temporary Norwegian workers had been well accepted, initial talk of a strike being resolved with 'a good old British compromise'. The infrequency of open discussion, and lack of information about progress and prospects were regularly commented on in island Council meetings. But there seemed to be little public impetus behind council demands for more co-operation. Perhaps both the apparent absence of interest in Lewis Offshore since construction and production began, and the positive absence for two years of information about the terms of the lease, can be attributed to the same source — the desperation of the workforce in an economically depressed region. The people of Lewis seemed to be suspending judgement on the Arnish development, fearful alike of a repeat of previous boom/ slump developments, and of causing any trouble which might precipitate the cessation of operations by Lewis Offshore. The Stornoway Trust was equally sensitive to the idea of trouble, which might indicate to industrialists that the Lewis labour force is unreliable and thus that the island would be an unsuitable site for other branch factories or developments. The company itself was concerned to limit information on industrial action, because this might prejudice future orders. However it appeared to be assuming a position of power. Having obtained a favourable lease it was able to assume an implicity threatening posture with respect not only to its own employees but to the Lewis labour force as a whole, while maintaining the outward role of benefactor. This appears to have been at the base of the 'British compromise' reached over the Norwegian workers. Thus the company could for a while manipulate the employment situation to its advantage. This included not paying mainland wage rates. The import of discussions over the Norwegian workers seems to have been that if Lewis gained a poor reputation for labour relations and delivery dates, not only would no further industrialists seek sites on the island, but also Lewis Offshore itself might be compelled to cease production. The force of the company's argument lay in the ability to evoke both the fear of unemployment and also the 'good of the community'. Lewis Offshore became temporarily the custodian of the Lewis public image.

There is little doubt that it was in the interest of the company, like that of any manufacturing enterprise, to maintain not only good industrial relations but a *reputation* for good industrial relations. In order to secure this the company set about building a structure of union/management communication on the Norwegian model. However I would argue that the attempt to impose such a model derived from the highly centralised Scandanavian union/management framework, to the decentralised negotiation structure of British Trade Unions, was never entirely successful. This was due in part to the rather unusual industrial situation in Lewis. It was also connected to an increase in industrial action by the Lewis proletariat as a whole, which indicates that Lewis Offshore did not suddenly introduce capitalist relations on to the island but simply reinforced those which were already present.

One Lewis Trades Union official, an incomer to the island, remarked in the course of an interview, that the absence of class consciousness on the island made his work particularly unrewarding. This might be regarded as surprising if one considers that the category of crofter in its present form came about within the political framework of the labour movement in Scotland, through the work of the Highland Land League. In the early history of socialism in Scotland the land issue was as important as the labour issue, and John Maclean described land raids in which crofters staked out plots on sheep farms, as the Highland equivalent of industrial strike action (Hunter, 1975 p. 201). Yet an element of nationalist feeling was always present in the early Scottish labour movement. The labour and nationalist movement have since become largely separate and islanders now tend to channel their feelings of deprivation, through SNP rhetoric towards the English. Conceptually the English have become the middle class, and the class struggle has been subverted by the nationalist struggle. Alongside this confusion of class consciousness at the level of political activity, is a noticeable absence of the 'class' gradation is social relationships which typifies English rural and urban life. Although there is a certain rural/urban antagonism, and although Stornoway itself has well defined residential areas, there is a generalised egalitarian ethos over the island as a whole. This is often overtly expressed in the nature of terms of address. The prefixes 'Mr' and 'Mrs' are seldom used to superiors except where they are newcomers. Individuals are referred to, and addressed by, their Christian name, or even a nickname. Nicknames, particularly, in country areas, are common, because of the small range of Christian names in customery use. This use of familiar modes of address persists in the workplace, and is reflected in the attitude to industrial relations, particularly in the Tweed mills. Thus a shop steward in one of the Stornoway mills stated confidently that he could go directly to 'the gaffer' with problems, adding 'I think the world of him for that'.

Mill workers are members of the TGWU, as are weavers who belong to a special category usually concerned only with periodic peaceful wage negotiations. I enquired about labour relations in discussions with Stornoway officials and businessmen. I was given the reply that industrial conflict was unknown on the island, except in the case of the dockers. This response is of course related to the need to represent the island as a trouble-free zone in industrial relations, as an incentive to possible incoming industrialists. A report in an American newspaper shows this clearly. It describes local 'boosters' (officials and businessmen) seeking American industrial interests, who 'pile each other up in a scrimmage of prose and passion to describe the island's untapped resources', including the fact that there are 'no chronic symptoms of industrial strife' (CI 10.12.72).

The small group of dockers at Stornoway harbour, have borne for some time a reputation for labour problems. In view of ever increasing redundancies this is hardly surprising. The number of dockers has dropped from 200 to 28 in recent years, and the work for those remaining is minimal. The despair felt by the dockers at this situation was somewhat alleviated by the prospect of additional work at Arnish, which is situated on the South side of Stornoway harbour. 'We were building our hopes on that' commented one docker. Yet these hopes proved unfounded. According to the dockers, Michael Thompson gave a verbal undertaking in 1974 that unloading work at Arnish would be available. Yet in 1976 Lewis Offshore was denying any such agreement. They claimed that Arnish was outside the harbour area, and that their own operatives could be used for unloading. There was also some disagreement about the size of gang which would be needed. Lewis Offshore disputed the necessity for the traditional 14-man gang. One factor in the argument was the Lewis Offshore insistence on having only one union involved in the enterprise. Dockers were not members of the AUEW which was the union involved at Arnish. During 1976 the dockers blacked cargo intended for Lewis Offshore, which was being landed at Stornoway harbour. The dispute was only settled after arbitration by a panel appointed by the National Joint Council of the Port Transport Industry. As a very small group the dock workers could apply no real pressure, and their sense of helplessness was almost tangible. Negotiations, one man complained to me, were all 'done by word of mouth. You learn about it later'. It was clear that they felt they had been tricked by Michael Thompson. 'He's smart alright. He's turned it around'. By 1976 some islanders were expressing disappointment that Arnish had not meant instant prosperity for all, but the group of dockers felt it bitterly. 'Arnish was going to do a whole lot, but it hasn't done it. It was all to be local labour, he promised that. But if twenty men are idle when a boat comes in, that isn't employing labour.'

Whatever their history of industrial action, the dockers' recent problems were largely caused by external exigencies, like the advent of a roll-on-roll -off ferry, and the 1975 Dockworkers Bill. As a group they have little negotiating power. But contrary to popular Lewis opinion, they are not the only group of island employees to be involved in recent industrial action. One other group of workers on the island seldom features in descriptions of the economy which concentrate on Harris Tweed and fishing, the 'traditional mainstays' of island economy. Yet in 1971 fishing and fish-processing accounted for only 1.1% of employment in Lewis and Harris, and Harris Tweed for 17% while the construction industry, employing a total of 910 men and women represented 16.4% (Russell op. cit. p. 71). Many of these workers are jobbing builders who are self-employed, but the majority are employed by the council or three large locally operating construction firms.

In many ways it appears that what might be called the new wave of industrial relations on the island started with this group of workers. Significantly one issue which crystallised industrial action was a national one, the use of workers 'on the lump' (self-employed contract labour) on construction sites. The membership of the construction union UCAAT had grown from eight to ninety over the three years preceding 1975, and its members took action in January of that year. One local left-wing newspaper was not slow to make the point that it was the arrival of the oil industry which had precipitated a new era of class consciousness, ending its report with the words 'Gaelic had become a language of industrial action — and not a moment too soon' (WHFP 31.1.75). Although the growth of UCAAT on Lewis did occur while negotiations to commence the Arnish development were taking place, it seems unlikely that the mere promise of oil-related development should produce industrial action as a direct result.

Certain of the subsequent problems within the construction phase at Arnish, and the issues which arose, were a preview of industrial action at Lewis Offshore itself. The two firms subcontracted by Lewis Offshore for the construction phase were the mainland firm Bovis, which won the £2 million contract for building the fabrication shed and offices, and William Tawse which was subcontracted for building the two miles of road to the site. As neither of these firms were subject to the clause in the lease regarding local labour, it was not surprising that some problems arose. Bovis did import some 'foreign' labour, but the islanders were aware that this was temporary. The only real concern was that these temporary migrants might be housed in 'labour camps' which would bring to the island the type of social problems associated with such camps on mainland oil-related construction sites (WHFP 23.8.74).

Nevertheless the most interesting industrial action on Lewis during the first phase of Lewis Offshore's construction and development took place in the Harris Tweed industry. As mentioned above, the weavers form a special branch of the TGWU for negotiation purposes. It is also a 'closed shop' situation in which weavers cannot get on to the distribution lists at the mills without being union members. Officially the weavers have self-employed status, but far from being an independent producer the weaver is in effect the employee of the mill. But neither employment nor a regular wage are guaranteed. From the moment that the mills purchase the requisite wool from the Scottish Wool Marketing Board they are in control of the production process. The weaver is virtually one mill employee amongst others, paid on a piece rate, despite his classification as self-employed. The mills only temporarily lose control while the unwoven tweeds travel back and forth across the island to weaving outworkers. Moreover mills are unable to monitor quality directly, or to control the time spent weaving.

It was over recent 'double width' proposals that weavers, the most important facet of the industry, were given the power to speak and act as a body for the first time. The proposed introduction of double-width power weaving to replace single-width 'hand' weaving shows up some of the anomalies of the weavers' situation while trying apparently to solve them. Harris Tweed production is usually described as hand-weaving, craft production. Yet the looms have automatic shuttles, and are powered by a foot pedal. Although the weaver works by himself in a small shed, he has no part in the design process or even choice of design, nor is any great degree of traditional skill required. From the spinners' point of view the introduction of power weaving is one step in the progressive rationalisation of the industry. It would enable them to gain control over the entire production process. The weaving population could be contained in small factories, called workshops, at three points on the island, and quality control as well as efficient output could be maintained. From the weavers' point of view, double width was a problem which arose suddenly and unsought. But it gave them the power of veto, the first power they have ever had in an industry which has supposedly been run for their benefit for seventy or more years. Despite the fact that double-width proposals were drawn up by the TGWU, HIDB, Harris Tweed Association and spinners it was thought that the Board of Trade would not consent to change the specification of the famour Harris Tweed Trade Mark without the consent of the weavers. Given the power to act as a coherent body against what they conceptualise as the power of the mills the weavers voted an uncompromising 'No' to the proposals. Although this took place in 1976 it cannot be argued that it was precipitated by the arrival of the oil industry. The proposals had taken 5 years to draw up. They were the result of planning towards modernisation and rationalisation, but they were not the result of the introduction of capitalist relations on the island. One small mill of the West side of Lewis is still in the hands of a single family. But both this and the major mills in Stornoway have been involved in both capitalist production process and capitalist market for many years.

The decision to site Lewis Offshore itself at Arnish can only be regarded as the result of decisions taken at the level of international monopoly capital. It is the outcome of what came to be known as the 'oil crisis' of the early 1970's, and of British and Norwegian energy and labour policies. With respect to industrial relations on the island it was announced in May 1976 that the single union on the Lewis Offshore shop floor would be the AUEW. The expressed desire of the enterprise to negotiate with only one union was rational in that it could be presumed to facilitate wage negotiations and avoid demarcation disputes. This rational decision was probably influenced by the Norwegian origins of Lewis Offshore. Scandinavian countries have a reputation for smooth labour relations, despite having experienced their share of industrial strife in the past. They have tended to develop a highly organised system of collective bargaining governed by a well defined and widely accepted body of rules (W. Galenson, 1949, p. 1). The main distinction between the Norwegian and British systems of industrial relations is the degree of centralisation exhibited by the former. Both labour and employers are centrally organised for the purpose of collective bargaining (ibid p. 3). Moreover, because Norwegian labour swiftly achieved a degree of hegemony with the ruling labour party, it had by the 1940's espoused a form of compulsory governmental arbitration of disputes which would meet with opposition in the British setting (ibid, pp. 2 and 4). In 1945 the Norwegian Labour movement gained an absolute parliamentary majority. It was thus forced into a position of responsibility for economic planning (ibid, p. 316). This was combined with the stringent planning policy which was responsible for the Norwegian post-war revival (A. Bourneuf, 1958). The result was a labour force which was obliged to assume responsibility not only for wage and price control, but also for production and social welfare. Gradually an ethos developed in which strikes are regarded by workers as counter-productive with respect to national welfare (Galenson, op. cit. pp. 319 - 229). This contrasts with the decentralised British system of industrial relations typified by demarcation disputes, and an underlying system of shop floor bargaining (R. Hyman, 1972, pp. 36 - 7). It also contrasts with the Lewis system of industrial relations. Despite the ethos of egalitarianism and lack of industrial strife it is characterised by paternalistic control, and in part at least, by a lack of proletarian power and action.

One of the first objectives of the company was to secure a single-union shop floor, which would both avoid demarcation disputes and enable it to negotiate at one time, on an annual basis, with all shop-floor employees. These were referred to by management by the single term 'operative'. Management also appeared committed to establishing a pattern of equal responsibility. To these ends it came to an agreement with the AUEW, (in preference to the TGWU and the Boilermakers' Society), and made certain symbolic statements about egalitarianism in the workplace. Principally these consisted of building a union room next to that of the Personnel Manager, and having a single dining room for all employees including staff. It is possible that management expected no trouble once such precautions had been taken, particularly in view of Lewis' reputation as a relatively strike-free area. But a subtle attitude of 'them and us' remained. A further factor in industrial unrest at Arnish was that many of the workforce were expatriates who returned from working at Nigg Bay, or one of the other mainland construction yards. In the course of their employment there, many had gained their first real experience of Trades Union activity, usually with the TGWU of the Boilermakers' Society. The atmosphere of labour relations in the mainland construction yards is militant, and many Lewis expatriates returned with the knowledge of the potential of union power, but little knowledge of the processes of negotiation. Whatever the causes, the AUEW at Lewis Offshore was particularly active, despite a high initial turnover of personnel at shop-steward level. Interest in union affairs was strong and meetings well attended. Some disputes led to strikes or threatened strike action. They exhibited the same concerns which arose in the construction industry. Travel-to-work problems were an initial cause of annoyance, for public transport on the island is very poor, and does not in any case cover the two miles of road which lead out to Lewis Offshore. In the early stages there were grumbles about conditions before the site was fully operational. However the main source of contention was the disparity between island and mainland rates of pay, despite the fact that Lewis Offshore wages were high by island standards. Frequently the course of a dispute was marked by misunderstandings. A conflict of attitude between company and labour highlighted the inherent antagonisms outlined above. The company policy anticipated a more co-operative 'responsible' attitude from labour, while operatives were used either to the paternalism of Lewis employers or to the more direct confrontation of British industry.

What is clear is that the situation in Lewis is not one in which a new set of capital/labour relationships have intruded on a pre-capitalist form with the arrival of Lewis Offshore. Unionisation has proceeded apace over the past few years in a situation which was previously typified by capitalist relationships with a disorganised workforce. It cannot be argued that the arrival of Lewis Offshore created a new proletariat. Nor can it correctly be stated that the process of unionisation was accelerated by oil-related industry. Gaelic may well have become, symbolically at least, the language of industrial relations. But it was a language of political rhetoric in the nineteenth century for the Highland Land League, and for the Labour party on Lewis in the twentieth. A new Gaelic-speaking proletariat has not been created. But unionisation, as capitalist activity on Lewis becomes more intense in all spheres, has made the already existing proletariat more effective.

The long term effects of large-scale capitalist industrial enterprise in the shape of oil-related industry are not in any case in the realm of industrial relations. Events seem to have followed the relentless Lewis pattern of boom slump which has characterised the economic life of the island for 200 years. In 1977 it became clear that Lewis Offshore was having difficulty filling its order book. By the end of that summer employees were expressing grave doubts about the future. The effects of the enterprise on employment figures had been minimal. Although the percentage of registered unemployed had fallen to 12% the Department of Employment considered this to be due to an increase in Tweed production, and the success of the Government's Job Creation Scheme.

Finally management was forced to admit that further production at Arnish seemed unlikely. In April 1978 redundancy notices were issued to all employees. The degree of solidarity achieved by the workforce in the short life of the company was then revealed. Immediately upon receiving the news the shop stewards announced their intention of keeping the workforce together. An Action Committee consisting of shop stewards, members of Comhairle nan Eilean and the Stornoway Trust was formed. It pledged itself to the task of finding further orders for the company.

In view of the lack of activity in oil-related fabrication as a whole, the task of the Action Committee was impossible. There was little it could do to delay the collapse of the Arnish Development. The Committee seems to have lost impetus in the face of an implacable economic situation, and the workforce has inevitably dispersed. Island reaction appears to be muted. The *Stornoway Gazette*, as is its policy, stated the 'facts' of the case without comment. There were no subsequent letters in the press, although almost every other island event usually heralds lengthy correspondence. Perhaps the people of Lewis feel relieved that they suspended judgement, and now find no necessity to write an epitaph.

NOTE: Since this article was written there have been further developments. Lewis Offshore has secured a contract for limited service work. Yet this does not affect the argument put forward here. The company is importing skilled labour to the island for this contract and only a small proportion of the previous, local labour force is being re-employed.

*REFERENCES*

(a)   *Newspaper abbreviations*
      CI —    *Cinncinnati Enquirer*
      SG —    Stornoway Gazette
      WHFP — West Highland Free Press

(b)   *Unpublished Sources etc*
      Comhairle nan Eilean          *Aithnis na Roinne* (Regional Report) for Submission to the Secretary of State under Section 173 of the Local Government (Scotland) Act, 1973.

      Comhairle nan Eilean          Social Work Committee 1976: *Home Help Services in the Western Isles.*

      HIDB: 1973:                   *Offshore Industry Supply Bases in Lewis and Harris.* Study by Babtie, Shaw and Morton, Consulting Civil and Structural Engineers, 95 Bothwell Street, Glasgow.

      Hunter, J, 1976 (A):          *The Social Impact of Oil Related Industrialisation on the North of Scotland, Lewis, the Current Situation.* Type script report prepared for the Scottish Office.

      Manpower Services             *The Discovery of North Sea Oil and Gas.*
      Commission, 1975:

      Pease, G, 1974:               *Impact Study on Planning Application by Messrs Fred Olsen at Arnish Point, Stornoway.* Ross & Cromarty C.C.; County Offices, Dingwall.

      Shipping Research             *Stornoway Offshore.* Report from Fred Olsen, Ltd.
      Services, 1974:

(c)   *Published Sources*
      Bourneuf, A, 1958            *Norway, The Planned Revival*: Harvard University Press.
      Ennew, J, 1977.              The Changing Croft: *New Society.* 16th June.
      Galenson, W, 1949           *Labour in Norway*; Russell and Russell.
      Headrick, J, 1800.          *Report on the Island of Lewis*: London.
      HMSO, 1973                   *North Sea Oil and the Environment.*
      Hunter, J, 1975             The Gaelic Connection; *Scottish Historical Review* Vol. 54, 1976 (b) *The Making of the Crofting Community;* J. Macdonald.

      Hyman, R, 1972              *Strikes*, Fontana.
      Janes, 1977                  *Janes European Companies.*
      Newett, P, 1977             Occupational Pluralism in Crofting, *Scottish Journal of Sociology*, Vol. 1 no. 1.

      Russell, W, 1972            *In Great Waters*; HIDB.
      Thompson, F, 1968           *Harris and Lewis*, David and Charles.

# 5 Local Authority Accommodation of Oil-Related Developments in East Ross

*Isobel Grigor*

The early work I did in this area was concerned with the implications for Local Authority housing policy of recent oil-related developments in Easter Ross.

The question of housing is a particularly interesting one in this context, representing as it does a fairly clear indication of the attitude of Ross and Cromarty County Council towards the county's apparently rising prospects of industrial development.

When it became clear that, through HIDB promotional efforts and negotiations at Central Government level the provisions of regional economic policy and local apsirations of development for the Moray Firth area were to begin to be realised by the construction, starting in 1967, of an aluminium smelter at Invergordon, the main task facing the County Council was the provision of infrastructure sufficient to support increased commercial, industrial and population pressures.

At this point, the County's housing policy was defined by the requirement of meeting needs which would arise in the event of the smelter starting production — i.e. the anticipated, identifiable shortfall in housing resources measured against housing demand had to be met. As it turned out, the smelter began production just as a world excess in production and a consequent decline in world demand began to bite. Thus BA Co. opened only at half-production, with the result that around 65 houses intended for permanent workers at BA Co. were not immediately required. A Council furrore ensued, the excess housing providing ammunition for those who had opposed the Council's unreserved welcome of the Smelter. Subsequently, the Local Authority house-building programme was stopped, pending the allocation of excess stock or the identification of an alternative clear case of housing need.

As no further developments appeared to be in prospect, which would build on the basis established by BA Co. at Invergordon, or on the new industrial credibility germanating in the Moray Firth area, the County Council, in late 1967, embarked on a policy of self-help and set about systematically promoting the advantage and opportunities waiting in the area for industrial investment. At this point the Council declared as its stated objective the introduction of "major industrial developments". Thus an approach towards the promotion of industrial development was formed, for the Moray Firth, generally, and in particular forEaster Ross:

1) at National level, by Central Government's work in directing BA Co. to Inver-gordon, and by the inclusion of the Highlands and Islands in specific policies for regional development (principally; Inquiry into the Scottish Economy, 1960 - 1961: Report of a Committee appointed by the Scottish Council (Development and Industry) under the Chairmanship of J. N. Toothill, and; The Scottish Economy, 1965 - 1970 — A Plan for Expansion, Cmnd. 2864).;

2) by the subsequent establishment, under the Highlands and Islands Development (Scotland) Act, 1965, of a specific agency whose task was "for the purpose of assisting the people of the Highlands and Islands to improve their economic and social conditions and of enabling the Highlands and Islands to play a more effec-tive part in the economic and social development of the nation" — and, then, the identification of the Moray Firth as one of three growth areas singled out for special efforts as the sites most conducive to development from which centres benefit would spread, in time, to other areas (whether the identification of these growth centres represents the recognition of on-going industrial location patterns or of an intended policy of directing future investment remains another ques-tion);

3) by the County Council's stated intention of promoting major industrial develop-ment in Easter Ross, which had followed earlier statements, of a general nature, in preparation of the 1964 County Development Plan concerning the perceived need of establishing a strong industrial manufacturing base in the County. After the arrival of BA Co. at Invergordon and the feeling that HIDB had dis-charged its responsibility as far as Ross and Cromarty was concerned, at least for the time being, the Council was united in its support of the proposal to engage in a reinvigorated promotional effort. The East Ross Working Group was form-ed, comprising a planner, an architect and an engineer who liaised with the full Council through one single member, and whose task it was to identify com-panies whose requirements would be most completely met in the East Ross area. They would then approach the company directly and all subsequent negotiations were carried out by the Working Group on behalf of the County Council. In this way it was possible to co-ordinate the responsibilities of different Council departments in terms of the companies' stated requirements. This arrangement aroused the professional jealousies of the departments within the County Coun-cil, who saw their powers transcended at a time when the challenge was greatest, so the group was disbanded.

One major avenue through which the Council can articulate this general policy intent is through its responsibility for the provision of housing. By the late 1960's, in addition to zoning excess land for industrial development — so to avoid "un-necessary delay" in the event of serious enquiries being made by potential develop-ers (industrialists) — the Council repeatedly stated its intention that programmes of house building be undertaken which would serve to (a) be seen to serve the needs of current enquiries, and (b) grant the area a new legitimacy in the eyes of firms which might in the future consider East Ross on a shortlist of sites favourable for investment.

In line with this general promotional exercise, in 1967, the County Council set up a Development Department, and the HIDB commissioned the Jack Holmes Planning Group in Glasgow to produce a "sub-regional plan which will demonstrate the development potential and population capacity of the Moray Development Area'. This report, 'The Moray Firth – a plan for growth', has been severely criticised for its failure to examine the feasibility of even likelihood of this area ever achieving the level of growth on which its proposals of settlement size and organisation were predicted. Yet this was never the Planning Group's task. They were to produce an end-of-the-century-type plan describing how the population should be arranged given a future of economic growth. The figures of population growth based on projections assuming a factor of 30 jobs per acre in all except large scale process plants are inevitably hypothetical. By 1972, with the added credibility won by the decisions by M. K. Shand, pipe-coaters, and Highlands Fabricators, platform contractors, to settle in the area, the hypothetical calculations of Jack Holmes concerning the population increase which could be contained in the Moray Firth region had become the basis of County Council forward planning strategy on the zoning of land for industry and housing. 'The main factors which may act against it (the attainment of target employment levels taken from Holmes) are the rate at which housing and other infrastructure can be made available and the level of 'community satisfaction' which is achieved.'

Broadly speaking, then, the housing policy which had earlier been addressed to meeting the needs of a specific industrial enterprise (BA Co.) now evolved to represent an articulation of the Local Authority's attitude towards industrialisation – that infrastructure be provided in excess of existing needs thereby to enhance the locational advantages of the East Ross area and to legitimist this area as a site for industrial investment. Put crudely, one could say that for Ross and Cromarty County Council, houses means jobs. Once the houses could be guaranteed now or in the future, then there was every possibility that the desired levels of employment could be achieved.

Yet I would argue that this policy, characterised by an attitude of accommodation on the part of the County Council was never actually executed. Instead, events arose, concerning the unanticipated arrival on the scene of major oil-related developments which transcended any ideas the County Council had had concerning the direction developments should take.

The argument I hope to advance will seriously question the control a Local

Authority can exercise over the means to be adopted towards the given end of industrial development.

I suggest that once the general philosophy of development via industry had been adopted, and thereby legitimised, and once the Council had taken the attitude of preparation, support and accommodation, thereafter it could only wait to see who was interested in buying the local resources which were up for sale. The Council's commitment to building an industrial future meant that the merit in the long term of any potential developer remained unquestioned. Far from the Council examining proposals of different firms to consider how they might contribute to the objectives of development found in the County Development Plan or subsequent statements of Council policy, instead, by 1972, the original Development Plan had been altered in order to meet the needs of whichever firm said at the time that it was interested in settling in Easter Ross, but not within the limits of statements in the Development Plan. The general line of thought seems to have been that it wouldn't do anyone any good to turn down a proposal simply because objections could be found to its acceptance in a Plan prepared in 1964. The County needed industry. The firms making application for planning permission wanted to come to this area, therefore it would accomplish little good to force them to look for an alternative site. By 1973, so many revisions had been made to the original Development Plan that the Secretary of State for Scotland who had to arbitrate every proposed amendment, asked Ross and Cromarty County Council to undertake a complete reappraisal of its development plans in light of past events, by which future movements could be assessed.

It is interesting to note that whereas the proposals of the 1964 Development Plan concerning details regarding the most appropriate siting on amenity, environmental, social and economic grounds were regarded as being of lesser consequence than the benefit accruing to proposed developments of an alternative location, yet the decision arrived at in each of the Public Inquiries was made on the grounds of whether it would be in accordance with the principle of the Development Plan — the pursuit of 'major industry quickly'. Thus, although the specific detail of amendments to the Development Plan was stimulated by the companies' interests, it remained to be justified by the County Council on the grounds that it constituted 'major industry'.

In 1971 and 1972 two major decisions were made which announced the arrival of oil-related developments on the shores of the Cromarty Firth. First of all, in 1971, just as construction activity tailed off at the Invergordon smelter, a new opening seemed to present itself with promises from Highlands Fabricators of jobs in platform construction at Nigg for 600 immediately and for 40 or 50 years. Then in the spring 1972, M. K. Shand, a pipe-coating firm, were granted permission

73

to use 50 acres of zoned land, previously leased by BA Co., for coating pipes to serve the North Sea oil fields — offering jobs 'for approximately 120 men for 15 years'. Crucially for Easter Ross, the activities of both of these firms enter the production phase immediately. There is no preliminary phase, except in ancilliary areas, of construction during which time is in hand when preparations can be made for the accommodation of the workforce to be employed during production. This is unusual for industries starting production in a green field site.

A discrete break between construction (during which temporary accommodation is usually provided for the duration of the job by the contractor) and production had occurred in the case of BA Co's smelter — allowing the Council sufficient time to meet anticipated housing need. But with the arrival of Hi-Fab at Nigg and M. K. Shand at Invergordon, Ross and Cromarty County Council found on its doorstep two extremely large employers which were starting production immediately and a serious shortage of housing for the workforce.

Early in negotiations with the County Council, representatives of M. K. Shand made it clear that the Local Authority should not consider their labour force when assessing housing need. It was clear from the start of their involvement in the area that employment would be fluctuating and cyclical, always depending on their winning a contract. The company employs men on a short-time, contract, basis. They recruit men, often from the industrial centres in the South and lay them off when the contract is completed. Shand initially used a caravan site to house their workers for as long as they were in the area. Then they brought a work camp into use. Soon they were employing 600 men, and with cyclical peaks and troughs this has fallen as low as the maintenance core of around 100. This core, employed more or less permanently now, are mainly resident in the area in conventional housing. They are a mixture of men who have come into the area and settled down and local (i.e. Highland) men who either previously lived in the Invergordon/ Alness area or have moved from elsewhere in the Highlands — many from the Islands.

This was the first job of this sort undertaken by M. K. Shand for the North Sea oil fields. The high numbers employed in early days and the extreme nature of labour fluctuations are attributed by the company to their lack of expertise. 'We could do as much work now with half as many men in half the time.'

With Highlands Fabricators, the County Council faced à dilemma. The County Council were vitally concerned that this, the only industry in prospect, be a means to the realisation of their stated intention of introducing large-scale industrial development to the area, not a temporary intrusion, not a passing fancy. Yet, in essence, its nature was not very different from that of M. K. Shand. Its contracts, being physically and technically of greater magnitude, it presents a different scale of the same phenomenon. Greater numbers are employed at any one time — 3,000 at its peak, and the fluctuations in the course are more sharp. Like M. K. Shand, Highlands Fabricators were novices in the field, learning as they went along, and as they learnt, becoming able to increase efficiency and trim off surplus employment so that the head-line-screaming days of 1974 will never be repeated. Now, as with M. K. Shand, a relatively small local labour force is employed for the unskilled or semi-skilled work, and numbers of skilled men on a short-term basis from the industrial centres of the South as their skills in shipbuilding and sheet-metal working become more valuable at different stages in the production process.

As far as the County Council were concerned, in 1971 - 72 there occurred a huge escalation in industrial activity. As a means of gaining a new creditability for the future of the area as an industrial centre Highlands Fabricators and M. K. Shand, the only large-scale concerns on the horizon, were vital. Any suggestion that these works represent a stop gap (in recognition of their transitory nature) in the movement towards establishing a viable industrial sector must be a post hoc rationalisation — although it is in this light that these events are now commonly regarded. No. For the Council, this was development in the making. On the basis of these developments, future industries would be set and others would surely follow now that the Cromarty Firth had been put on the industrialists' map.

This attitude becomes most clear in the course of Council housing provision. We have seen how, after the County Council began to increase its efforts to promote the Cromarty Firth for the introduction of industry on a large scale, its housing policy was dictated by the desire to build in excess of existing, identifiable needs in order to attract industry in the future.

In fact this policy could never be carried out since, almost before they could draw breath, Highlands Fabricators and M. K. Shand had started production at their respective sites. Accommodation of the Shand workforce confirmed as the firm's responsibility, the Council had had to decide, only months earlier whether to consider Hi-Fab's employees as permanent residents in the tradition of production workers (therefore the responsibility of the Council) or as a temporary construction labour force. Conditioned by the Council's insistence that Hi-Fab be not a temporary intrusion but a herald of things to come, the housing policy evolved, as an extension of the policy of building in excess for the future, but now in response to the real, perceived, need which had arisen at Nigg, that as many houses be built as quickly as possible — first of all for the Hi-Fab workforce, then for the added needs which would result from subsequent development (starting, if we remember, from virtually no reserve since the house-building programme had been stopped after completion of the smelter construction showed up an excess of housing). Up

75

until this time the policy of building in excess for the future had never gone beyond the point of rhetoric. Now, when the Council reopened its building programme it was to find that before it could begin to build as a hedge for the future it had first to meet the immediate needs it perceived at Nigg. Concerned by the Highland Local Authorities' apparent inability to meet housing needs, which had been compounded by the loss of large numbers of building workers to platform construction, the Scottish Office stepped in to co-ordinate efforts and to guarantee the provision of finance in special cases. So far as the Cromarty Firth was concerned, Scottish Office intervention made little impact on the general 'build as many as quickly as possible' philosophy — so that in October, 1974, the following statement was made by the HIDB in a report to this liaison between the Scottish Office and the Local Authorities, the Moray Firth Working Party:

' . . . information collected by SDD from potential employers and housing factors, indicates a reasonably firm demand for 7,200 houses in the area. This includes the additional needs for committed industry up to the end of 1976. In addition, there is a possible demand for up to 1,400 extra houses in the Easter Ross area to serve industry that may come to the area. The timing of this possible extra demand is difficult to predict: it is unlikely that the full amount will be needed in the near future; on the other hand, some of the demand could materialise almost overnight if the use of approved industrial sites suddenly commences.'

The Scottish Special Housing Association were recruiting by the Scottish Office and with the blessing of the Local Authorities to provide houses for key workers. So, too, was the Albyn Housing Society, by BA Co., consent of the County Council, to build additional needs at the smelter now that it had begun full production with a rising demand for aluminium. Thus, the situation at this time (1973 - 74) regarding housing provision was one of organized chaos. The Scottish Office, Local Authorities and BA Co. directing a build, build, build programme to be undertaken by SSHA, Local Authorities and their contractors and the Building Society.

In May of 1973, it was estimated that of the expected new job opportunities (total 12,700), 9,100, or 75%, would be taken up by incomers to the area. Allowing for natural increase and normal rates of migration, this amounts to a population increase of 21%. The demand for housing generated by the 9,100 incomers was calculated to be 5,000 dwellings; one house for every 1.8 new jobs.

At this time, which was during the building of the platform at Nigg, and included developments for pip-coating at Invergordon, various supply industries, an increased demand for labour in the building and construction trades and an estimated increase of 1,800 jobs on the service sector, it was calculated that from 1973 to 1975, at best, the number of houses which would become available to meet all categories of need was 2,025, while estimated maximum needs for incoming workers, alone, would be a total of 4,300.

Great efforts were made to help ensure that the shortfall in housing provision could be met. There was a significant shift in the allocation of finances by the SDD for capital expansion, so that East Ross could enjoy a greater rate of progress in its capital works programme than other areas of the County.

Normally, it takes at least 2 months to process initial preparatory work for a building project — and even then the proposals are often returned by the SDD for revision. During this period, however, approval for projects was being given by the SDD within 24 hours. Money was no object. Crises in the building industry were by-passed. Workers were imported from the South. The area was made exempt from restrictions imposed by the 3-day week which resulted from the power crisis and the miners' action. A national cement shortage was rendered ineffective. The SDD paid for imported cement. It had been difficult to interest Scottish builders in East Ross contracts. They naturally gravitated towards the concentration of lucrative contacts in the South. So the County Council bought 400 - 500 wooden, rapid construction houses from Norway. As an exercise in management and organisation and in the terms demanded by the Councillors, this was excellent. Yet any questions of social factors appear not to have been considered.

In Balintore, for instance, a small village on the East Coast, 176 houses were grafted onto the existing community. This not only induced the very kind of mushroom development which is normally avoided at all costs, and expansion beyond the community's natural containment area, but in addition, no interest was shown in the requirements of a new community by the provision of recreational facilities.

In order to ensure the greatest speed, only two types of houses were built — 4-or 5-apartment. The consequences of this could be serious. Others, who do not qualify for a 4/5 appartment house are selectively not catered for; and the risk is high of creating an artificial social mix with the development of separate communities.

In admittedly difficult circumstances the County Council were interested in houses and the numbers thereof. Now there is little money available to compensate for past social and environmental deficiencies in these rapid-construction — high-density estates.

If expediency defined the direction that housing provision should take, and it would be a mistake to underrate the financial and other pressures experienced by the Council at this time, then it was an expediency informed by pragmatism.

A policy of catering for housing needs with temporary accommodation was rejected. Any plans submitted by the firms for the construction of workcamps were turned down although, latterly, this policy has been relaxed to cater for the needs of the men in large numbers who are 'travelling men' employed by M. K. Shand and Hi-Fab (these are the contract-hired men who return to their homes, and often their families when they are paid off). Yet this relaxation was only made after sufficient houses had been built to cater for these men if they had qualified for, or wanted, a house.

It was thought that the provision, on a wide scale, of workcamps or caravan site facilities would undermine the very possibility of developing a credible face of long term industrial opportunities or of a stock of infrastructure resources for the future Once committed to accepting the employment arising from oil-related developments as an essential component of their development policy, the building of large permanent settlements was a necessary consequence.

As it turned out, the public debate around this question was never expressed, as far as I can find, in these terms. Instead, the issue became translated into terms of being pro-or anti-development. The possibility of being generally in favour of broadening the base of the Highland economy by encouraging industry while still challenging the wisdom of building this development on oil was not entertained. It is interesting to note that in Ross and Cromarty one senior official asked to be allowed to retire prematurely, and another resigned on account of quarrels they had with the Council's administration of these events.

Some saw in this just as heavy and unbalanced a dependence on one industry as had been the Highland experience in times past — even more vulnerable to the influence of market forces and political factors than most. Thus, any pressure to regard oil as a special phenomenon — of current interest to the local economy, but separate from the reasoning applied to the construction of long term development plans, and to analyse its particular demands in detail — implying that the kind of permanent accommodation which had been provided was, perhaps, inappropriate to the nature of the existing, felt, need, was regarded as an attempt to undermine the very concept of development as it was understood for local policy.

The question of single men is an interesting one in this context. It shows clearly the way in which the Council's perception of housing need, its response to recent oil-related developments, is tempered by its commitment to establishing an industrial base in Easter Ross. There is no objective, unequivocal measure of housing need. Rather, it represents a choice of priorities made on political, economic and social grounds, concerning which groups are to be encompassed by the disbursing of Council resources.

In the case of East Ross, it was decided that no need existed to provide housing for single men. Single men are a mixed bunch. They comprise those now termed 'travelling men', who are permanently resident elsewhere but are employed on a contract basis in East Ross, and married men who have no residence elsewhere.

The Council declared that it would be their policy to provide family houses, but specifically not temporary accommodation in hostels or workcamps for single men — always assuming a single man inevitably regards his work in East Ross as temporary as does the Council. They said that when large numbers of single men had been employed by the Hydro Electric Board when bringing electricity to the Highlands they had had no accommodation problems. Many had rented properties. Many had taken lodgings in people's houses. Others had been housed by the HEB on site. The same should apply now.

An administrative distinction was formed, therefore, whereby single men became, for accommodation purposes, classed as temporary construction workers — and the responsibility of the company employing them. On the other hand, family men, on account of their marital status alone, were accepted as permanent residents and entitled to Local Authority housing. Whereas the Council perceived no need to house single workers, whom they considered to be temporary residents, with little potential so far as achieving a stable industrial population was concerned, the need clearly did exist that some group should consider these men sufficiently valuable to their ends to arrange for their accommodation. Highlands Fabricators commissioned two liners for this purpose.

Local Government reorganisation in 1974/75 brought an important change to Easter Ross. Around this time, there had been a change in national economic circumstances which brought cuts in public spending and higher interest rates. This coincided with a development slump and little sign of any building upon the industrial base within the County, or upon the infrastructure base.

With regionalisation, housing has become the main responsibility of the District Council, while the Regional Council is responsible for, among other things, Planning and Development (although minor, rural, matters can be disposed of at District level) and Finance.

The District Council found a large number of houses in excess of current or anticipated needs — a situation the County Council had talked about and striven for over the previous three years. Yet a large part of this excess can be attributed to

the failure of firms to build upon the present industrial base and to the greatly reduced employment levels of the two big companies.    From a peak of 3,300 in
1974, Hi-Fab had settled to an average of 1,700.    They now have accommodation
for 420 travelling men on contract work and many of these 1,700 commute daily in
transport provided by the firm.    Similarly, M. K. Shand, who employed 725 in
January, 1975, a year later employed 54 and currently employ 104,200 is a fair
average when they have a contract to meet.    This falls to around 60 when they do
not.    Subcontractors' numbers rise and fall accordingly.    Shands are finding that
there is at present a rundown in activities.    Falling demands has meant that finding
contracts is more difficult and the contracts are generally smaller, requiring labour
for a shorter time.    Even allowing for increased activity in the service and commercial sectors, it is clear that housing need has met and surpassed largely on account
of a dimenution in housing demand coincidental with a rise in housing resources.
On development issues, the policy of the District Council differs from that of the
County Council or of the Regional Council.    The District Council is keenly critical
of the County Council's commitment to development through oil.    They would
prefer to attract a 'humbler' size of industry for its 'intrinsically more human scale',
and, with, it is hoped, a longer life.    They oppose the policy of providing infrastructure generally, and housing in particular, as a carrot to industry, whereas this
had been the cornerstone of the County Council's development policy, that the
provision of infrastructure resources — of which housing was a major instance — be
an incentive to potential developers.

Having made a thorough assessment of the housing stock and building programmes in hand, the District Council resolved that to assent to proposed building
projects would be to ignore the fact that they were moving into a flat period for
expansion or development.

The building programme was cut, and the District Council's policy was framed —
that it should build for existing, identifiable needs, what it terms, 'real need'. The
District insists that, in the event of future industrial development occurring, the
SSHA should be asked to provide system-built units for the labour force.    It assumes that the gap will exist between the start of construction and production
which will allow two or three years for the provision of housing in line with accurate measurements of the number required.

The SSHA is well suited to large-scale developments on green-field sites, but
they, too, were nonplussed by the situation arising and developing so unpredictably
in Easter Ross.   Working almost in the dark, they built to the figures prescribed by
the various Town and Burgh and the County Council all of which has responsibility
for housing in their own territories.    The SSHA have felt the effects of falling demand most seriously.    Their rents being considerably higher than standard Council

house rents, it is their experience to be the first to find that they hold a stock of surplus housing. Some have been bought on an agency basis by the District Council since it took office, but many remain unoccupied. By contrast with the District Council, the Regional Council, comprising the most ardent supporters of oil-related developments from the old Ross and Cromarty County Council, through its planning and development functions, is working actively to attract further large-scale industrial development. In its latest policy statement, the Region described plans for a series of petro-chemical industries, with series employment of construction labour and concurrent industrial developments to be built between 1977 and 1991 — always keeping the construction force from exceeding 3,000, so that developments cause the same construction labour, and at no time implying a high proportion relative to permanent employment prospects. The provision of housing in line with development prospects remains crucial for the Regions. Indeed, there is considerable disquiet in some quarters over the lack of agreement on this point between the District and Regional Councils: There can be no guarantee that developments of the sort that arose in 1971/72 might not again occur. There may be sufficient slack in the existing housing stock to avoid a recurrence of the same kind of desperate build — or the Region may be forced to regard these developments, as the District would, like, as a temporary phenomenon. The District maintains that there can be no sufficient guarantee of development occurring in response to the Region's promotional efforts of the scale or in the time predefined in policy statements which can justify the provision of advance housing. The Region, in turn, insists that without this housing, then the chances of ever being successful in promotion of the area are considerably reduced by the disincentives of the delays which future firms investing in the area would inevitably meet.

We can see from the following quotation, taken from the recently published Settlement Policy of the Highland Region, how the Region regards the issue of housing and the way in which construction labour remains, strictly, a means to an end:

'The amount of permanent employment (c. 2,000 jobs, including services) created by the development of a petro-chemical complex . . . will not in itself lead to any substantial increase in the local resident population. This is because of factors such as the prospects for existing industry and numbers of school leavers requiring jobs. Population growth will depend in part upon the availability of housing and the extent to which commuters and construction workers are encouraged to settle down permanently in Easter Ross . . . The key factor, however, is policy towards providing accommodation for construction workers.

' . . . This accommodation is to be at the level of . . ."normal needs" plus, possibly, an allowance to retain the force needed to provide capacity for further population growth during the 1990's. . . . Where the construction force exceeds this second level however (that needed to provide capacity for further population growth during the 1990's), it *must* be housed temporary bachelor accommodation.'

For the Regional Council, it is vital that current proposals from Cromarty Petroleum Co. succeed in bringing an oil refinery to Nigg. Despite statements during the related Public Inquiry that the Company did not intend to extend its operation from refining into petro-chemicals works, the Region insists that is is on this basis that the future petro-chemicals industries will develop. The current situation in Easter Ross, where unemployment is higher than it has ever been, at 14.3, and where houses lie empty and more become unoccupied, is attributed by the Region to delays in the planning process met by the refinery proposals. The application for planning consent to build a refinery at Nigg was first submitted in 1973, and only finally approved in 1977. If it had gone ahead as intended, it is said, the hiatus in developments in East Ross would not have occurred. The criterion by which approval was finally given was the extent to which this proposal met the principle of development applied to East Ross. Supporters of the refinery project are angry that objections over points of detail should have forestalled the whole operation once the principle of development had been satisfied. Some would like to see this division between points of principle and of detail applied through the planning process so that once a proposed development was seen to meet the general principle of development then subsidiary points of detail could be thrashed out, not at a full-scale Public Inquiry, but locally, even by the Planning Committee. On the other hand, there is widespread anxiety throughout the area, as evidenced in the local press, that the promotion of industry is coming to be beyond question and that social and environmental issues are not represented in the debate over any case of industrial development. It is feared that any further moves to legitimise the principle of industrial development would exacerbate the present devaluation of questions of the implications of proposed developments for the welfare of the community.

Up to this point we have seen that, despite philosophical statements to the effect that housing be a resource to induce developments, the course of industrial events has meant that housing policy has been dictated totally by short-term expediency, albeit an expediency influenced by the intention on the part of the Local Authority that these provisions lay the basis for the future. Indeed, the Council's willing accommodation of these developments has probably meant that it was more prepared to meet the sudden, unanticipated, unpredictable housing needs which arose. Yet, in the long term, its uncritical welcome of these developments and its unequivocal philosophical commitment to an assumed permanency and the policy implications of this may be open to serious question.

The same attitude of accommodation is found in the old County Council's execution of the planning function. In many ways, an examination of the planning process may be more illuminating to the general issue of Local Authority reaction to proposed developments since decisions on housing policy only makes sense in the context of the associated planning strategy. In fact the above account of Ross and Cromarty's housing policy and the way in which it evolved reflects a parallel course of decision-making in the planning process. In Ross and Cromarty, from 1968 onwards, the stimulus for all significant planning decisions has been provided by the company making application for planning consent — albeit in parallel with statements of policy from the County Council emphasising and re-emphasising the Council's predisposition towards large-scale industrial development  and zoning actions by the Council to prepare additional land for industrial and residential use.

First on the scene was the Occidental Petroleum Corporation of Los Angeles who intended building an oil refinery. Following a Public Inquiry which found in favour of the proposed development, the Company proceeded with feasibility tests — only to disappear from the scene. It was later to emerge that the Company had been unable to find sufficient finance to turn their option on the land into reality. The next application of this sort came from Grampian Chemicals for a petro-chemicals products works at Nigg Bay. Approval was given to the company to proceed with this project, as they had requested on land different to that previously zoned, because of 'the importance of there being land in the Invergordon area which is ready zoned for industry, and . . . that the absence of such land can only act as a deterrent to an industrialist who wishes to come in quickly.' In fact the company subsequently failed to develop the site, having been unable to find sufficient money.

Thereafter, in the course of only two years, 1971/72, at least eight applications for planning consent for major new industrial developments arrived on the desk of the County Planning Officer. These included applications from firms to build a possible six sites for platform construction, two firms for marine related industrial development, an oil refinery and the ill-fated Cromarty Firth Development Co. (which subsequently went bankrupt — their ambitious plans being hitherto attractive to the County Council). Each of these applications was approved. In every case except one the company asked that an alternative acreage to that  presently zoned be zoned to their specifications since this would be more suited to its needs. Each time, the Council supported its approval of the company's request through the Public Inquiry stage, on the grounds of the contribution to be made by the company in question towards the achievement of industrial development.

Of these applications, Cromarty Firth Development Co. went bankrupt, the oil refinery is still, tentatively and with some apparent lack of enthusiasm, going through the planning stages and only one option has been taken up for platform construction (Highlands Fabricators). Of the marine-related industrial developments, the one bought over the other. In addition to these, there have been a number of other, lesser, applications for planning approval which proved abortive,

83

each of which has had to be considered on its merits.

The council has responded to these developments consistently, by supporting their applications and basing its subsequent policy accordingly. In the course of Public Inquiries this support was often in the face of objections to the effect that this support represented a complete volte-face by the County Council concerning previous policy declarations that the sites now proposed for industrial or residential development be avoided on social, agricultural or environmental grounds.

Throughout this period, each successive application has, by the accommodation of its own peculiar requirements by the County Council, brought revision to the Council's previous policy statements in detail of land use, settlement patterns and conservation. Each time new land has been zoned for housing or industry it is added to the previous total, and from the aggregate a calculation made using varying ratios of anticipated jobs/acre, which is used to form the basis for future statements describing the development prospects of the area — regardless of whether that zoning is ever taken up. From the early calculations of the Holmes report of 30,000 in Easter Ross these have been updated, in response to successful applications for planning consent, and the present zoning of over 6,000 acres to anticipate a future population of over 200,000, and it has been said that if the job densities and service factor of Holmes are applied then this could add up to 600,000. The more land that is zoned, the more people, it is assumed, there will be working and living in the area, and the greater the need for housing.

Yet this ignores the fact that the eventual decision as to whether to invest in the area lies with the company. In planning, as in housing, the County Council by its philosophical commitment to large-scale industrial developments being established around the Cromarty Firth has paved the way for an easy passage for any firm which declares an interest in making an investment in the area. Whether that firm will eventually take advantage of the opportunity, it cannot tell. Nor can it know whether it will remain in the area for five or fifty years. It cannot anticipate how many men will be employed when it starts production or a year further on.

It can only respond as it is philosophically disposed to — and that has been to anticipate the firms needs, and meet them before they have even arisen. In the case of too many firms the need has never developed for them to take advantage of the County's resources. The needs of others, like Highlands Fabricators and M. K. Shand, have arisen in ways not anticipated in the terms of Ross and Cromarty's policy for development. This has resulted in the past in a mismatch in the case we examined, of housing, between the nature of need and demand — a lack of temporary accommodation and a surplus of conventional dwellings.

84

The Regional Council continues in the tradition of the Ross and Cromarty County Council. The District Council steadfastly refuses to prepare contingency plans, which would allow for the promotional work of the Region.

It will be interesting in future to watch the working out of these apparently conflicting philosophies of the role to be played by the Local Authority in matters of development.

In closing, and remembering that it is on the proposed oil refinery that the Highland Regional Council are currently pinning their development hopes it is worth noting the justification presented to the Public Inquiry by Ross and Cromarty County Council for its support of the project:

'The future economy and social health of the area depended upon the existence of long-term development of a type to pin down the economy, and the refinery project was the only such in prospect at the present time.'

This account should be regarded only as a current working paper. As such it probably raises more questions than it answers.

## REFERENCES

| | |
|---|---|
| 'The Moray Firth a plan for growth' | Report to the Highlands and Islands Development Board: the Jack Holmes Planning Group. March 1868. |

Highlands Regional Council; Settlement Policy, 1977.

Ross and Cromarty County Council, County Development Plan, Dingwall, 1964.

Ross and Cromarty County Council; Council Minutes.

| | |
|---|---|
| Ross and Cromarty County Council: | 'Towards a Planning Strategy for the East Ross area of the County', 1972. |
| Ross and Cromarty County Council: | 'East Ross Demographic Study', 1974. |

Daily Transcripts of Public Inquiries into Amendments to the County Development Plan; Reporters' letters; Secretary of State's replies.

Inquiry into the Scottish Economy, 1960 - 61: Report of a Committee appointed by SC (D & I) — Toothill Report.

The Scottish Economy 1956 - 70:    A Plan for Expansion. Cmnd, 2864.

86

# 6   Oil Companies in Aberdeen: The Strategy of Incorporation

*J. D. House*

*Introduction*

Most discussions of oil and Scottish society refer mainly to the ways in which development related to the offshore oil and gas play in the British North Sea has affected Scottish society — upon how the society has adapted to and been changed by the advent of offshore oil.   Most of the papers at the conference for which this paper was originally prepared dealt with various aspects of that theme.   But the term, 'oil and Scottish society', could also be interpreted rather differently to refer to the way in which the international oil industry has adjusted to and been influenced by Scottish society.   This is the line that I intend to pursue in this paper.   As a central guiding theme, I will argue that in adapting to a new area that is already developed — in the sense of having a high degree of industrialization, mass literacy, and the kinds of skills acquired through formal education, and a basic cultural similarity to the Western home countries of the multinational corporations — the oil companies pursue a general strategy of *incorporation* rather than simply *exploitation* toward the local population.   As an unintended consequence, and despite local suspicions and various adjustment problems on both sides, this strategy (in the short-term) has proven quite compatible with local interests and aspirations.[1]

This perspective, I feel, should prove complementary to the main focus of the conference.   By investigating how oil adapts to the society, we should be able to understand better how the society adapts to oil.   I share with the rest of the contributors that ultimate interest, and the main thrust of my work in Canada now is to try to assess the likely impact of offshore oil-related development upon my home province of Newfoundland and Labrador.

*Method and Caveats*

The analysis which follows is restricted to oil companies as such, not to either drilling companies, construction companies, or the myriad of oil-related service companies that have moved to or sprung up within Northern Scotland since oil exploration began in the northern North Sea.[2]   And, among the oil companies, it is confined to those actively or potentially involved in exploration and/or production in the northern North Sea with branch offices in Northeast Scotland.   The concern is solely with the exploration and production subsidiaries of branches of the integrated international majors, and with smaller specialist exploring and producing companies; and not with the downstream activities of refining, transportation, and marketing. As a final caveat, it should be noted that most of the 'data' to be presented on oil company hiring practices and use of local supplies and services are those reported by the company representatives themselves; although I will try to compare these to some more 'objective' measures in a later section.

The basic source of our population of companies for the study reported on here is the North East Scotland Development Authority's Offshore Oil Directory, September 1975. We interviewed representatives of 15 of the 18 oil companies listed in the Directory, and 4 additional companies that we learned were active in or interested in becoming active in North Sea exploration, giving a sample of 19 companies. This includes all the important operators in the North Sea with the exception of British Petroleum with which we were unable to arrange an interview.[3] The analysis which follows is based upon interviews with 19 senior representatives of these oil companies, usually the operations manager or exploration manager. Most of the interviews were held in North East Scotland — 12 in Aberdeen, 2 in Peterhead — with 5 at the companies' head offices in London. All of the companies were subsidiaries, and all had their British head offices in London. The nationalities of the parent companies were: 11 American, 3 British, 1 French, 1 Canadian, 1 Dutch/British, 1 American/Canadian and 1 American/British. The nationalities of the interviewers were: 9 American and 10 British (4 English, 5 Scottish, and 1 Welsh).

The interviews were conducted by two research assistants, Ian and Carol Blackie, during the spring of 1976. They were semi-structured and aimed at checking whether my earlier findings for oilmen and their industry in Canada could be generalized to Britain, and at exploring specifically the kinds of adjustment procedures the oil companies follow and problems they encounter in becoming established in a new area. The interviews were all recorded and took from three-quarters of an hour to two hours. In general, the findings show that the basic patterns of oil industry organization, personal careers, collective beliefs, and job satisfactions are the same in Great Britain as in Canada, despite the differences in locale, in the phase of the development, and in offshore as opposed to onshore exploration and development.

Before focussing upon adaptation itself, I intend to discuss three background topics which help explain the processes and problems involved. First, I want to give some feeling for the oilmen's world and their attitude towards their work which I think are important for understanding their adaptation strategies and problems.

88

*Background: The Oilmen's World*

My earlier work in Alberta was essentially an ethnography of entrepreneurial, professional, and managerial oilmen.[4] Whatever one's political perspective and feelings about multinational corporations and contemporary capitalism, the data clearly shows that these oilmen enjoy fulfilling careers and a high level of job satisfaction. For the Canadian case, I have quantitative data from a mailed questionnaire to support the impression from personal interviews that oilmen thoroughly enjoy their jobs. Without exception, the managers interviewed in Britain were also enthusiastic about their work in the industry.

In the exploration and production side of the contemporary British oil industry, we can distinguish three types of career patterns by social background and recruitment: expatriots, returning natives, and local recruits. In the rest of this section, to try to give some feeling for what it is like to be an oilman in Britain today, I will quote at some length from an interview representing each of the three types.[5]

1 *An Expatriate American*
   I was born in New Jersey and went to college there, and then went to graduate school in Louisiana. After I got my degree in geology I went to work in the oil business, about 32 or 33 years ago. I went to work for one of the predecessors of this company, and worked for them for some 25 years in Florida, Mississippi, Louisiana, Oklahoma. I was Chief Geologist at the time of the merger with (a large American multinational) in 1969. I moved to be on the staff in Dallas, and then came over here in 1973 — my first job in the international division . . . I tell you this has been, you can almost say a lifetime of doing what I enjoy doing. So there has been very little in the way of dissatisfaction with work. It has been like a lifetime long vacation, just doing what I'm really interested in. I'm in a profession which I really enjoy working at, geology. Just the activity, the changes from day to day that occur, the competitiveness and the chance of being a part of something that can be of major importance . . . I love working in England, I'm very happy with it. My wife and I are just over here enjoying everything that London has to offer.

2 *A Returning Native Welshman*
   I was born in 1924, I joined the oil industry in 1948. I went to the Middle East as a roughneck, then became a driller. And then I went to the states to become trained as a chemical engineer, and then went back to spend the best part of 12 years in the Middle East, during which I had training periods in Canada and the States. Then I became the director of a drilling contract company in Rome, so we operated in 11 different countries out of Rome. I then set up a chemical company for a French organization which I ran for three years. Then I rejoined (an American major) to come back to the UK. In 1971 I was made a director, and then in 1974 came up here as managing director . . . Having worked in the oil industry since 1948, I'm very happy in it. I think it's a growth industry, it's a very creative industry, it's highly political which I enjoy, and it's full of constant change . . . Well, I've had 5 moves in the last 10 years and I've had 15 moves in my career in the oil industry, and of all the places I've worked in, even I'm sorry to say Canada, Aberdeen is the best place I've ever been to — for many reasons, first of all

it's a delightful community, the Aberdonians are really great people, it has a very fine infrastructure here in Aberdeen, and it has a hinterland which is remarkable in its beauty.

### 3  A Local Scottish Recruit

Basically I'm not an oilman, I've only been in the industry for three years. I'm an administrator.  I was born in Glasgow, but in fact my home town is Edinburgh because I've spent most of my life there.  I was in the British army for some time, and was all the way around the world there.  For the past 12 years I've been in Scotland working on two local authority projects, one in Edinburgh and one in Glasgow.  So when I came to (a French oil company) three years ago it was my first time in the private sector and my first time in the oil industry . . .  My main satisfactions are to work in an industry where there is always the unexpected, and there is a genuine interest because you never know whether the particular operation you're involved in at the moment is going to be a success or not.  I don't like a humdrum life, and therefore I find that the exhilarations of the oil industry, the up's and down's, happen to suit me.  For the administrator, of course, the oil industry can be infuriating because you think you've planned everything and then it just goes in the opposite direction, so you have to start again.  So it can be frustrating.  On the whole, if you want a straightforward 9 to 5 job, then don't work in the oil industry.  If you want something that has a little more stimulation, and that involves you in a personal involvement almost all the time, then it's a very good industry to work in . . .  I like working with the French, I think they're charming and it's very interesting to work with them.  And I also like working in Aberdeen, but of course I have the advantage of being a local, almost a local, and it's very pleasant to be at home.

Although not all oilmen (or fledgling oilmen) are as unhesitatingly enthusiastic about working in the oil industry and in Britain as the three men just quoted, their statements are nevertheless an accurate representation of the general attitude toward work of managerial and professional oilmen.[6]  This attitude contrasts sharply with that of a large proportion of the British working class which has a historical heritage of alienating and oppressive work and has managed to organize itself to place formal restraints upon the extent of its own exploitation in a capitalist society.  The oilmen's positive attitude toward work, based upon their more favourable work experience, combined with the industry's organizational imperatives of flexibility and efficiency, are more important in accounting for their frustrations with an opposition towards the union movement and increased government regulation (see below) than simply material greed for the uninhibited right freely to exploit labour.  But before examining this mutual adaptation between the industry and the society in more detail, I want to outline the way in which the industry is organised in Britain, and to discuss some general principles of organization that help explain the adaptive strategies and problems.

### The Administrative Organisation of the Petroleum Industry in Great Britain

In this section, it is illuminating to compare the British case with the Canadian, In

Canada, the financial, refining, and marketing centre of the industry is, as one would expect from dependency theory, in the metropolitan region of southern Ontario and Quebec. But, partly because of sheer geographical distance, partly because of the less developed state of transportation and communication at the time of the discovery of major oil fields in western Canada in the late 'forties and early fifties', and partly because of the emergence of direct administrative links between the Canadian hinterland and American metropolitan centres, the city of Calgary in Alberta has become the exploration and production centre of the Canadian oil industry. Two-thirds of the oil companies and subsidiaries operating in Canada have their head offices in Calgary, and important government and business organizations, such as the Alberta Energy Resources Conservation Board and the Canadian Petroleum Institute, have their headquarters there. Even the large integrated companies with their head offices in Toronto and Montreal locate their exploration and production managers, and their large staffs of professional geologists, geophysicists and engineers in Calgary. Calgary is firmly established as the administrative centre for oil and gas exploration in Canada, even for the newer exploration plays in the northern frontier and east coast offshore areas. It promises to continue as a vital petroleum centre when reserves in Alberta itself are exhausted, and its emergent importance in the Canadian energy scene has helped strengthen the hand of Alberta's Premier Peter Lougheed in dealing with the Federal Government.

In Great Britain, however, the distribution of administrative power is rather different in that it is solidly centred in the metropolis, London. London was a major international oil centre before the North Sea discoveries and it became the exploration and production centre when that development got underway in the southern sector. Hence, nearly all the British exploration and production subsidiaries have their head offices, most of their senior management, and most of their professional staff in London. For the oil companies Aberdeen, and to a lesser extent Peterhead, has become the operations and service centre specifically for the northern North Sea development. The senior person in Aberdeen is typically an operations manager, although the number of managers and professionals does increase markedly when a company moves into the production phase of its operations. Of the oil companies we interviewed, only about one-fifth of the total number of employees worked in North East Scotland, although the proportion increased to about one-half for the largest producers.[7] This suggests that in the longer term Aberdeen, unlike Calgary, will decline in importance as an oil centre as the northern North Sea play runs its course. It also suggests that, despite geography, oil is less powerful as a bargaining tool for Scotland in negotiating with London than it is for Alberta in dealing with Ottawa. Administration control is fundamental, and in Britain this is firmly established in the metropolis.

To understand the processes and problems encountered by the oil companies in adapting to Aberdeen, I have been suggesting that we need first to know something about the oilmen's attitudes toward their work, and about the role of Aberdeen in the administration of North Sea petroleum exploration and production. It is also important to know about the organization of the oil industry itself and the principles by which it operates. In this section I will outline those general organizational principles that relate to the present analysis, and in the next focus upon the companies' approach to adapting to a new area which fits with these principles. We will then be in a position to consider the Aberdeen case in particular.

It is instructive to view oil industry activity as a competitive game in which each of the players, the oil companies, attempts to maximize its growth rate and profit picture as compared to its competitors. This competitive drive is, I think, not fully appreciated by those who focus upon explicit or implicit collusion in such areas as price-fixing and maintaining a united front to governments and the general public. The competition is not a zero-sum game, and there are important areas of co-operation and alliance among the companies — in maintaining prices, dealing with outsiders, sharing information, sharing technology, conducting research, and in joint exploration and production ventures. But these should not obscure the equally important areas of competition, which are particularly strong at each end of the industry's integrated chain of activities, for control of raw materials on the one hand and for markets for refined products on the other. The former, which is our main focus, takes the form of a fierce competition for a favourable 'land position', in other words for control of promising exploration permits. Once the land position within a particular exploration play becomes set, relations among companies becomes more benign and co-operative. But even co-operation should be viewed as self-interested alliances among competitors. Oilmen also agree, and this continues as important aspect of their moral order, upon the basic rules of the game — for example, that contracts should be honoured and so should informal agreements. The collective belief in fair business dealings and the rule of contracts is sanctioned by ostracism and thereby business failure for known offenders. We will see that this code is important for understanding oilmen's objections to some forms of government intervention and regulation of the industry.

Success in the competitive game means improving one's position in the standings compared to other companies. This, in turn, implies a number of secondary drives as means toward this end — for growth, for profits, for markets, for control over new sources of raw materials, for new techniques, for innovative organizational forms, and for stability and security within their operating environment. All of this implies that the oil companies strive to be efficient in finding, producing, refining, transporting and marketing petroleum. In terms of their own limited objectives, and despite the prelevance of certain inefficiencies that one might expect within such large organizations, they have proven remarkably successful in achieving this efficiency.[8]

In striving to achieve their ends efficiently, the international oil companies over the years have evolved highly flexible, adaptable, and pragmatic forms of social organization. Flexibility is promoted, for example, in their practice of contracting out much of the work involved in petroleum exploration, even in such core activities as geophysical data gathering and analysis, drilling, and platform construction. This saves on overhead, reduces the likelihood of 'labour problems', promotes the case of moving into or out of a new area, and serves as a kind of buffer against market and political instability. It is the drilling contractor and small service company, not the oil major, that finds itself burdened with excess capacity during exploration slow-downs. Adaptability was displayed, for example, in the recent oil crisis, when the oil companies successfully took on the task of allocating crude oil among consuming countries (Stobaugh, 1975), and in their transforming themselves into profitable contractees of the state producing companies of many OPEC countries following nationalization. The oil companies pragmatic approach to governments tends to be two-fold. On the one hand, they resist proposed changes for all they are worth, and can be counted on to produce a barrage of 'evidence' indicating that such changes would make life impossible for them. On the other hand, they have shown an almost uncanny ability to adapt to change and to turn a profit under new conditions. In their dealings with new government regulations, a recurrent phrase among oilmen is: 'We don't like it, but we can live with it'.


*Adapting to a New Locale: The Principle of Incorporation*

In line with the above considerations, I would like to suggest, as the main theoretical point of this paper, that the oil companies pursue a strategy of *incorporation* rather than simply *exploitation* towards a local population. It is the resource, crude oil and natural gas, that the companies wish to exploit; and their aim in this exploitation is to gain the co-operation of the local communities in which they must situate themselves.

In the small scale capitalist enterprises of the nineteenth century, and indeed in much of contemporary capitalism, the main *means* for successfully exploiting a resource or set of resources for realizing a profit was through the exploitation of labour. The decision-makers within the major oil companies are in the enviable position of not having to pursue such a policy to nearly the same extent as their predecessors. This is partly because much of the manual labour in the industry is performed through contractees. But, more importantly, it is because we are dealing with a capital intensive, high technology industry. In a perceptive passage in the *Grundisse*, Karl Marx anticipated the importance of such a development:

> To the degree that large industry develops, the creation of real wealth comes to depend less on labour time and on the amount of labour employed than on the power of the agencies set in motion during labour time, where 'powerful effectiveness' is itself in turn out of all proportion to the direct labour time spent on their production, but depends rather on the general state of science and on the progress of technology, or the application of this science to production (Marx, 1973: 704 - 5).

This means, to put it in terms of a simplified Marxist economics, that the decision-makers within the oil companies can afford to distribute a sizeable share of their economic surplus to their own employees and still realize large profits; and the competitive nature of the industry ensures that they must do this to attract their share of scarce professional, managerial, and clerical talent. The bargaining positions of these different categories of workers, of course, vary. It is the secretarial staff of the major oil companies that most closely resembles an exploited labour force, but even here the oil makers are able to pay higher salaries then most other industries and administrative organizations. In pursuing a strategy of incorporation, I mean that the oil companies attempt to persuade and induce the local population of a new locale into serving the industry's interests, into providing what the oil companies require. Practically, for an offshore operations centre such as Aberdeen, this means harbour and docking facilities, warehouse space, office space, housing for incoming employees, and various forms of infrastructure — transportation, medical services, educational facilities, shopping districts. Also, ideally, the oil companies would like to be able to acquire the goods and services that they require locally, and to hire new personnel at all levels locally.

There are sound business reasons for preferring local services, supplies, and manpower. It is more convenient and more economical. With respect to personnel, this is true in both a direct and an indirect sense. Expatriates are paid by a different, higher salary scale than are locals and they have to be transported to the new locale and housed when they get there. As one American oilman explained in blunt business terms:

> I think that any company that's responsible to shareholders has got to be thinking about building a local work force, it is the only way that you can get the cost down, it's very expensive to have U.S. people in here, you have to provide things that you don't have to provide for local people. I believe it's, you know, the economic incentives are there for the companies without legislation to really force it on anyone.

Expatriates also encounter adjustment difficulties, both in accommodating to local business practices, and in their (and their families') adaptation to a new culture and life-style. To cope with these difficulties, expatriate oil people tend to live in the same areas, to organize special schooling arrangements, and to constitute an identifiable 'oil community' within the new locale.

The oil companies' attitude toward hiring locals is, however, purely pragmatic. They hire them if they are available, but their main concern is to find somebody skilled and competent for the job that needs to be done. Since most of the locals in the new area are not trained oilmen, the industry employs a high proportion of outsiders, particularly at senior managerial and technical levels. The extent to which locals become incorporated in the literal sense, as company employees, depends partly upon the initial educational level and availability of local people, and partly upon the rate at which the petroleum resources in the region are exploited. Oil subsidiaries in Britain employ a higher proportion of locals than did subsidiaries in third world countries at a similar phase; but the proportion of natives in the Canadian oil industry is higher than in Britain, because the industry in Canada has grown gradually over a 30 year period. The current patterns in Scotland, as reported by the oil company representatives, is that expatriates, mainly Americans, fill the senior managerial and technical positions, returning natives (mainly Englishmen) fill many middle managerial and professional positions, and local Scots fill most of the clerical and unskilled and semi-skilled positions. The proportion of Scots in senior positions will increase over time; but because of the rapid pace of resources exploitation, and because company head offices are situated in London, it is unlikely that this will reach a majority position (although I think it likely that, for most companies, the majority *will* be British).

The same logic applies to the provision of goods and services. The companies encourage locals to produce what they need, and buy locally when supplies and services are available at competitive prices. In Britain the Offshore Supplies Office monitors the companies' performance in this regard, and threatenes to take poor performances into account in subsequent rounds of licensing. But OSO recognizes the companies' need to import certain specialist equipment, and has not to date forced them to buy British at noncompetitive prices. It is noteworthy that the nationality of the parent company is not an important factor. If anything, foreign companies may be more sensitive to public relations pressures. Two American majors reported that OSO had informed them that their record in buying local was better than either BP's or Shell's.

It is striking that, particularly in a literate, industrialized area, the self-interests of the oil companies mesh remarkably well with those of many people within the local communities. Locals want jobs and, if they are qualified, the oil companies want to hire them. Local businesses want opportunities to supply and service the oil industry; and, if they are competent, competitive, and willing to adapt to the industry's pace of operations and irregular work routine, the oil companies want to deal with them. Local communities like to have their infrastructures upgraded and, within limits, the oil companies are willing to contribute toward this, as they share the same desire. This meshing of interests is, however, purely co-incidental. As the above quote from an American oilman indicates, the companies' first duty is to their shareholders, which I take to be their rhetorical way of saying to themselves. It happens that, in many ways, the interests of locals, oilmen, and foreign shareholders are happily coincidental as long as the oil and gas play lasts. The more developed the area initially, the more is this the case. The interests of less developed regions, lacking the skills and materials the companies want, do not mesh as well with the oil companies'. Oilmen resist attempts to make them alter their accustomed pattern of behaviour in the interests of local communities. This can be seen in the current negotiations between the companies and the government of Newfoundland and Labrador. In this less developed region, lacking the skill, industrial, and infrastructural base of North East Scotland, the government has been asking the companies to contribute toward local training and research before development occurs. The companies have objected strenuously, but are gradually beginning to accede, on paper at least, to the government's terms.

The companies' position, then, is that local areas should gear themselves up for oil-related development, and should gratefully accept the benefits that accrue spontaneously as an unintended consequence of the companies' pursuing their own economical self-interests. These benefits will be greater the more developed the areas initially, and the more oriented it becomes toward meeting the industry's needs.


*Oil-related Employment in the Aberdeen Area*

The incorporation thesis as proposed above is grounded in a substantial number of interviews with oilmen in Scotland and Canada. It is, unfortunately, difficult to test the thesis systematically against more objective, quantitative data about employment and the success of local firms within the Aberdeen area. The national UK figures are not well broken down by region, even by England versus Scotland; and oil-related employment is poorly specified by industry sector. The data available are, however, consistent with the argument in a general way.

The level of oil-related employment in Britain as a whole in 1978 has been estimated at around 100,000 (Scotsman, 1978). In Scotland, overall employment has been estimated at 56,000 - 65,000 in mid-1976 compared with 43,000 - 50,000 in 1974 (Scottish Economic Bulletin, 1977). Although this does not constitute a lot of jobs in terms of the overall UK economy, and has had little effect upon the unemployment problem in southwest Scotland, it has had a marked effect upon employment in the Highlands and Islands and Grampian regions, where oil jobs represent some 7.3 and 9.3 per cent of total employment respectively (Scottish Economic Bulletin, 1977). In the area in which Aberdeen is the hub (the Grampian region), some 77 per cent of the jobs created have been in the non-manufacturing sector. It is reasonable to assume that most of these have had to do with servicing and supplying offshore rigs and platforms. Aberdeen has become a service but not a manufacturing centre for the oil industry.[9]

It is in this service and supply capacity that the oil companies have most needed locals in the Aberdeen area. The success of their incorporation strategy can be seen from information that, whereas the UK content in overall oil-related orders received increased from 40 per cent in 1974 to 52 per cent in 1975, the increase in the category Other Services was from 68 to an impressive 89 per cent.[10] This category 'includes such items as food, fuels, logistic support and insurance',[11] most of which would have been supplied from within the Aberdeen area. From the community's point of view, these figures suggest that Aberdonians have successfully captured most of the service business related to offshore oil, but they have not established a long-term manufacturing base in the industry. I will now examine in more detail the dynamics of industry-community relations that these figures reflect.

*The Adaptation Process in Aberdeen*

As the above considerations would lead us to expect, the oil companies on the whole have enjoyed a highly successful adjustment to Aberdeen. Despite an array of minor problems, the overall adaptation has been smooth and to the oilmen's liking. In terms of my thesis, I would argue that they have been highly successful in their strategy of incorporation.[12] Largely, this has been due to Aberdeen's having been already provided with much of what the oil industry wanted even before the northern North Sea development got underway. And largely it has been due to various segments of the local community's having perceived their own interests as coincidental with the oil companies'. In serving themselves, they have served the oil companies; or, to reverse a well-known aphorism, what has been good for Aberdonians has been good for the oil companies. The local harbour board has planned and executed the transformation of Aberdeen harbour to the oil companies' liking; the local authorities and private developers have — if somewhat delayed and chaotic at first — provided the housing and office space the companies wanted; local businesses, again perhaps with something of a lag, have geared themselves up to provide for the industry; and the local labour force, including returning natives and other migrants from various parts of the UK, have fulfilled many of the industry's personnel needs. In the words of the district superintendent of one multinational company:

> Fortunately for us, Aberdeen has been the right place, I think. It is probably one of the best physical set-up's I have ever had, you know, your own frontage, your own dock, your office right on the dock. The logistics of it are really quite easy. Plus we had some background in UK personnel. The fellow whose job I took had been with one of our joint interest companies for 20 to 35 years and was English, as was our materials man. One of the original engineers was an American but the number two man was British. Now he is the District Engineer, the senior engineer here. So, there was a sound basis to make a very easy move and I think this was true of most companies. It is not hard for an international company to move, and this is probably one of the easier moves really. This town probably has the best support of any boom town in existence short of, maybe even the Gulf Coast. Maybe even as good as that, in some areas maybe better because there was more twentyone and a quarter ten thousand equipment workin' out of Aberdeen than any other place in the world. They've seen more of it go through one shop than anybody in the world. They're gettin' pretty good at it. Your wire rope rigging companies have done an excellent job, the Aberdeen Harbour Board hasn't done badly. In general, they're doing a pretty good job.

This almost patronisingly favourable appraisal nicely captures, I think, the oilmen's view of a successful process of incorporation. From their perspective, it essentially means that the locals have done their best to gear themselves up for and to accommodate to the industry. There have, nonetheless, been some adjustment problems, many of which the experienced international oilmen forsaw and were prepared to deal with.


*Adaptation Problems in Aberdeen and Great Britain*

From the oil companies' perspective, the biggest problem in moving to a new area, and Aberdeen is no exception, is to placate and hopefully dispell local suspicions about the industry. In general, oilmen believe that they are misunderstood and unappreciated by governments and the public. The problem is compounded for them by the steps through which they typically move into a new area. In keeping with the flexibility principle, they start out on a small scale, renting office and warehouse space on short-term leases. This gives a temporary, almost fly-by-night appearance to their operations. One interviewee contrasted this to the coming of a large industrial plant, where the construction of a large factory immediately gives the impression of a permanent commitment to the area. The oil companies do not have such a commitment at first. If the exploration play fails, they are free to leave with a minimum of cost. Once they make a commercial discovery, however, they move to more permanent-looking quarters, increase their staff, and begin to settle into a long-term relationship with the local community.

Experienced international oilmen expect to be treated with suspicion, and this helps fortify them against it.    In the move to Aberdeen, the larger oil companies tried as far as possible to use such men in the initial stages, and were fortunate in having a number of experienced British oilmen at their disposal for this.    This also helped alleviate a second common problem in adaptation, culture shock.    Although Aberdeen was, in the oilmen's term, more 'civilized' than most places in the international oil scene, its similar-but-not-quite-the-same aspect was disconcerting to some.    Whereas in a middle east locale it was natural for oilmen to establish their own separate community, and this also  happened to an extent within Aberdeen, there was a feeling that one should try to assimilate more with the culturally similar  Aberdonians.    Decisions on schooling reflected this same ambivalence. One American, for example, sent his two brighter  children to local schools and was very  pleased at how they fitted in; but he sent his 'slower' child to the American school because he thought the British standards were too high for that particular child.    As a trivial but perhaps illustrative example, an Englishman complained that Scottish pubs and Scottish drinking habits were less 'congenial' than the English. On the whole, however, cultural differences were not a serious problem for the oilmen.    Only one of the 12 interviewers in Aberdeen was openly looking forward to finishing his assignment there.

A common complaint was that, although they eventually 'came around', the Aberdonian authorities, businesses, labour and general public were slow to appreciate the benefits of offshore oil and were therefore slow to gear up for it.    A representative of a small company expressed this rather strongly:

> They're starting to build new houses in Aberdeen now, but I mean this is 4 or 5 years too late.    I think if they had built their houses up, and built the harbour at the same time, they could have got enough income from the harbour and from the rights to the industrial estates that they could have subsidized houses for the locals.    It was a small harbour just  tottering along, and when the oil companies came, they started saying: 'Well, it can't be done, this costs money, that takes time', instead of thinking: 'Well, if I do this, what can I get out of it?'

As the comment suggests, the high cost of  housing and of inflated prices generally caused problems for the oilmen.    This was so in both a direct and an indirect sense.    Directly, like everybody else in Aberdeen, they had to pay high prices for housing and some other consumer goods.    Oilmen admitted that they could afford this more easily than most locals;  but some of them resented the way in which, as they perceived it, many local vendors would increase their prices if they knew the prospective buyer was an oilman.    One man stated that: 'It is, after all, common knowledge that if you  want a good buy on something you certainly don't state that you're an oilman'.    He gave an example of his (British) company's wanting to rent a flat for visiting colleagues.    A professor from the university had had the flat previously for 40 pounds a month.    When the company took it over, the rent was immediately raised to 60 pounds, the following week to 80 pounds, and the next month to 120 pounds; Indirectly, the oilmen feel that they are unfairly blamed for the escalation in housing prices, pointing out that it is, after all, local people who charge the higher prices. Neither the oilmen nor the locals seem to recognize the problem is due to the inadequacy of a market system in distributing real estate in a community faced with a sudden influx of money and people. The complaint that locals sometimes tried to exploit oilmen took another form as well. Some local services and supply companies have reportedly attempted to drum up business by threatening to inform OSO officials if the oil companies choose a foreign firm instead of themselves. Such blackmail attempts have failed because OSO has refused to comply with that kind of pressure.

In discussing adjustment problems, the oilmen inevitably shifted the focus of the conversation from the local to the national level. From their perspective, there were two basic difficulties to operating in Great Britain: uncertainty about government intentions and regulations, and the labour and union 'problem'. Both of these can be related to our earlier discussion of work attitudes and organizational principles within the industry. The most common complaint about government involvement was that is was *unpredictable*. Oilmen could 'live with' the red tape OSO's scrutiny of their contracting practices, and with various forms of taxation, royalty agreements, and participation schemes. But they objected to the way in which the British government kept changing the regulations, particularly when this involved renegotiating agreements that had already been signed. This offended their belief in the sanctity of contracts, a deeply held percept in the oilmen's moral order for internal business dealings. More pragmatically, it also caused problems for long-term planning; although, I would suggest, these flexibily organized companies were able to adapt successfully to such changes more easily than they cared to admit, or perhaps even recognized. Nevertheless, to pursue my earlier analogy, it is clear that, as intensely involved participants in a competitive game, the oilmen become frustrated when governments, as 'referees', change the rules of the game while it is in progress.

The foreign, particularly American, oil companies came to Great Britain reconciled to the prospect that they would have to deal with what, from their perspective, seemed to be unnecessarily powerful unions and unsatisfactory industrial relations. Again, the oilmen's position is essentially pragmatic, rather than narrowly self-interested or ideologically determined. The union movement's mandate to exercise control over the hours, conditions, and spheres of its members' work conflicts directly with the oil companies' imperatives of flexibility and efficiency, and with oilmen's attitudes towards work as an engaging, fulfilling activity. In other parts of the world, including North America, the industry has been quite successful in thwarting the union movement by anticipating its demands in advance — it

100

has offered highly competitive wages, fringe benefits, and working conditions.[13] In Canada, they even sponsor company unions as advisors to management on safety and working conditions. The aim of this co-optive policy is to forstall strikes and other forms of restrictive labour practices, and thereby to keep the industry humming. In Great Britain, however, the labour movement was too firmly established at the time of the petroleum discoveries for such a strategy to work. The oilmen recognized this and accepted it reluctantly. Again, their position is pragmatic: the unions are there, so we have to deal with them. This acceptance, however, is tinged with resentment, frustration, and even a feeling of moral superiority towards the 'problems' of British industry. Oilmen believe that, wherever the fault may lie, industrial relations and organization of labour in Britain produce inflexibility, inefficiency, and an unhealthy attitude toward work. Many of the interviewees cited specific examples, such as the following:

> We're having our production platform built in Briatin, but I would really prefer to have it built some place else. The labour situation in this country is so unreliable. The capabilities are here, the craftsmanship is here, but it's almost to a point where the reliability of the delivery almost precludes using it. It's not the workmen. We have had stuff go into shops on critical crash projects and I have been extremely pleased with the workmanship, with the way the company went about doing their business, recognizing our requirements, getting the job done and then the union gets a strike organized after the work is completed, but ties up the trucks so we can't get it out. To try to get something that's unrelated to what we've been doing . . . it's involving an entirely different plant, they are trying to get a mess hall or something in another plant, so they tie up a critical job. It's blackmail.

Needless to say, the oilmen show little understanding of or sympathy toward the motivations and points of view of organized labour. Nevertheless their experience may shed some light upon a basic conundrum in the contemporary British economy — how to ensure fair conditions and returns to labour, while at the same time preserving productivity, reliability, and continuity within the industrial system.

## Conclusion: Oil-related Development in a Partially Developed Area

Before the advent of oil, North East Scotland could be viewed as a partially developed and partially underdeveloped region. Some of its characteristics, such as a highly skilled and literate labour force and mechanized industry, would fit an ideal type of development; others of its characteristics, such as gradual depopulation and generally low level of industrialization, would fit an ideal type of underdevelopment. Deirdre Hunt has raised the important question as to whether offshore oil will likely lead to further development or underdevelopment (Hunt, 1977). Her own work on the Aberdeen business elite suggests that offshore oil has led to a decreasing proportion of local ownership and control in the industries and businesses of the area. On the other hand, local businesses have been profiting by the boom, many new jobs have been created, the population flow has been reversed, local infrastructures have been improved, and the general standard of living has increased. It seems clear that, on balance, we are viewing a dynamic of development, at least for the duration of northern North Sea exploration and production.

The oil companies' perspective, as presented in this paper, helps to account for why and how this positive dynamic has emerged. The companies have been successful in incorporating the local community to serve their interests. This is mainly because, in this already partially developed region, the interests of many locals have meshed with those of the industry. The industry has acquired goods and services cheaply and efficiently, while the locals have enjoyed business and job opportunities. In a sense, the local community has ridden to prosperity on the coat-tails of the international oil companies. This is similar to the process of development in Alberta since 1950. In Alberta, however, Calgary promises to continue to be an oil capital after the local petroleum reserves run out; it is the provincial rather than the federal government which has managed to capture the lion's share of petroleum revenues; and the local government enjoys more political power than does North East Scotland. The dynamic of development in Alberta appears to be securely established for the foreseeable future.

This brings us to the central issue for North East Scotland, the oft-repeated but nevertheless vital question: what will happen when the oil runs out? The happy coincidence of interests between the oil companies and the local community will be terminated dramatically. For the companies this merely entails the minor adjustment problems of moving out of North East Scotland for greener pastures. For the local region, however, it may well mean the reversal of the dynamic of development into a new dynamic of under-development. In other words, the strategy of incorporation within a partially developed peripheral area may be more benign than naked exploitation, but may nevertheless give rise to major economic and social dislocations in the long term. As the oil companies move out, they take their best people, foreign *and* Scottish, with them; service and supply companies, including local firms, either fold up, follow the oil companies, or find new kinds of business; average incomes decline; depopulation recurs; the bottom falls out of the real estate market; local authorities are left with unused and decaying houses, dock facilities, and warehouse and office space; The situation may be worse than in pre-oil days, as the business elite has given up control over local businesses; and the local labour force has lost its traditional skills. This gloomy picture is, of course, merely a likely possibility. Whether or not it becomes a reality depends upon the local area's ability to establish alternative development dynamics, either through traditional or new industries. Planning and executing these alternatives will be the central challenge facing Aberdeen and North East Scotland when the oil companies complete their adaptation by pulling out of the region, and the local petroleum service industry finds itself rudely disincorporated.

## NOTES

1 I do not mean to play down the sorts of environmental damage and the long-term appropriation of part of the economic surplus produced from North Sea petroleum, but these do not appear to be major concerns for most of the population of North East Scotland.

2 Our research did deal with these companies as well. The findings will be reported in subsequent papers. For a discussion of the reaction of the local business community to offshore oil, see Deirdre Hunt, 'Responses of Industry Within Aberdeen to Oil Related Change: Some Implications for Urban Planners', *International Journal of Environmental Studies, 1976.*

3 This is consistent with our more general finding that the foreign-owned subsidiary companies were more concerned than the British to give the appearance of full co-operation with local people. Note that the Exxon Corporation is not represented in our sample, because Shell UK Exploration and Production Ltd, is the operator for the Shell/Esso consortium's substantial North Sea interests.

4 This is scheduled for publication by Macmillan of Canada next year, tentative title: *The Oilmen of Calgary: The Sociology of the Petroleum Industry.*

5 These are edited slightly to make them read smoothly but the meaning has not been affected in any way.

6 Note that the present analysis makes no claims abour nonprofessional oilmen, who are probably less enthusiastic about and less involved in their work.

7 Excluding British Gas Corporation, the 17 oil companies had approximately 6,000 employees in Great Britain, and approximately 1,100 in North East Scotland.

8 For a more extended discussion of the organizational principles underlying oil industry efficiency, see J. D. House 'The Social Organization of Multinational Corporations: Canadian Subsidiaries in the Oil Industry', *Canadian Review of Sociology and Anthropology,* 14 (1), 1977: 1 - 14.

9 See Dierdre Hunt, 'Organizational Strategies and Technical Diffusion: The Case of Oil-Involved Engineering Companies in the City of Aberdeen 1977.'

10 'Offshore 1975: An Analysis of Orders Placed', London: Department of Energy 1976, pp. 1 and 7.

11 *Ibid.*, p. 8.

12 Literally, of course, 'incorporation' is too strong a term. The oil companies do not make the local community part of themselves. Only a small proportion of locals are incorporated in this literal sense. But the logic of the process, in a more general sense, is to incorporate locals into serving industry interests. I have used the term to contrast it with 'exploitatation', which implies a direct conflict of interests, without wishing to deny that some degree of exploitation also occurs.

13 I am not suggesting that oil companies are model employers. Their safety record, for examply, has no doubt often been poor, particularly in third world countries.

# REFERENCES

Hunt, D, 1977  'The Sociology of Development: Its Relevance to Aberdeen'. *Scottish Journal of Sociology*, Vol. 1, pp. 137 - 54.

Marx, K., 1973  *Grundrisse: Introduction to the Critique of Political Economy.* Harmondsworth, Penguin.

Scotsman, 1978,  March, 19.

Scottish Economic Bulletin,  1977.  'The Impact of Oil Related Activity on Employment in Scotland.'

# 7 The Sociology of Development: Its Relevance to Aberdeen

*Deirdre Hunt*

Much of the information produced on Aberdeen has either been derived from short stay journalistic visits or consists of merely factual descriptions of overall changes (e.g. Gillman & Rosie, 1974).    Generally it pivots around three main points, Aberdeen has become the major centre of offshore activity in the North Sea, the housing market has been under extreme pressure and traditional moral standards have been rudely assaulted.    If information on the changes taking place has developed little beyond this despite massive media coverage, I would suggest this is because of a failure to ask the appropriate questions, given the ready access to an abundance of relevant research areas existing within the City.

This situation reflects a lack of knowledge of and or interest in constructing change models for those urban areas in peripheral regions within mature economies which have been affected by the development of offshore oils, e.g. North West Europe, North East Canada.

Up to the beginning of the current study not even the simplest mapping exercise of the changes taking place within the City of Aberdeen had been undertaken.[1] No attempt had been made to develop a base line description of the City before it was affected by the experience of oil related activity, let alone to ask the simple, but necessary questions:   'What firms have moved into the City in response to offshore development?', 'What effect has oil related activity had on the service and professional sectors of the City, that is on tertiary activity as opposed to manufacturing?', 'What geographical, technological and organisational paths have been followed by local firms moving into new industry, outside firms moving into the area, and outside firms moving into new areas of manufacturing?'[2]

Given the absence of such questioning there were no attempts made to seek answers.

This meant that the more complex questions which were posed such as 'What are the criteria for determining and promoting the long term viability of the offshore oil industry within the local region?' could not be answered, but could only raise anxieties.

Nor given the absence of initial mapping was it possible to explore such theoretical questions as 'How far and in what way can Aberdeen be seen as an archetype of offshore development in mature economies?' or 'How far can models derived from Aberdeen provide insights into similar developments in immature economies?', or vice versa, yet the City houses the majority of industrial, servicing and professional, oil related activity engaged in UK offshore development.

This absence of sociological analysis has meant that no attention has been paid to already existing models of development which have concerned themselves with such questions.

The central question put forward in such models is how far does movement into a region of foreign externally controlled companies consistute the development of development, or the development of underdevelopment.

The criteria for the development of continual underdevelopment in those models are the draining out of surplus capital, thus ensuring no possibility of reinvesting back into the area of its locally generated wealth, (Gaskin, et al, 1969) the insulation of alien industrial presences from local influence in two ways: by preventing local recruitment to the new career patterns developed by the incoming companies; and by preventing the transferences of new technical knowledge from the in-coming companies to local individuals and firms. The end result, it is argued, is that the local economy remains essentially intact with the means of improving or changing its situation, through the investment of locally generated capital and the development of or the application of new knowledge, perpetually denied. (Frank, 1972: Cardoso, 1972).

Continuity of previous economic activity, the draining out of locally generated capital, the non-transference of new technology to existing or new locally generated companies, as well as the recruitment patterns of local labour to in-coming companies are all areas requiring analysis in any attempt to determine to what extent development, as opposed to the development of dependency, has occurred or is occurring in Aberdeen. Currently I can only comment – and somewhat superficially – on the effect on local recruitment patterns.

Within the City one is concerned to learn how far the traditional pre-oil industries, fishing, paper-making, food processing, marine repairing, shipbuilding and plant handling machinery, have remained unaffected.

Here one can distinguish between effects on labour supply, both short and long term, effects on development, unionisation and technology transfer.

Preliminary work suggests that the remoteness of the area and the tightness of the housing market (Jordan, 1976): initially meant that labour could not be easily supplemented, so that, in-coming firms, offering higher rates of pay, stripped local firms of labour.

As this occurred during a period of national wage freeze existing firms were unable, at least legally, to retaliate by raising wages. A variety of ingenious attempts designed to do precisely this, however, can be identified. Some companies altered shifts worked from alternative to split shifts, others changed job descriptions, renamed jobs and paid a new salary. Meanwhile, vigorous lobbying of Central Government by the Chamber of Commerce was taking place with an eye to making an exception of Aberdeen in respect of the wage freeze policy.[3] This effort failed and the resulting bitterness was increased when later in the year Ministry of Labour officials visited the area and fined local companies who had broken the pay code. (Hunt, 1975). Here was yet another example of an inappropriate response from Central Government to local needs. In attempting to solve a national problem government activity only served to crush local initiative and made local companies more vulnerable to external competitions and the area therefore more dependent on externally controlled employment.

The main occupational groups transferring to in-coming firms seemed to have been secretaries, clerical workers, time-served engineers, junior managers, technicians and following the slump in fishing of 1973, auxiliary fish workers, fish porters and drivers. Labour has continued to be drawn off, if in a slightly less obvious way, for example, apprenticeship schemes much sought after pre-oil now have difficulty attracting sufficient recruits. Pre-oil companies have lost both existing and potential workers.

Managers in such local companies also complain that they are unable to attract the same quality of labour as before. One such firm specialising in heavy plant handling machinery had pre-oil impact restricted applicants to its apprenticeship scheme to grammar school boys. Currently it is unable to fill its apprenticeship scheme from any source.[4]

The labour force, it is also argued, became more volatile and militant (Aberdeen People's Press 1976) whilst at the same time wage rates moved from below the national average (Gaskin, 1969).

Two main effects of such changes can so far be distinguished. The areas in North East Scotland in which oil related developments are now taking place had earlier been penetrated by externally controlled industrial groups attracted to those areas by low wages, abundant stable, high quality labour with a record of low militancy, such companies might have been expected to remain in the areas as long as such wage and labour advantages persisted.[5] These advantages were particularly important in industries with a high labour component, e.g. food processing, or continuous manning, e.g. paper production.

Once these advantages went the movement of investment elsewhere within the company, with a consequent slow run down of activity and cancellation of long term investment in the Aberdeen subsidary, could be expected.

There is evidence that this is occurring, large scale redundancies have been announced in the food processing and paper-making industries, though this is complicated by the simultaneous effects of a down turn in the market for these products. Though a down turn in the market for such goods may well have led to a decline in local activities it is interesting to note that difficulties in labour supply have been mentioned by the managements concerned as a reason for retrenchment (Grieco, 1975).

In terms of locally controlled existing companies the effect of oil development has been one of slow haemorrhage with loss of labour, accelerating labour costs; higher costs given the disappearance of locally generated services which are also suffering from higher labour costs and lack of labour, etc. Combining these pictures of pre-oil branch plant and locally controlled industrial activity the overall prediction has been one of the gradual withdrawal of the external company and the run down of the local company.

Given that oil is a non-renewing resource, the effect of oil related activity coupled with the decline in traditional industrial employment may lead to the swapping of long term industrial dependency, with branch plants offering low wages but stable employment, for a small sector of the population, for a shorter period of higher wages for larger sectors generated by externally controlled but more mobile companies attached to the area during the period of offshore development and production only. The end effect following the run down in oil reserves being, after a brief era of highlevel wages and employment, an overall decline in industrial employment within the area.

Such industrial decline could be expected to affect the overall economic activity level with paralleled declines in the service and professional employment sectors. (Mackay and Mackay, 1975).

Within the peripheral regions of mature economics the effect of the entrance of extractive industries based on depleting resources, in a manner reminiscent of the picture depicted by Silva Michelena in his study of Venezuela, (Michelena *et al*, 1975) may, far from leaving the existing economic structure intact, destroy the range and level of activity and employment instead, so that on withdrawal the area is left with a far less varied and viable industrial vase than before. But industrial development even in third world societies rarely occurs in a vacuum, within mature economies one ignores at one's peril historical antecedents to impact as well as

108

local patterns of co-operation and collaboration.

*The Social Context of Change*

a) The construction of base-lines.

One of the aims of the study is to examine strategies involving locals, in-comers and return migrants and to become aware of the implications of the different choices made. Developing this approach it would seem that any study of industrial impacts must work from a pre-oil base line which provides pre-impact information on existing local industrial organisations, career patterns, levels of technology, investment, share-holding, decision making patterns within companies, co-operation between companies within the area and their external and business institutional linkages. (Hunt, 1976). Without this there would be no criteria against which to evaluate subsequent change. The construction of such a base, with the unit being the individual enterprise, has been an obvious necessity in the current project.

b) Rate of Change

Equally little attempt seems to have been made to distinguish between different types and rates of industrial entrance. Even restricting the examples to oil related change in Europe can one distinguish different effects due to slow rates of development, e.g. Norway, particularly north of Trondheim, small scale development, e.g. Southern Ireland, and large scale rapid impact, e.g. The North East of Scotland.

It is possible that local enterprises have responded in different ways due to differences in scale and the speed of change.

c) Brokerage

Another type of analysis, which to my mind has not yet addressed itself explicitly enough to the question of under-development is that represented by anthropological studies of rural entrepreneurs and economic brokers. The main force of this research is the study of those individuals who play a major part in connecting local production systems with the wider socio-economic framework and who control the crucial set of relationships involved.

Depending on the researcher's theoretical interests, this work either tends to stress the entrepreneurial function (the management of capital and other sources invested in an enterprise) or it discusses the question of economic brokerage (the control of the important sets of relationships that provide the main links with the regional or national economy), occasionally it deals with both. (e.g. Long, 1975).

Such studies are of central importance for the analysis of under-development since they identify the groups and individuals holding strategic positions in the system of linkages between local rural economies and the wider regional and national structure. Through this we may gain further insight into the devices by which economic surplus is extracted and can establish to what extent it is invested in local production. It also enables us to describe the social characteristics of economic brokers (e.g. whether they are 'locals' or 'cosmopolitans', whether they run enterprises and invest in agricultural production, the extent of their urban experience and contacts, whether they hold local or extra-local political office, etc) and examine the networks or social relationships used by them to consolidate their positions and gain some insights into their perceptions.

Concentrating on such individuals appears to me to counterbalance the overlay, passive victim model so prominent in impact statements which, whilst perhaps some relevance to Third World societies, may serve to obscure the realities of development in the peripheral regions of mature economies.

Two contrasting descriptions of the local responses of such individuals occur in the literature (Long, 1975). In the first model, decision makers are bribed by the incoming companies either through direct appointments or a variety of sub-contracts to act as spokesmen for the company locally, regionally and even nationally: they are paid to counteract negative, indigenous responses and supply relevant local intelligence, such individuals act as front men of the interface between the national/multi-mational, yet their presence denotes no more than that, they are rarely given executive powers.[6]

To the host society their involvement, particularly if employed, apparently denotes the open non-discriminating employment policies of the incoming firms. This proves, however, to be largely an illusion as foreign employees rarely have access to the same career prospects as co-nationals of the parent company. Lack of executive power may appear, however, at least initially, to be compensated for by income levels which give access to a life style otherwise unobtainable. For such individuals traditional life styles are devalued and abandoned and the new life style acquires a high status ranking within their own society. This domination of executive positions is seen and accepted as evidence or lack or native ability, rather than the retention of power positions.[7]

In the second model, in a declining or industrially underdeveloped area, the locals actively welcome the entrance of new manufacturing plant. According to Davis (Davis, 1973, 1974), this initial welcome quickly turns to panic as local manufacturers experience labour and wage competition. They then attempt to discourage further entrance or local expansion of incoming firms. However, at this stage, incoming firms are no longer concerned with local opinion, having made contact with wider government agencies which they now tap for information, technical and financial backing.

This also focuses on one of the central questions of the research: has an urban highly educated population (whether its educational base is appropriate or not is another question), with a strong positive sense of its own identity, been able to react more vigorously to impact than scattered, low income populations in developing societies?

When examining the differences in industrial impact between third world and mature economies, it may be that one is looking, in particular, at differences in the responses of local brokers and industrial decision makers in the areas affected.

If one wishes to explore the two main hypotheses examined in the review of the development literature: namely that the role played by local brokers critically affects the organisational style of new industry entering the region and that the differences between regional growth in underdeveloped and developed economies are due to differences in the *expertise* of such brokers, Aberdeen would appear to be an excellent area in which to carry out research.

In 1970 industrial and commercial structures in the City were dominated by a highly integrated, self-recruited industrial, commercial and professional oligarchy.

Unlike other UK cities, ownership and decision making control pre-oil had been largely retained by this local group. Inshore fishing, building, printing and investment trusts remain entirely under local companies, a local board with local directors having been retained. The reason for this remains currently obscure. Popular explanations focus on the remoteness of the area, coupled with the assessed quality of existing directors (Hunt, 1974).

Equally obscure is the degree of decision making control retained by such subsidiary boards. Directors within the City showed a high degree of interlocking, with lawyers playing a prominent part in such linkages. It may be that such linkages prior to 1970 enabled common stands to be taken on wages and manning within the area. Certainly many such linkages connected local industries with the substantial investment trusts in the area, such trusts acting as alternative local sources of risk capital. But overall industrial activity in Aberdeen had been for many years of less importance than its commercial, legal, medical and educational activities, the City acting as a professional, educational and administrative centre for the North East of Scotland, Orkney and Shetland. Both industrial, service and professional sectors were largely self-recruited. It is scarcely surprising that de-

111

cision makers in 1970 were not only local but saw their area as inferior to none, an appraisal so well summed up in the local phrase 'Aberdeen and twelve miles round'.

The Aberdeen industrial decision makers of the early 1970's saw successful employment trends as reflecting their own personal ability. Industrial decline, or stagnation in the economy was due to the remoteness and indifference of central government, i.e. located in a metropolitan centre which was also foreign, and the dominance of lines to Westminster by the Edinburgh and Glasgow lobbies.

This sense of a district remote from government control meant that loca decision makers faced with declining industrial activity during the 1960's attempted to:

1  analyse the factors contributing to this decline;
2  set up local organisations to stimulate regional growth.

In these attempts local industrialists and academics acted as advisers to the Scottish Office, which in turn, seconded to them two full-time civil servants to carry out whatever research and administrative duties they required. These undertakings involved commissioning economic research into the area from the University, arranging meetings between producers and manufacturers in processing, fishing and light engineering and setting up the North East of Scotland Development Association as a permanent body.

One aim of my current work is to examine the industrial relationships of local decision makers and their role as brokers both externally and internally prior to 1970 and subsequently, their attempts to retain industrial control, penetrate and affect the entrance of new firms to the area. This I hope will throw light not only on the inter-relationships between local companies and their boards and branch subsidiaries (either joint venture or entirely owned) and their managers.

A second aim of the proposed study is therefore, working at the level of local industrial decision makers, to examine their responses to changes in the local economy following the development of offshore activity. This double interest in both the responses of companies and the responses of industrial decision makers echoes the interest of Firn in his work in the Strathclyde area. Criticising theories of regional development within the UK developed on the two foundations of neoclassical economic theory or geographical determinism (Christaller and Losch), Firn argues that the 'only meaningful way that any deep and perceptive understanding of regional change can be achieved is to focus attention on the change that occurs at the level of the individual enterprise or firm . . .' (Firn, 1975). What is important is the realisation that a region is composed of a collection of individuals and enterprises, each one of which is facing certain problems and each one of which is able to adjust to such problems. Further Firn found in the Glasgow area that it is the presence or not of individuals with the experience of strategic decision making (such individuals be called entrepreneurs) in the region, which determine the formation or not of new indigenous enterprises.

Seemingly unaware of the sociological material on development, he nevertheless reiterates the same message, that the degree to which individuals have opportunities to engage in entrepreneurial as opposed to managerial activities affects the long term vigour of the local region, particularly the degree to which local companies will enter new industries and take to new techniques.

Certainly this is an interesting hypothesis to explore in the Aberdeen region where the material would suggest that, to an extent unparalleled in UK urban literature, there was a remarkably high degree of local control. In 1969 sixtyeight percent of local companies were locally owned. Such local industrial decision makers had also in the previous decade shown many examples of vigorous attempts to articulate the local economy. At this point it becomes clear that one of the aims of the research is to examine the ways in which groups within the North East of Scotland have articulated the local economy post-offshore developments; echoing O'Brien when he states 'an economic process is a social process in which economic groups establish or try to establish a system of social relationships which permits them to impose upon society an economic form compatible with their interests and objectives'. (O'Brien, 1975).

But the interest of the current project within the North East is obviously not solely focused upon those groups already existing before the advent of oil, but also on incomers. The research is concerned to map the paths of entry, organisational structure, career patterns developed, location of strategic decision making, manufacturing, warehousing, research and development, training programmes offered and to whom, technology, industrial activity spread, shareholding and financial linkages of incoming companies, both in manufacturing service and professional sectors. I am particularly interested in delineating those developments which would enable local groups to learn and become competent in a new industry and local individuals to gain both experience of strategic decision making and entrance to new careers. Latterly the project will examine the interconnections between incomers and local companies.

A review of the literature would suggest that research into the effects of the regional movement of companies within a political entity has rarely been undertaken. (Roig, 1976). Research on the movement of multinational companies has been at the aggregate level of analysis, with the exception of Stoppard (Stoppard and Wells) and Francko (Francko, 1971) (and they write in the aggregate) the behaviour of subsidaries has rarely been considered. Almost no material exists on the business policy situations which occur between existing companies and incoming subsidiaries, either joint venture or wholly owned, or of multi-national companies whose previous arena of operations were based in ther regions.

It should be that the material will throw light on patterns of movement into the area of UK national, multi-national companies and subsidiaries of local companies, whether as clients, supplier or competitors. Semantic difficulties suggest the field is uncovered. Currently it is difficult to distinguish between companies operating purely within national boundaries, operating worldwide with headquarters in the national boundary within the research is taking place, companies operating internationally with headquarters outside the society in which the research is taking place, and joint venture subsidiaries with more than one parent being located inside/outside the society or both.

*Research Parameters*

Drawing from a large number of sources, the task has been to develop an overall list of all companies operating in Aberdeen immediately prior to the discovery of offshore oil, such a list provides the base line against which to evaluate subsequent developments. Secondly, I have been constructing a list for the year 1976, to provide an initial comparison. Working at the level of the individual company I have identified:

> Its existence within the area, the area being defined as the City of Aberdeen and five miles around which enables me to include Dyce airport and industrial estate. Other characteristics collected have been the range of activities engaged in, industrial classification, board membership, geographical location of headquarters and registered office, equity and board control of these companies. Where possible the numbers employed were also determined, but here in such a vital area there have been problems of access. (Firn, 1975).

It might be argued that the determination of organisational structures was purely butterfly collection; a time consuming, busying activity which told us nothing. I would argue, however, that organisational patterns demonstrate choices, choices to enter a new technology, buy up, control, influence other companies.

Any examination of organisational structures will therefore illuminate the business policies and strategies of the companies involved, the identification of which will explain differing reactions to the same opportunities. For example my material will through examination of funding and shore-holding patterns enable us to identify access to, criteria of visibility, developed and changing sources of, finance

114

and control. For given that skilled men and management have been at a premium it has been to the advantage of incoming firms to gain share control of an already existing company which with retooling and minor skill modifications could form a viable base for offshore engineering. (Grieco, 1975). Such companies have been rendered easy pickings through loss of skilled manpower to incoming companies aggraveted by wage freeze restrictions in 1970, loss of orders due to the inability to deliver on time, given loss of labour, coupled with years of low capital investment which led to little or no research and development and aging plant. A strong accountancy influence at board level of local companies seems to have led to a short term appraisal that either sale or absorption of the company was the only business strategy available. Thus the boards sold out. I hope to look at the make-up of boards in order to examine in greater detail the influence of lawyers and accountants in Aberdeen in the early 1970's.

*Initial Research Findings*

Comparison of the 1970/1976 lists allow me to identify the presence of new companies and the disappearance of old as well as change along any of the dimensions covered in the indices. Already work on the 1970 index has dispelled some firmly held myths. Firstly by identifying the presence of oil related companies at the end of 1969 we are forced back to 1968 as the final year of non-oil economic structure, that is two years before most commentators would place the initial impact. From my work it would seem that the initial three years saw not just the entrance of drilling and seismographic companies but also catering and a wide variety of service companies.

By 1972 a full range of oil-related enterprises were present in the Aberdeen area, diving companies, diving equipment suppliers, diving equipment manufacturers, oilfield equipment manufacturers, oilfield equipment suppliers, steel stockholders, specialist engineering sections, systems builders, tele-communication services and equipment suppliers, management consultants, translation services, consultant geologists and cartographic services, specialised personnel recruitment services. Of the 24 catering firms known as at present in Aberdeen in 1976, 20 were present as early as 1972. Similarly, of the 53 service companies present in 1976, 43 were already present in late 1971/early 1972.[8] Of the service companies which left, two were closely connected with particular rigs which moved elsewhere and which they followed to a new location. It may be that certain local service companies and catering outfits fulfil a stopgap role for incoming offshore operations, providing services to the rigs while they await the arrival of their services proper, however, in the present the exact pattern remains unknown.

115

There is no reason, however, to prevent one moving the lines backwards or forwards through time, thus focusing on the different phases of development. For by moving the indices over time one can identify organisational structure which reflects differing appraisals of the viability, time scale and nature of offshore development in the North Sea. So one can identify companies establishing an outpost, either a new agency or a man and a telephone, in an offshore supply centre moving into warehousing, servicing and manufacturing, spreading risks through operating several firms in unconnected industrial areas, developing integrated services and controlling back through acquiring suppliers and moving from the local to a world market which will sustain higher capital investment (Penrose, 1976).

If incoming companies, particularly multi-national companies, have the advantage of knowledge of the required technology, large research and development departments and access to liquid capital, local firms have the advantage of an intimate knowledge of local companies, whether viable or not, services, planning regulations and industrial infrastructure. In the opening period of oil development many local companies realised that they had access to two assets, those of industrial premises and skilled men. In the longer term the supply of both commodities would increase but in the short term the economic rent that could be demanded was high. Certain Aberdeen companies sold out and used the capital thus acquired to obtain new plant and premises on the developing industrial estates to which as locals they had first priority. This particular strategy involved no need to tap alternative sources of liquid capital and rendered the companies less rather than more vulnerable to external control. It also circumvented the problem of wage restraint legislation operating in that period, for newly defined jobs in a new company could be completely funded.

Though the 1970/1976 indices are not yet completed, it is already possible to demonstrate interesting patterns both of entrance and industrial spread. Selecting out drilling, engineering and catering companies for my initial comment it is possible to chart geographical movement by identifying geographical location of company headquarters and registered office. This shows that geographical movement of companies into the City has occurred along several routes.

Movement from outside the UK has been dominated by movement from North America. Taking drilling services and engineering companies operating in Aberdeen in both 1972 and 1976, ten such companies had registered offices in the States, five being located in California. These companies already engaged in oil exploration elsewhere brought with them highly developed skills and already established less obvious but equally salient customer contacts. More numerous have been the movement of UK companies. Among Scottish companies the move has been overwhelmingly a Glasgow-Aberdeen movement. Taking the same group, drilling ser-

116

vices and engineering companies, 17 such companies have headquarters in Glasgow. Glasgow firms have developed in the area in two main ways; expanding or changing the function of minor depots in Aberdeen or setting up entirely new ventures, based on existing engineering knowledge.

Though oil related manufacturing activity has spread to the Glasgow area our material would suggest that offshore developments have also accelerated the withdrawal of industrial activity from that area relocating it in the North East. Minor movement in from Dundee and to an even lesser extent Edinburgh has also taken place. Within the rest of the UK the main move has been from London and surrounding towns in the South East of England. Currently I have identified 24 such companies among the industrial group selected from these areas. A smaller West Midland group – 7 companies focused on Dudley – also exists.

Whereas in 1968 the majority of companies in Aberdeen were locally controlled by 1973 control had passed to three main areas, Glasgow London and the States, particularly California. Our investigation into share control will, I suspect, further increase the % of out controlled companies.

Nor was the early arrival a simple presence in the area, for if we look at the service companies even as early as late 1971/early 1972, they present a bewildering variety of organisational forms and services.

In common with engineering, catering., drilling companies, etc, entering at the same time the geographical movement of service companies saw the movement of Scottish firms predominantly from the Glasgow area, English firms prodominantly from the South East of England, and foreign companies, the largest group being from the USA in which category we have so far identified 8. The companies fell into three main groupings. At the simplest level, particularly in the early stages, some companies offered little more than warehousing and office space, yet other companies acted as matchers obtaining equipment, offering agency and hire services for helicopters, supply boats, light aircraft, hiring out office equipment services, secretarial staff, as well as acting as interface agents between customs and excise and the company client. A third group offered a wide range of highly specialised services each focused on an area of special knowledge, expertise or equipment.

One firm offered core services centred on steel fabrications, pipelines and accommodation modules. Another offered offshore helicopters, refuelling tanks and equipment for transportable fuels, a third developed an underwater marking system, a fourth digital well control systems and well blow out simulations for training and estimating purposes, a fifth, internal x-ray equipment.

Other companies offered package services centred around their specialism, one company focused on the production of core leads and gave its customers access to cost comparison programmes.

Movement cut which occurred between 1970 - 1976 seems to have two main features. As drilling further north and as more space was required companies moved either to the Shetlands or Peterhead. Yet other companies, survey ships and supply boats, remained in the area only for so long as survey ships were engaged there and initial contracts for supply boats had not been made. Once this occurred they withdrew back to their home base.

I can also begin to identify points of entry into the offshore industry which affect technical competence, services offered, structures and organisation. So one can distinguish between companies both UK and non-UK, national and multinational with associates or wholly owned subsidiaries who have been involved with such oil related activities for some considerable time, and UK companies or subsidiaries who initially became involved i.e. started to learn, in the smaller gas fields in the south. (SEB, 1976).


*Conclusion*

The wealth of material uncovered, even at this preliminary stage, suggests that abandoning an impact victim model in preference for a development approach has proved illuminating, dispelling some widely held myths on the entry and organisation of oil related industry.

The change in perspective has led to identification of different entrance paths, geographical, organisational, cognitive and temporal, allowing evaluation for the first time of the implications for local companies of the speed and complexity of entrance of those firms already involved in offshore activities.

The research highlights the confusion arising from the failure to analyse company behaviour other than in terms of the entry of non-UK firms. The material shows that for locally controlled enterprises the entry paths, organisational structures and market penetration of English companies already involved in offshore activity in Norfolk, was indistinguishable from non-UK, oil involved enterprises.

Geographical path analysis also indicates that attempts to locate offshore manufacturing activity in the West and Central Belts has been partially circumvented by firms in those areas shifting manufacturing activity to previously held warehouse outlets in the North East.

Such information is not retrievable from the listings held by government agencies, which given their static presentation necessarily fail to reflect the dynamic nature of the changes occurring. Yet such listings, largely provide the basis for both statements on the geographical dispersal of oil related manufacturing activity within Scotland and forecasting of developing trends. Compiling material in this way has led the authorities to interpret figures showing a low percentage involvement in oil related manufacturing activity in comparison to total manufacturing capacity in the West Central area as 'a pointer to the scope for further involvement by West Central Scotland industry in North Sea oil related work', rather than a sign of shifting activity to the North East (Lang, 1975).

The research findings also suggest that local government agencies with little previous knowledge of oligopolistic trans-national infrastructures have lacked the theoretical base which would have allowed them to evaluate the developments occurring from an experiential background of long term unemployment, high migration and small scale industry activity there has been a tendency to confuse short term servicing and warehouse activities with long term employment generation.

Overall three main facts are obvious:

1 That decision making at both national and local levels has been based on either macro-economic material or local aggregate listings.

2 That defining oil impact as occurring within a mature economy (again the usage of a macro-analytic framework), there has been a tendency to dismiss development literature as inappropriate to the North East of Scotland, a tool exclusively for use in the developing world.

3 That personnel with training in the behavioural and organisational aspect of offshore infrastructures have been largely absent from North East planning structures.

However, recent shifts of focus have been occurring in both sociological, economic and planning literature in Scotland, with an increasing interest in Scotland as a separate, if dominated, society and in local factors involved in promoting or retarding regional growth. This has been paralleled by the emergence of a devolutionary political climate which focuses on two main concerns, who controls oil revenue an who benefits? It is interesting to speculate that development models in tune with these wider currents may be seen as increasingly relevant by those involved at all levels in the current changes.

# REFERENCES

Cardoso, F., 1972. *Dependency and Development in Latin America.* New Left Review, No. 72, 1972.

Davies, R., 1973. *The Impact Process: The Problem of Dynamics* Working Paper, Department of Social and Environmental Planning Central London Polytechnic, October, 1973.

Davies, T., 1974. *Some Aspects of the Impact of a Large Plant: the first preliminary visit.* Working Paper, Department of Social and Environmental Planning, Central London Polytechnic, February, 1974.

Firn, J., 1975. *External Control and Regional Policy in The Red Paper on Scotland.* (G. Brown ed)., EUSPB, 1975.

Francko, I., 1971. *Joint Venture Survival in Multi-National Corporations,* Praeger New York Publishers, 1971.

Frank, A. G., 1969. *Capitalism and Underdevelopment in Latin America,* Monthly Review, New York Press, 1969.

Gaskin, *et al.,* 1969. *A Survey and Proposals,* HMSO, 1969.

Gillman, P and Rosie, G., 1974. *The Oil Rush,* The Sunday Times Magazine, 28 April, 1974.

Grieco, M., 1975. *Peterhead: Preliminary Report,* Institute for the Study of Sparsely Populated Areas, University of Aberdeen, May 1975.

Grieco, M., 1976. *Return Migration,* Unpublished Paper, July 1976.

Grieco, M., 1976. *Oil Over Troubled Waters,* Aberdeen Peoples Press, 1976.

Grieco, M., 1977. *Towards a Sociology of Industrial Development in Peripheral Areas,* Monograph, Robert Gordon's Institute of Technology, 1977.

Howard, Permuller and Thoselli, 1971. *Towards a Theory of the Multi-National,* Harvard business Review, January, 1971.

Hunt, D., 1974. *Oil Related Research Activity in Aberdeen,* Norwegian Ministry of Finance 1974.

Hunt, D., 1975. *Aberdeen and The Oil Boom,* Personnel Management Review, Vol. 7, No. 2, February, 1975.

Hunt, D., 1976. *Responses of Industry, Within Aberdeen to Oil Related Change: Some Implications for Urban Planners,* International Journal of Environmental Studies, 1976.

Jordan. *500 Top Scottish Companies.*

Long, N., 1975. *Structural Dependency, Modes of Production and Economic Brokerage in Rural Peru* in *Beyond the Sociology of Development* (ed Oxaal) Routledge, Keegan and Paul, 1975.

Mackay, D and Mackay, G., 1974. *The Political Economy of North Sea Oil,* Martin Robertson, 1975.

Michelena, S, *et al,* 1975. *Social Impact of Oil on Vene uela,* Institute of Development Studies April, 1975.

O'Brien, R., 1975. *A Critique of Latin American Theories of Dependency* in *Beyond the Sociology of Development* (ed Oxaal), Routledge, Keegan and Paul, 1975.

Penrose, E., 1976. *Ownership and Control* in *The World Divided,* Cambridge University Press, 1976.

Roig, B., 1976. *The Challenge of the MNC to Spanish Local Firms,* Institute de Estudies Superiores de la Eurpressa, 1976.

SEB, 1975. *'Oil Related Employment in Scotland'* in *Scottish Economic Bulletin,* No. 71, February, 1975.

Stopford, J and Wells, L., 1972. *Managing the Multi-National Enterprise,* New York, Basie, Books Inc, 1972.

# 8 'Inauthentic' Politics and the Public Inquiry System: A Discussion Based on the Moss Moran Controversy

*John J. Rodger*

Since the late sixties, the number of major public inquiry controversies connected with North Sea oil activities has been notable. The unfortunate necessity to encroach upon exceptionally beautiful rural sites for large scale developments has been an attendant factor that has increased the intensity of reaction against the initial planning applications. In the Highlands particularly there have been several well publicised conflicts between multi-national companies and locally organised Action Groups. Easter Ross, for example, has been the scene of two controversial inquiries, one in 1969 into the Grampian Chemicals application to build an oil refinery at Nigg, and again in 1975 with the application from Cromarty Petroleum also to build and operate a refinery at Nigg. Then with the push for oil in the early seventies there became a need to find sites to facilitate the construction of large oil production platforms. There followed a public inquiry at Dunnet Bay into the application by Chicago Bridge to construct steel platforms on a site renowned for its exceptional qualities to geologists, geographers and botanists. This was followed in 1974 by the most famous of these types of inquiry, the Drumbuie public inquiry into the application by Mowlem and Taylor-Woodrow to construct concrete platforms on Loch Carron. Additionally, public inquiries were held into the Portavadie and Portkill sites. In May 1976 the forerunner to the Moss Morran inquiry started in Peterhead; the subsequent withdrawal of Shell UK from that inquiry and their shift of attention to sites in Fife provides the starting point of the case study to be discussed later in this paper.

The insistence by the Secretary of State for Scotland to be informed of all oil related proposals has perhaps had the effect of politically charging many of these planning controversies, and has meant more public inquiries into the specific issue of onshore oil developments than might otherwise be expected for other, less strategic, construction projects.[1] However, regardless of how many significant political controversies there have been in recent years connected with the public inquiry system, and the widespread disrepute the system has fallen into over the years, there has not been any serious interest shown about this subject. The references to the Nigg and Drumbuie inquiries in some recent sociological writing on the Highlands for example, have concentrated discussion on the salient arguments of the conflicts and so have failed to engage the question of the influence the public inquiry process has on the formulation and presentation of those arguments. Neither David Taylor, who has described the Drumbuie inquiry as a 'charade' and a 'network of lies', (Taylor, 1975) nor Maurice Broady, who discusses the achievements of the Drumbuie inquiry in terms of David's defeat of Goliath, (Broady, 1975) seriously addresses the problem of the nature, purpose and influence of this institutional apparatus in the contemporary political arena. Their description and discussion of the local community disruption, internal community conflicts and disenchantment with the fairness of the existing planning framework, does suggest however that a more adequate exploration of the public inquiry system in the context of major planning controversies needs to be undertaken, (Varwell, 1973).

The overwhelming consensus view which has resulted from all the controversial public hearings in Scotland is that the system is restrictive. Individuals and objectors groups are constrained to accept many of the premises of the developers case. The question very quickly becomes one of what ways can the development of a particular site be made more agreeable to objecting parties rather than should this site be useful for this purpose at all. The political interaction inherent in the public debate over planning issues invariably gives way to a celebration of technical details. This tendency for the inquiry system to reduce the political to the technological has consequences for the possibilities that are open to interest groups and third parties to select information and organise opposition campaigns. It seems to me to be a mistake to view the inquiry hearing in isolation. It does in fact exert an influence which shapes the very formulation of objections to a particular proposal. Indeed the centrality of the inquiry hearing becomes quickly established in most cases. The task of mobilising local people, petitions, demonstrations, and the organisation of Action Groups has as its object to ensure a recorded public debate, and this can only mean a local public inquiry hearing within the confines of our existing planning framework.[2]

The emphasis which I want to give therefore is that the planning system, in the context of major oil related onshore developments, invariably involves a public inquiry at the centre of the controversy, and that it should be viewed as a *system* which embraces the totality of the opposition process. Once the option is taken by individuals and interest groups to fight a public inquiry there are obvious implications for the input into formulating and presenting an opposition case. The type of information and knowledge that can be utilised must adapt to the logic and limitations of the local inquiry system. Following on from this proposition it seems significant to examine this system within the context of a theoretical framework, sharpened by a vocabulary, that highlights the nature of the discourse often overlooked in planning controversies. Thus it becomes a question of probing beyond apparent open and hostile political reactions against large scale industrial projects to an examination of the impact of the public inquiry institution on the articulation and evaluation of knowledge and information, and further, to specify the consequences for the political process that such an examination reveals. The focus of our concern must necessarily turn to the social and political limits on rational discourse within the public sphere.

122

In this paper I will argue that what is characteristic of the current planning inquiry system is its 'inauthenticity'. By this I mean, following Etzioni (1968), 'a relationship, institution or society is inauthentic if it provides the appearance of responsiveness (i.e. to social actors) while the underlying condition is alienating' (Etzioni, 1968: 619). The problem of 'inauthenticity' within the public inquiry system, I will argue, is determined by the nature of three related problem complexes:

a) The relationship between *expertise* and *political practice* and the *political role of the public* mediating in that relationship. This reveals the degree to which the public sphere is an open and democratic arena in society where political will and public opinion can be formed and be influential in directing and controlling political processes.

b) The configuration of power presupposed by the *classification* and *framing* of knowledge and information considered to be relevant for evaluating a given public issue, particularly, the relative power between non-state interest groups and individuals, and the political-administrative centre of the state in controlling the direction and character of that evaluative process.

c) The dominance of alternative modalities of grounding decision-making determined by the nature of (a) and (b) and the emerging conception of the 'political' following either the logic of a *systems rationality* on the one hand, or a *discursive rationality* on the other.


*The Idea of Inauthenticity*

The idea of 'inauthenticity' is at the heart of the contemporary problem in the political institutions of the advanced industrial societies. It is a specific case of a set of possible relationships between society, its institutions and the social actors who populate those institutions. Amitai Etzioni, for example, treats the idea of 'inauthenticity' as a sub-category of the broader and more abused notion of alienation. His intention in employing such a concept is to specify a particular instance of alienating experience in contemporary society; the exclusion of people from controlling the quality and direction of their social existence. 'Objectively both alienating and inauthentic conditions are excluding, but *inauthentic structures devote a higher ratio of their efforts than alienating ones to conceal their contours and to generating the appearance of responsiveness'.*[3] He further makes the distinction between alienation and inauthenticity in terms that the former encompasses the experience of 'not belonging and to feel that one's efforts are without meaning', whereas 'to be involved inauthentically is to feel cheated and manipulated'.

This argument which Etzioni develops lays particular stress on the growing 'inauthenticity' of political processes. The characteristic of contemporary political institutions, for example, is that they absorb and institutionalise protest without seeking to resolve the underlying causes of the protest. Thus political institutions must, to be 'authentic', create the conditions whereby human needs and goals can be established by active participation within them of affected people, rather than that participation being utilised to manipulate and negate genuine influence.

The use of the local public inquiry system in the context of North Sea oil related developments has brought this problem of 'authenticity' into close perspective because of the wider national and economic importance of the oil and gas developments it has processed. At a time of national economic urgency in terms of Britain's relationship to the trading world, and internal economic crisis with high national unemployment, North Sea oil onshore projects have brought with them both the hope of internal economic regeneration and national solvency. However, a planning institutional system with a local focus is being used to process development proposals of national relevance. The gap between national policy formation with respect to planning issues, and local objection and participation in planning disputes is being filled by a political-administrative system which embodies and displays the tension between realities of national and local planning perspectives. While it may appear that the influence and significance of the national planning perspective is constrained within the structured specificity of the local public inquiry process, this has often seemed to be contradicted in reality. Local objectors at many recent controversial public hearings have felt that national dilemmas have given priority within a planning inquiry process supposedly constituted to mediate in problems relating to the pattern of land use in a given locality, and paradoxically, the broader connections between local developments and national problems are prevented from being made by the 'localness' of planning inquiry remits.

A recognition of this apparent contradiction of the local inquiry system was made by the Action Group opposing Shell and Esso in Fife: 'While claim "national economic importance" for the project, the bureaucrats decreed that its future should be decided by the narrowly confined process of local public inquiry, on the basis of indefinite proposals and on a cursory investigation of both the preferred and alternative sites. The national issues were not open for examination'.[4] The frustration of the objectors at the Moss Morran public inquiry has led to various strategies to combat the 'inauthenticity' of the system, which they believe has failed to be responsive to the arguments and fears they expressed at the public hearing. The principles of 'openness', 'fairness', and 'impartiality' of the Franks Committee it seems, obfuscate an underlying manipulative and ritualistic process which promoted the Action Group chairman to denounce the hearing as a 'charade' on the opening day in June 1977.[5]

I will now explore the problem of 'inauthenticity' through drawing on some ideas developed by Bernstein (1973), Habermas (1970, 1971, 1974, 1976) and Luhmann (1971, 1975), before returning in the latter part of the paper to describe the consequences of the inquiries alienating condition for local opposition to Shell and Esso in Fife.

*The Public Sphere: Expertise, Political Practice, and the Public*

The writing of Jurgen Habermas has displayed a continuing concern with the 'political' as an authentic dimension of social existence. Through his early analysis of the *public sphere* the guiding idea central to his conception of democratic politics was established.[6] The public sphere was conceived as a realm of society distinct from the state and civil society where public opinion was formed and mediated in political processes in an institutionalised way. His argument is that during a period from about the mid 18th century to mid 19th century the incidence of bourgeois clubs and journals represented, for a period, a specific historical example of the 'bourgeois public sphere'. At that time people discussed political issues of contemporary importance and, through club journals and newspapers, opinions were formed and developed through free public discussion among the franchised bourgeoisie which were publicly disseminated to countervail the actions and power of government. This significant idea from this early study was the identification of an 'open and free communicative community' for influencing and directing political and social life. The opening up of an exclusive public sphere, occupied only by a privileged franchised minority, with the coming of universal suffrage, and the blurring of the distinction between public and private in modern mass democracies with the interventionist state and corporatist tendencies, has resulted in a bypassing of the public sphere and/or a degeneration of its fundamental processes. The conditions and possibilities for the establishment of a rational public sphere in modern society has remained central to Habermas' entire intellectual project since writing *Strukturwandel, der Offentlichkeit* (The Structural Transformation of the Public Sphere).

In his later consideration of the role of science and technology in contemporary decision-making processes Habermas identified a fundamental political problem which relates directly to democracy in planning in the public sphere, namely, the relationship between the 'expert' and 'political practice'. His analysis suggested a discernible move towards the 'scientisation of politics and public opinion'.[7] This denotes the tendency for decision-making to be underpinned by the knowledge and technical information of the scientist or professional technologist. 'The dependence of the professional on the politician appears to have reversed itself. The latter becomes the mere agent of a scientific intelligentsia, which, in concrete

FIGURE 1

THE RELATIONSHIP BETWEEN 'EXPERTISE' AND 'POLITICAL PRACTICE'

| | Technocratic Model | Decionistic Model | Pragmatistic Model |
|---|---|---|---|
| Direction of Communication | From 'Expert' to Politician | From Politicial to 'Expert' | Interaction between 'Expert', politician, and the Public |
| Criteria for determining Social and Political Problems | Imperatives of the Political-Administrative systems capable of 'technical' solution | Sectarian interests and Political values of representative political elites | Publicly determined needs grounded in social values and norms of community |
| Bases for validating information | Scientific and technological expertise | Scientific and technological expertise selectively interpreted in accordance with 'political objects of elites | Public debate |
| Political role of Public | Formal legitimation of administrative personnel on base of professional qualifications | Formal legitimation of political elites | Active mediation of public influence through debate and influence in 'authentic' public institutions |
| The Public sphere is: | By-passed and/or Restricted to formal elections | | Open and Unrestricted |

126

circumstances, elaborates the objective implications and requirements of available techniques and resources as well as of optimal strategies and rules of control'.[8] The relationship between the 'expert' and the politician is regarded only as a tendency now being displayed in the more advanced industrial societies towards technocracy. In contrast to this *technocratic model* of the relationship between the expert and political practice it is instructive to point up alternative models; first, either decisions could be made by representative politicians who selectively raid the store of information of the technical expert according to sectarian political values and programmes, this is the *decisionistic model* second, the identification of needs and programmes of action comes from below, from the communities and people directly affected by a specific social or economic change, this is the *pragmatistic model*. In the *pragmastic model* the relationship between the 'expert' and the politician is characterised by a critical interaction and not by strict separation, as it is in both the *technocratic* and *decisionistic* models. And it is only in the *pragmatistic model* that a political role for the public is allowed for. The obvious tendency to bypass the political public sphere by employing technical experts as the only legitimate way to validate information and ground decision-making is a significant problem in contemporary industrial societies confronted by major planning and industrial development projects. A range of crucial questions are raised about the translation of social and practical problems into scientifically formulated questions from this analysis by Habermas however the limitations of this paper prevent a closer examination of them.[9]

The three models set out in Figure 1 neither represent static, mutually exclusive categories, nor are they specific enough to indicate how these relationships are realised in concrete social and political contexts. However, Habermas' initial formulation is instructive and can usefully furnish an overall framework within which empirical studies of public action and the decision-making process may be developed at the institutional level.

Within the general typology two main points can be stressed with respect to grounding our analysis in the specific institutional setting of a public planning inquiry:

a) The emergence of the idea of 'public participation' in planning in recent years has given rise to a situation where the disjunction between public expectations for influencing the decision-making process and the existing institutional structures for the realisation of that influence, has created an inherent tension, particularly within the public inquiry system. The political role of the public in this situation is an empirical question which will vary depending on such factors as the value orientations of those affected, the political issue at stake, and resources to move a 'social base into a social force'. (Pickvance, 1977)[10]

b) For the analysis of the public inquiry system it seems appropriate to combine elements of both the *technocratic* and *decisionistic* models. (We refer to this as *techno-decisionism*). The public inquiry remains an instrument of government with the ultimate power of decision lying with the Secretary of State, but relying on 'expertise' and public discussion to determine a 'rational' technological or scientific basis for decision-making.

I will now turn attention to the institutional level where the relationship between 'expertise', 'political practice' and the 'public' takes form. The problem becomes one of exploring the configurations of power which are possible within the inquiry setting itself given certain variable patterns in the *classification* and *framing* of knowledge considered to be relevant for evaluating a given public issue.

*The Classification and Framing of Public Inquiry Knowledge*

Basil Bernstein starts his seminal paper 'On the Classification and Framing of Educational Knowledge' (Bernstein, 1973) by emphasising that 'how a society selects, classifies, distributes, transmits and evaluates the educational knowledge it considers to be public, reflects both the distribution of power and the principles of social control' (Bernstein, 1973: 227). It is my argument that this equally applies to the evaluation, selection and articulation processes integral to the public inquiry system. The two concepts of *classification* and *framing* developed by Bernstein in his paper articulate the relationship between discrete areas of knowledge, expressed as the problem of boundary maintenance between the different contents of units of knowledge (classification) and the degree of control, and so the relative power between teacher and taught in the pedagogical relationship (framing).

In the context of a planning inquiry into a major industrial project, like the petrochemical development proposed for Moss Morran in Fife, different areas of knowledge and information may be brought to bear on the evaluation of the project. These can range from highly complex and specialist scientific and technological knowledge at one extreme, and everyday commonsense knowledge and fears at the other. Additionally, the categories of people seeking involvement in the public debate over a controversial development proposal ranges from scientific and technological experts to laymen such as elderly people who may be afraid or annoyed about an impending physical intrusion into their lives. It is the subsequent determination of the parameters of relevance between areas of knowledge and the relative power to initiate consideration of *what is to be known* that reveals the configuration of power within the public hearing.

The degree of openness or closure between different realms of knowledge, and between different states of knowing may vary. So, for example, the relationship between technological and design knowledge for the siting of a petro-chemical plant, on the one hand, and social, political and environmental knowledge on the other, may be characterised by an open relationship whereby the socio-political and environmental factors feed into the purely technological. Based on some relational idea a site would be selected which sought to achieve a compromise but maintain the maximum effectiveness of the different criteria.[11] Alternatively, such different realms of knowledge could be in a closed relationship whereby techonological and economic knowledge, for example, is not compromised to some relational idea and the realms of knowledge are hierarchically evaluated such that economic and technological factors predominate over factors relating to the physical environment, to mention a possible example. The receptivity of the public inquiry to different states of knowing between experts and laymen can also be characterised in the same way. Here it is useful to introduce a distinction between *engaged debate and disengaged debate*. As modern public inquiry hearings sit to consider matters relevant to a very specific remit, a subtle, and often unspoken, differentiation is made by inquiry Reporters between evidence that directly engages the inquiry remit, and this is invariably carefully selected technical evidence, and evidence which does not engage the specific technical problem directly but instead introduces broader or more personal factors into the evidence. This latter type of *disengaged debate* is invariably undertaken by local third party objectors. The relationship between these different states of knowing can be characterised in terms of the terms *open* and *closed*, when the Reporter sustains the latter relationship the layman's evidence will be less effective.

Given that the degree of openness and closure in the relationship between *classification* and *framing* of public inquiry knowledge can vary independently it is possible to represent four general configurations of power within a public hearing setting. In Figure 2, I have made the distinction between the individual and administrative institution levels of *framing* knowledge and information to show the relative power between (i) individual and third party objectors; (ii) technical experts*; (iii) an independent adjudicator, and (iv) an inspector controlled from the political-administrative centre, implied whenever the relationship between areas of knowledge is treated in terms of open or closed boundary maintenance. The two levels are, of course, related and the public inquiry system today can be generally characterised in terms of cells 2 and 4.

* The Developers in public inquiries are largely re]resented by 'experts' who give evidence on the various aspects of the proposed application: the Developers therefore have no independent role within the inquiry from the technical witnesses representing their case.

NB 'technical expertise' refers to specialists regardless of who they may represent in Fig. 2.

FIGURE 2

## CLASSIFICATION AND FRAMING OF PUBLIC INQUIRY KNOWLEDGE

### CLASSIFICATION

Relationship between contents of knowledge and states of knowing (technological, ecological, political etc. 'expertise' and 'commonsense' etc)

| FRAMING | Locus of power to initiate and determine the parameters of relevance of knowledge | | Open | Closed |
|---|---|---|---|---|
| | | *Individual* 1 | Power disseminated, institutional mediation of power suspended | Power centres with 'experts' 2 |
| | | *Administrative Institution* 3 | Power with independent adjudicator | Power with pol-admin. centre which determines remit. 4 Reporter agent of pol-admin. centre |
| | | Description | Quasi-Judicial | Political-Administrative |

From the above typology the balance of power within a given decision-making process will alter from cells 1 through to 4. Cell 1 represents a situation where the exercise of power to control and determine what will and will not be discussed is suspended by the institutional apparatus of the political-administrative centre in favour of a free public forum where any individual or social interest can initiate or call into question information or problematic statements. In cell 2 power falls to those individuals who can marshall the most specialist or esoteric knowledge and bring that to bear on the evaluation of a highly specified issue; power is with the 'expert'. In cell 3 the relationship between contents of knowledge and states of knowing is left indeterminate, but the power to determine the parameters of relevance within that open relationship lies with an adjudicating official(s) independent of the political-administrative centre, and presiding over the public discourse of a controversial issue. In cell 4 power lies at the political-administrative centre of the state to both predetermine the issues, and select knowledge, and so, expertise', in accordance with the dictates of the problems and pressures facing the political system generally.

The descriptions 'Quasi-Judicial' and 'Political-Administrative' are used to distinguish the relative autonomy from the State of cells 1 and 3, and the fact that cells 2 and 4 are inextricably linked to the State by functioning as an instrument of government.

130

*Complexity Reduction and the 'Ideal Speech Situation' : System*
*Rationality versus Discursive Rationality*

So far I have suggested that two main elements characterise the public inquiry system as an 'inauthentic' structure, namely, its techno-decisionistic tendencies in relating 'expertise' to political practice, and the institutional concentrationn of power to control public debate about major planning issues in the political-administrative centre of the state.   However, it is necessary to develop further the fundamental problem which 'inauthentic' political structures present; the fact that they 'devote a higher ratio of their efforts . . . to conceal their contours and to generating the appearance of responsiveness'.   Through an outline of the central ideas of the recent debate between Niclas Luhmann and Jurgen Habermas (1971) I want to highlight the theoretical dilemma which is presupposed by the 'inauthenticity' of the public inquiry system, and round out my discussion before examining the Moss Morran controversy briefly in terms of this theoretical dilemma.

German systems theorist Niclas Luhmann has developed an analysis of contemporary industrial societies based on what has been described as 'one of the few coherently argued theoretical justifications of the demise of democratic institutions', (Mueller, 1975: 136).   It is my suggestion here that Luhmann's analysis identifies tendencies now at work in the political-administrative systems of the advanced industrial societies and is cogent for theorising the function and underlying rationality of the public inquiry process.   Habermas reacts against the political and social implications of Luhmann's analysis, stressing instead the necessity to establish and sustain a freely accessible public communicative community for grounding policy and decisions.   Habermas' most recent exploration of the grounds for rational discourse will provide a normative model against which the democratic nature of the public inquiry process may be judged.

The starting point of Luhmann's thesis is that modern industrial societies are now too complex with the result that participation and communicative reasoning by laymen about the condition and direction of change in society is futile.   The pace of change is now so fast that the political-administrative system must be able to respond immediately to the salient issues and conflicts which arise.   As societies become more complex and conflict-ridden its institutional systems must of necessity maintain their own complexity at a level which corresponds to their environment.   For example, a given institutional system should be structurally adjusted to its environment in terms of the information it can incorporate: 'Complexity should be understood as the totality of possible events — the complexity of the world as the events of the world, the complexity of the system as the events that are compatible with the structure of the system', (Luhmann, 1975: 10).   It becomes imperative therefore that a given system maintain its own internal complexity to enable it to incorporate and process a wide range of alternatives, variation, dissent and conflict. 'For this purpose, the structure of the systsm to a certain degree has to be undetermined, contradictory, and institutionalised in a flexible way. It has to be kept open artificially and remain underspecified against the natural tendencies of concretion and absorption of uncertainty', (Luhmann, 1975: 10). However, the flexible structure of a system, as indicated here by Luhmann, means that institutions today tend to be 'judged by a degree of complexity which is extremely difficult to live up to', a point Luhmann recognises. However, following on from the proposition that the complexity of a given system cannot be less than its ability to reduce complexity in the world, an axis of conflict in our existing political-administrative institutions, is pointed up namely, the frustration of 'radical' information and demands which fail to penetrate our *inflexible* institutional structures. Political administrative controversy revolves around the *actual* conservatism and lack of sensibility in modern administrative systems which are in reality much less adapted to the complex world than they *try to appear*, and Luhmann prescribes. This problem of 'inauthenticity' is not the political problem complex explored by Luhmann however, the problem should be resolved by less policital participation more he argues.

Within the theory propounded by Luhmann politics becomes sharply separated from administration, or more accurately, politics becomes administration as the political-administrative sub-system in the modern complex state becomes the steering centre of the social system towards specific goals. Central to this formulation is the idea of information selection by political-administrative systems out of a world regarded as contingent and threatening to modern society by its very complexity. The fundamental problem becomes one of counteracting this boundlessness by constructing 'a plurality of overlapping islands of lower complexity, of manageable, bounded sets of selected aspects of reality', (Poggi, 1976: 61).

Now in relation to the subject matter of this paper, the essential problem revolves around this task of complexity reduction in the contest of an open and democratic public debate over a highly complex industrial project. The orthodox conception of democratic politics comes into question, as Luhmann states:

> 'Decision processes are . . . processes of eliminating other possibilities. They produce more 'nays' than 'yeas' and more rationally they proceed, the more extensively they test other possibilities, the greater becomes their rate of negation. To demand an intensive engaged participation of all in them would be to make a principle of frustration. Anyone who understands democracy in this way, has, in fact, to come to the conclusion that it is incompatible with rationality'.(Luhmann and Habermas, 1971: 319)[12]

There has therefore to be a disconnection of decision-making for the collective values and motivations of the political community through any form of institutional participation in the public sphere. (As this is a statement of potentialities considered by Luhmann to be essential in the future evolution of modern societies, it can only be treated as an articulation of tendencies now being discerned in the practice of contemporary politics and in the functioning of modern public institutions.) The *techno-decisionism* referred to earlier finds it theoretical justification in Luhmann's argument. Like Habermas, Luhmann recognises the influence of science in modern society but he interprets its role differently.. The project for society is to achieve an altered conception of politics. Politicisation amounts to 'linking scientific self-investigation to structural selection' this places in question 'the classical differentiation of experience and action, knowledge and decision, truth and power'. Science becomes the dominant 'sense' system whereby the world comes to be known.[13]

The emerging problem for the political-administrative system is that of establishing a basis for decision-making which reformulates questions in terms capable of 'scientific' or 'technological' resolution. Participatory politics, with its complicating normative and value claims, must be systematically limited. The political-administrative system must seek to transform conflicts in society 'from an immediate conflict into a regulated, verbalised struggle for influence on decision-making centres'. (Luhmann, 1975: 11). This is done by channeling conflicts towards specific decision outcomes by processes similar to public inquiries:

'At the beginning, real uncertainty with regard to the result has to be structurally guaranteed, this means power has to be suspended in order that participation can be motivated at all. The participants have to assume roles which require complementary behaviour, as, for instance, to be answerable for their position; they also have to be requested to give binding accounts of their position of which their opponents can depend. Only in this way can a process of controversial communication occur in which issues can be defined better and alternatives can be eliminated to the extent that the final decision can take place with a minimum of selectivity and, therefore with little social impact' (Luhmann, 1971, 11).

Luhmann is here articulating the framework for decision-making which contemporary public inquiries adhere to. It is premised on the idea that debate must move toward the reduction or shaping down complex arguments, of limiting and closing off alternative formulations of problems which might be dysfunctional for the objectives of the political system as a whole, or put differently, demands which are not in accordance with the existing hierarchies of power controlling the political system are systematically screened out. The problem is that invariably such demands are seeking basic responsiveness, rather than seriously threatening the systems ongoing function, and 'inauthenticity' results.

Habermas develops his argument from a similar position of symmetry between participants in a decision-making forum, but deviates markedly on the direction in which discussion should flow. There are two essential notions in his approach to free communicative action; first, his basic model reposes on the idea of a consensus of truth arrived at through argumentation, and second, the notion of an 'ideal speech situation' which is counterfactually based on the background assumption that there are no structural limitations placed on the selection and use of 'speech acts". As the parameters for obtaining a free communicative process are established, Habermas provides us with a methodological aid for examining the actual 'systematically distorted communication' in public institutions.

Within Habermas' formulation, policy and decision-making should be based on submitting information, policies and statements, to discursive validation in an authentic public sphere. In order to be certain that any consensus arrived at is 'true' and 'genuine' conditions must exist to permit a progressive radicalisation of the argument. There must be the freedom to move from a given level of discourse to increasingly reflected levels. In addition to discursively evaluating theories, problematic statements, and norms there must also be the opportunity to 'call into question and modify the originally accepted conceptual framework . . . there must be the freedom to reflect on the systematic changes in these conceptual systems in an attempt to reconstruct the progress of knowledge (critique of knowledge) and to reflect on our need structures on the stage of our knowledge and our capabilities (cognitive-political-will formation)'. (See Habermas, 1970; McCarthy, 1976). Participants in this type of discourse must accept the force of the better argument. It is through argumentation and reason that a true from a false consensus can be distinguished, Habermas argues. He uses the 'ideal speech situation' to posit the structural parameters within which this distinction can be made possible. There has to be a forum free from constraint where all participants can 'at any time initiate and perpetuate a discourse', or 'put forward or call into question, to ground or refute statements, explanations, interpretations and justifications so that in the long run no opinion remains exempt from consideration and criticism'. The discourse must be open to those participants who are 'truthful or sincere in their relation to themselves and can make their inner nature transparent to others'. Finally all participants should be free 'to command, to oppose or permit or forbid so that one sided binding norms are excluded and formal equality to initiate discourse is made practical' (Habermas, 1970). In other words, the power to withhold information, or prevent information being given must be suspended.

This counterfactual model lays a heavy burden on the public inquiry system. However, interestingly the growth of the system has been based on two often contradictory principles; that of being an instrument of government for political decision-makers, and to sustain its basis in the rule of 'natural justice' (Franks, 1956: 534 - 563). In the post war years a publicly negotiated view of the system has been developing. It is no longer the case that inquiries are considered to be

134

arguments between people with a legal interest.    As Senior has interestingly re-marked, the public have consistently misconceived the purpose of public inquiries, and by so doing, 'the power of public opinion, without benefit of legislation, has been able to transform the whole nature and function of a piece of governmental machinery' (Senior, 1961).    An inquiry is now considered to be a dispute between third party interests and developers.    'A public institution is not what its creators intended, or the law lays down that it should be, but what it has become in the public mind'.    It is on the basis of this public misconception that many Action Groups demand democratic participation in the whole planning decision-making process, and feel 'cheated and manipulated' by the 'inauthentic' structure of the public inquiry system which is in reality an instrument of the political-administrative centre of the state to manage conflict and transform it 'into regu-lated, verbalised struggle for influence'.    Habermas interprets this as a process of 'systematically distorted communication' which sustains 'inauthentic politics' in the public sphere; accountability, symmetry and responsiveness are ideologically pro-claimed but structurally negated.[14]    And herein lies the inauthenticity of the public inquiry system; its appearance conceals the fact that a *discursive rationality* is consumed by a *systems rationality*; the 'ideal speech situation' gives way to 'complexity reduction'.


*The Moss Morran Controversy*

The basis of the Moss Morran controversy is the strong reaction against proposals by Shell Expro UK and Esso Chemicals Ltd to build natural gas liquid and ethylene plants on a site in Cowdenbeath in Fife, and in addition, to build and operate a tanker terminal on the north shore of the Forth which would receive processed feedstock by pipeline for export.    The Moss Morran site at Cowdenbeath has been designated for industrial development since the 1950's and is in the heart of an area plagued by industrial decay and high unemployment.    However, the proposed tanker terminal at Braefoot Bay lies in between Dalgety Bay to the west, which is predominantly a private enterprise new town development, and Aberdour to the east, which is an old established village used as a holiday centre.    Needless to say the main opposition to the oil companies' development proposals have come from the middle class areas by the Forth.

There are many issues involved in the controversy but for the purposes of this paper I will concentrate on the organised Action Group campaign against the development.*    Though opposition has the appearance of an open and hostile

---

* The Dalgety Bay/Aberdour Action Group have organised and fought their opposition campaign without any significant financial, political or intellectual support from politi-cians or national environmentalist organisations.

community directed campaign it is interesting to trace out the influence the public inquiry system has on the pattern of the opposition movement, and particularly significant is the influence of the system on the relationship between the Action Group and the communities it represents. I want to describe two processes that have become visible during the course of the opposition campaigns.

a) A process of 'autonomisation' which has taken place as the Action Group has become separated from identification with its community based support. This has been facilitated by an accompanying process that can best be described as 'personalisation' as the opposition has become synonymous with an inner elite of publicly known individuals who have come to be identified as the opposition rather than simply representing a wider constituency. It will be argued that the system rationality of the inquiry process forces debate towards highly technical issues to enable a decision outcome based on the evaluation of the technological process. Public debate is removed to the realms of the 'expert' and discourse within the community and between the community and the decision-makers is by-passed. The Action Group becomes 'autonomous' from the community at large adjusting to this situation.

b) The 'inauthenticity' of the public inquiry as a democratic forum obstructs or frustrates the objectors case to achieve a radical articulation. The failure of the system as an 'institutionalised ideal speech situation' leads to strategies by the Action Group to express their case fully outside the inquiry forum. The subsequent campaign to make their case known increases their autonomisation from the community and increases the extent to which the local community public sphere is by-passed.

In the early days of the proposed project the communities of Dalgety Bay and Aberdour were 'mobilised' over the issue. The local press covered the various stages of the planning application and published periodic comment from local politicians, oil personnel and various residents. The period from mid 1976 when interest was shown in the area by the oil companies, up until a few months before the start of the public inquiry in June 1977 was characteristically a burgeoning controversy, with letter writing to the press and to the local authorities, petitions against the proposals and a small one in favour, publication of newsletters, community public meetings and general debate in the vicinity.

Two Action Groups grew out of the existing community organisations, in Dalgety Bay the residents' association gave rise to a sub-committee which subsequently became the Dalgety Bay Gas Project Action Group, and from the Ratepayers Association in Aberdour a similar Action Group was formed. Importantly these groups were rooted in the wider communities in those early days. Both communities had originally held meetings to discuss the nature and implications of the

136

Shell NGL project before any Action Groups had been formed. In Dalgety Bay, where the newness of the township and the heterogeneous nature of the population gave rise to a less established community structure and network of relationships, there was great concern to establish an Action Group backed by a formally articulated community mandate. The neglect to obtain such a mandate during the course of one of the first meetings had caused a stormy end to the proceedings. The mandate was eventually given. In Aberdour a public meeting was held of the local Ratepayers' Association and was attended by many local residents. During the course of the meeting it became clear that the existing community leaders were against taking any action whatsoever until the formal application from the oil company had been lodged. The supporting argument had been that it was fruitless to object to something which had yet to be proved undesirable. This outraged many people at the meeting, especially when it was quickly brought to a close against the wishes of the majority of those assembled. The result of this was a series of informal meetings in local public houses and private houses of those anxious to form an Action Group. It was agreed at these meetings to form a community based group but to seek legitimation as a sub-committee of the Ratepayers' Association. The significant factor was that both groups were rooted in their local communities, and their task was to organise and orchestrate an opposition campaign and to keep local people informed.

Through the method of circulating a community newsletter to their respective areas, Dalgety Bay and Aberdour Action Groups announced public meetings, progress on the campaign activities, and sought help for the opposition cause. Petitions were organised and submitted to the planning authorities and the Secretary of State for Scotland, Exhortations to write official letters of objection were made. During this period the Action Groups were consolidating their organisation and there was a strong link established by these various public projects between the communities at large and the smaller group of Action Group members.

Given this structural location within the local communities of the Action Groups it is interesting to trace out the groups' subsequent development up to the public inquiry and after. How does the inquiry itself shape the formulation and presentation of the opposition case and the character of the Action Group?

The public inquiry system operates to shape down the information admissible for consideration by a series of formal and some informal mechanisms. First, major planning inquiries are invariably into *outline planning applications*, which often lack details about the actual working and subsequent development of a site, so discussion must be contained to general principles which by their nature lack the concretion for a thorough examination of the project being proposed. At the Moss Morran inquiry only the general principle of whether the sites should be used for petrochemical development was really under consideration, and the application by Esso Chemicals Ltd., for an ethylene plant had to be discussed not only with little in the way of detailed planning information available, but also without any assurance that Esso were actually intending to build their plant in Fife at all.[15] (This fact considered it is interesting to note the collapse of debate to issues integral to the technological process generally). Second, following the Drumbuie inquiry, SDD circular 14/1975 specified new *procedural rules* to 'cut down the length and cost of major inquiry hearings.' The Reporter's role in directing proceedings was given emphasis. The adjudicatory role of the Reporter can rule out certain moves to initiate discussion and allow others in accordance with his remit given to him by the Secretary of State. His role therefore is to insure that debate is directed to the specific issues which the Secretary of State considers to be problematic and not what third parties, or even what the developers consider is problematic. Third, there has been a fashion in recent years to commission a comprehensive *technical report* to form the basis of discussion at the inquiry. The SDD commissioned the Sphere Report for Drumbuie, and Fife authorities commissioned technical consultants Cremer and Warner to prepare a report on the Shell/Esso projects for Fife. This factor in itself forces discussion toward the highly specialised details of the technological process. Fourth, the *lawyers* within the political-administrative forum assist in selecting information relevant to the specified remit. They invariably advise Action Group clients to fight the technical 'expert' with similar well researched technical information. The lawyers adaptation to the 'realities' of the public inquiry system makes them an integral mechanism of the system rather than a champion of their clients by seeking to extend the parameters of the system for their benefit.[16]

Faced with these same realities of fighting a public inquiry the Dalgety/Aberdour Action Groups advertised for technical expertise of their own and began to shape the various issues that had been raised against the oil companies. People in the community had raised rather vague environmental issues in their letters of objection, such as scenic value, leisure, bird and seal life, which the Action Group realised would be unimpressive in a technical public inquiry. Following the Qatar disaster in April 1977, when several people were killed and injured at a plant in the middle east state similar in design to the proposed plant for Fife, the hazard issue was seized on as the one with most leverage. The result was that the more widely understood themes were subordinated as the arena was taken over by the intricate complexities of petrochemical fires and explosions. It is significant to note that the logical structure of the opposition case became altered at this point. Initially, the objectors wanted to accomplish a broad based evaluation of alternative sites which would incorporate a national assessment of environmental, economic, social and cultural factors. And in order to obtain this they had consistently pressed for a Planned Inquiry Commission (PIC). However, to argue on the level of the technology of the plant and whether or not the technology is proven and safe is to implicitly accept the problematic issue as one of assimilation of the project into the environment, and importantly, it is an acceptance that the issue is debatable and re-solvable in accordance with 'rational technical criteria'. This shift of attention to technological issues rather than the broader one of the politics of site selection dis-torts the significance of the issues involved, and removes the controversy from the community to the 'expert'. The environmental, and less tangible issues which are generally comprehended and passionately felt, are devalued.

The Action Groups united their resources and delegated individuals to undertake research into the various complexities of petrochemical processes and shipping in-flammable gases. The pressure of constructing such an involved case against the oil companies meant that 'technical expertise' because the main input requirement for direct involvement at the centre of the opposition campaign. An obvious gulf emerged between the community and the Action Group stemming from the general feeling that the basic issues were too complex for most people. Helpers who had contributed to the campaign by leafleting and collecting money became detached from the remainder of the campaign as it focused on the public inquiry. Professor D. J. Rashbash, an expert on fire and petrochemical hazards, became the key wit-ness for the opposition case. His evidence, along with the Cremer and Warner consultants, became the central exchange during the course of the inquiry. The pressure to formulate a highly technical case manifested itself in repeated requests from the Action Group to postpone the inquiry to enable them to adequately pre-pare their case with their obvious limited time and resources. The equally repeated refusals to postpone led the Action Group Chairman to state: 'It is difficult to escape the feeling that everything is being carefully planned to make it as difficult as possible for the objectors to present their case effectively . . . there should be full allowance for the fact that objectors have limited resources and time to prepare their case. Sadly, it appears the boot is firmly on the other foot and no oppor-tunity is wasted to put the boot in where it hurts.'[17]

The public inquiry system places the onus on laymen to find the intellectual and financial resources to challenge wealthier, more powerful developers, and through its own institutional procedure tends to confirm the autonomisation of the Action Group from the community. (This appears to be the case with the Moss Morran controversy). Due to the extremely involved nature of the issues local Action Groups have to invest a great deal of their spare time in preparing and researching their case. The newsletters perforce stop being produced and once the last possible scrap of money gas been collected from door to door collections, then the link be-tween an Informing Action Group and an informing community tends to become severed. The Moss Morran controversy characteristically resulted in the actual inquiry system prematurely closing off the fundamental link between the commun-

139

ity and its active representatives.   As the Action Group was a community directed organisation initially, without formal political association with political parties and the like, there remained no formal link whereby information and support could be channeled.

In the eyes of the oil companies, and the local politicians who unanimously supported the development project, and the Scottish Office, the tendency to view the opposition group as an inner elite of knowledgeable individuals who are publicly known rather than a vocal community reaction, becomes a reality.   In conversations with non-Action Group principals involved in the controversy the author became aware of the tendency to discount the opposition case in private as a few 'alarmist', 'middle-class', 'agitators'.   Two factors emerging from the public inquiry hearing itself exacerbated this tendency.   First, individual Action Group members became strongly identified with the opposition case by receiving media publicity, especially for their frequent headline quotes, and statements.   Second, the orderly technical formulation and presentation of the Action Group case meant few local people took the opportunity to comment or support from the floor of the inquiry with symbolic or vocal assistance.   The chances for an open public forum was lost and the scenes reminiscent of the English motorway inquiries never materialised. The Action Group were left in splendid isolation.

The logical structure of the public inquiry is based on the techno-decisionistic idea of a discussion between 'experts', as I have suggested throughout this paper.   It was this structuring of the proceedings around specialist knowledge rather than issues which fundamentally blocked an open discussion and destroyed the hearing as potentially an 'institutionalised ideal speech situation'.   However, the frequent attempts by objectors to expand rather than reduce the scope of the debate created a situation of frustration within the Action Group which subsequently led to a continuing campaign to articulate and amplify their case outside the inquiry forum, but very much conditioned by it and aimed towards a re-opening of it.

The oil companies carefully constructed their case around the evidence of a large number of specialists.   Each specialist was expert in one particular aspect of the highly complex project and was unwilling to encroach upon anyone else's territory.    The lines of demarcation between one specialist's remit and that of another was used to withdraw from attempts by objectors to radicalise the discussion.    For example, the different experts from Shell and Esso Chemicals were difficult to question on the interaction of the two separate plants because they were prepared only to speak for their own particular companies.   Points were lost to the objectors as they failed to cover specific issues with one expert and found a general unwillingness by the Reporter to recall witnesses who had already given evidence.    Another interesting example of how the inquiry setting frustrated attempts to expand the scope of debate and 'move to levels of deeper reflection' was on the area of non-technical questioning of technical experts. The objectors tried at one stage to initiate a discussion about the 'morality' of the oil companies and their assembled experts and their apparent technocratic, clinical, commercial interest. A witness speaking for Shell sought the protection of the Reporter after a short line of questioning dealing with 'commercial pressures and the quality of life and which was more important'. After an initial attempt to answer the question in terms of the necessity to tolerate some risk in life for a 'good quality of life' the witness enquired if he had to answer that *sort* of question and it was indicated that he did not by the Reporter who commended him for his tolerance to have answered as much as he had. The issues of career an commercial pressures on safety standards and the role of the scientist within a commercially oriented enterprise were generally not pursued very far, mainly due to impatient interruption from the Reporter enquiring 'where that line of questioning was leading.' And the explicit challenge to 'expertise', when it was made to the academic who had selected the site, met with a hostile display of injured dignity, assisted by timely interjections by the oil companies lawyers.

Since the conclusion of the public inquiry in July 1977 the Action Group have been attempting to overcome what, for them, was the failure of the inquiry to address itself to the broader issues which they felt crucial. In particular, the national dimensions on some issues was felt to be excluded, and it was felt that an international comparative perspective on the safety and siting of petrochemical plants near to residential areas was seriously neglected. Failing to obtain a PIC to examine these wider matters the group have systematically organised information research and collation for a sustained campaign of amplifying their original case on the safety issue with the hope of convincing the Secretary of State to re-open the public inquiry. It is particularly significant that the public inquiry system still continues to be influential as a focus for Action Group activities, and as setting the trajectory for the development of the ongoing controversial issues.

The discovery of the danger of radio waves as an ignition source for inflammable gas vapour clouds at the Ministry of Defence station at Crimond nearby the St Fergus gas installation, prompted the Action Group to compile their own report on similar dangers in the Forth area. That report, along with 'an exclusive advanced copy of a US Government safety report', which embarrassingly nobody else in this country had a copy of except the Dalgety Bay/Aberdour Action Group, was submitted direct to the Secretary of State. In addition, the objectors produced two sopisticated brochures which they sent to all MP's and some members of the House of Lords (Dalgety Bay/Aberdour: 1977, 1978). The two main points to be made about these post-inquiry activities is the persistence of the group to obtain a broader consideration of their case because the original inquiry format was inadequate and unresponsive to some crucial problems, and secondly, the strategy of engaging the political-administrative centre directly in a technical dialogue is ironically by-passing the public sphere and an open public discussion. The practice of communicating directly with the Secretary of State for Scotland follows logically given the structural limitations of the inquiry system. There is no provision for an ongoing publicly oriented discussion about major industrial developments, such as the one being proposed for Moss Morran. As I have argued in this paper the power to control public debate about major industrial and economic changes lies at the political-administrative centre. The Secretary of State has the power to re-open a public inquiry or create a Planning Commission, but instead of either of these alternatives being chosen a corporatist style exchange between representative elites is the automatic option taken within the confines of the present system.


## Concluding Remarks

I have argued that the public inquiry system is characterised by a *techno-decisionistic* structure. Prominence is given to technical expertise within that structure to define the problematic issues in terms of 'technical criteria' for subsequent political decision at the political-administrative centre. The concentration of power to regulate public debate at the political-administrative centre of the state means that public discussion can be contained to a technical discourse. The social, political and broader environmental values of the community are relegated to the periphery. It is the imperatives of the political-administrative system and the sectarian interests of political elites which determine the outcome of the conflict and not the publicy determined needs grounded in the 'value beliefs' of the community.[18] Having stated this, a large question remains to be answered: how is it possible to ensure a rational public debate within an open and free public sphere given the constraints of time and resources which accompany major planning developments and industrial projects? It is not possible to address this fundamental question here. Indeed part of this far reaching problem is the task of translating social and practical problems (problems of social values, norms and beliefs) into scientifically formulated questions, but this is of course beyond the scope of this paper. The debate between Niclas Luhmann and Jurgen Habermas, briefly presented earlier, specifies the critical dilemma for politics and the publics role in political processes which forms the framework within which this problem must be resolved. This paper has sought only to highlight that dilemma.

# NOTES

* The research for this paper was supported by a research contract from the SSRC North Sea Oil Panel held at the University of Edinburgh. I am grateful to Brian Elliott and Professor Gianfranco Poggi of Edinburgh University and Douglas Wynn of Stirling University for comments on an earlier draft of this paper.

1 See SDD circular 23/1974 reminding local authorities to inform the Secretary of State of all oil related developments. The subsequent procedure of 'calling-in' oil related applications has increased the likelihood of the public inquiry instrument.

2 Existing planning legislation allows for the alternative use of a Planning Inquiry Commission (PIC) to evaluate major planning projects, however, to date this instrument has never been used and will only be reluctantly used in the future due to the cost in time and money a PIC would incur through combining, as it does, local inquiry hearings with a planning commission of up to five people sitting for an extended period considering broader issues.

3 Etzioni (91968: 620).

4 Dalgety Bay/Aberdour Joint Action Group (1977: 12).

5 See SDD Circular 14/1975 for a recent official statement about public inquiry procedures and the principles of the Franks Committee (1956).

6 Jurgen Habermas Strukturwandel der Offentlichkeit Neuwid, Luchterhand, 1962. See Habermas (1974) for a summary of the main themes from this book.

7 Habermas (1971).

8 Habermas (1971: 63 - 64).

9 See Habermas (1971: 50 - 122), especially 'Technical Progress and the Social Life-World'.

10 The formation of Action Groups and the strength and vociferousness of organised opposition can obviously create an environment within which authoritative decisions by government departments can be more or less easy to deliver. However, such groups are structurally constrained by the institutional parameters of the planning system which today is characterised by a technocratic and decisionistic bias.

11 Such a relational idea could be that of locating petrochemical plants in areas already developing a petrochemical industry so maximising the use of skilled labour and reducing costs for the developer while minimising the spread of a polluting industry, and satisfying the environmentalists.

12 See Habermas (1976: 130 - 142) for discussion and quotations from Gesellschaft oder Socialtechnologie.

13 Cf. Sixel (1977) Luhmann in addition argues that the complexity of society means the 'legitimation of political power can no longer be left to presupposed morality'. The urgent problem for power in this situation is to institutionalise its own process of legisimation. In regard to this the establishment of *procedures* as mechanisms for foundling meaning becomes crucial. *Procedures* act to divert attention from the actual reasons or principles underlying decisions. The public inquiry could be conceptualised as a 'political ritual' in this formulation. See Lukes (1975).

14 In terms of Figure 2 in this paper, cell 1 would be representative of the 'ideal speech situation' and cell 4 of a decision-making forum mediated by the political-administrative system following the logic of complexity reduction and systems rationality 'Inauthenticity' within the public inquiry can be conceptualised in terms of the systems apparent 'Quasi-Judicial' structure concealing its actual 'Political-Administrative' contours. See Figure 2.

15 The limits on open discussion were revealed by Shell's advocate. 'If you accept that the amount of hazard, pollution and visual impact on surroundings of the scheme will depend on the ultimate design of the plant . . . the objections on these grounds are out of place at the plant are known' Public Inquiry Dunfermline, 18 July, 1977.

16 Two interesting points emerged at the MM inquiry. Firstly, the Action Group advocate advised dissociation of the group from the politically ambiguous arguments of the Conservative Society, and advised on giving the impression of not being anti-petrochemical developments. Second, an editorial in the Dunfermline Press, 1 July, 1977 criticised the lawyers 'sharp advocacy' and stark black and white formulation of questions of deeper complexity.

17 Dunfermline Press, 10 June, 1977.

18 The notion of 'community' here would include not only areas objecting to the proposed Moss Morran development but also areas in the wider vicinity which would experience its impact. So people in the Cowdenbeath areas who are generally in favour of the project should also be directly involved in communication regarding the proposed project. Their views should be open to public scrutiny rather than being filtered through representative politicians. There should be a move toward a *Pragmatistic* rather *Decisionistic* model of political practice.

# REFERENCES

Bernstein, B., 1973. *Class, Codes and Control*, London: Paladin.

Broady, M., 1975. 'David and Goliath in Scottish Rural Development' *Community Development Journal* Vol. 10, No. 2.

Dalgety Bay/Aberdour Joint Action Group, 1977. *Hostage to Hazard*.

Dalgety Bay/Aberdour Joint Action Group, 1978. *Nought for your Heritage*.

Etzioni, A., 1968. *The Active Society*, New York: Free Press.

Franks Committee on Administrative Tribunals and Enquiries, 1956. *Minutes of Evidence*, London HMSO.

Habermas, J., 1970. 'Towards a Theory of Communicative Competence' in Hans Dreitzel (ed) *Recent Sociology No. 2*. Collier-MacMillan.

Habermas, J., 1971. *Towards a Rational Society*. London: Heinemann.

Habermas, J., 1974. 'The Public Sphere: An Encyclopedia Article' *New German Critique* No. 3, Fall.

Habermas, J., 1976. *Legitimation Crisis*. London: Heinemann.

Lukes, S., 1975. 'Political Ritual and Social Integration'. *Sociology* Vol. 9, No. 2.

Luhmann, N, and Habermas, J., 1971. *Theorie der Gesellschaft oder Socialtechnologie?* Frankfurt: Suhrkamp.

Luhmann, N., 1975. 'The Sociology of Political Systems' in Klaus Von Beme (ed) *German Political Studies*, Sage.

McCarthy, T. A., 1976. 'A Theory of Communicative Competence' in Paul Connerton (ed) *Critical Sociology*, Harmondsworth: Penguin.

Mueller, C., 1975. *The Politics of Communication*, New York: Oxford University Press.

Pickvance, C. G., 1977. 'From Social Base to Social Force' in M. Harloe (ed) *Captive Cities*, London: John Wiley.

Poggi, G., 1976. 'Review Article: Luhmann's 'Match', Stuttgart, 1975' *Contemporary Sociology*, Vol. 5, No. 1.

Senior, D., 1961. *Architects Journal*.

Sixel, F., 1977. 'The Problem of Sense: Habermas v Luhmann' in J. O'Neil (ed), *On Critical Theory*. London: Heinemann.

Taylor, D., 1975. 'The Social Impact of Oil' in G. Brown (ed) *The Red Paper on Scotland*. Edinburgh: Edinburgh University Students Publications Board.

Varwell, A., 1973. 'The Highlands and Islands Communities' in M. Broady (ed) *Marginal Regions*. London: Bedford Square Press.

145

# 9 Oil Related Development and Shetland: The Institutional Framework

*Margaret Grieco*

This paper has three major aims, the first is to explore the reasons why Shetland attempted to gain control of the oil related developments taking place within its area of jurisdiction; the second is to explore the reasons why and the manner in which it was successful in obtaining such control; and the third is to indicate the problems inherent in having obtained such control given the specifics of the Shetland situation.

## 1 *The need to control the developments*

Much of Shetlands' perceived need to control the oil related developments within its area of jurisdiction flows from the geographical location and the island character of the site.

The impact of oil related development on a group of islands far distant from a major land mass is different from that of the impact of oil related development on a mainland site in a number of respects.

It is our intention to explore here only those areas of possible difference which would appear to have been areas of major policy concern.

It is then in terms of being an island site as well as a major land-fall for pipelines that we will discuss Shetland's attempts to gain control of the developments.

a) *The presence of a large constructed force: the possibilities for integration*
As a major land-fall for the pipeline, Shetland could be certain of the presence of a large construction force on the islands for some considerable duration. (Grieco, 1975). Thus from the beginning of the exploration period Shetland expressed some concern as to the *social impact* of oil related development.

As an island site Shetland could be certain that the employment generated by oil related activities in the area would be largely of a temporary character, the majority of the employment generated being in the construction sector. The local labour should become dependent on employment of such a temporary character was not considered desirable on two counts, firstly, the loss of labour by indigenous industry to the oil related sector was regarded as having an adverse effect on the island economy, and, secondly, the problems of *replacement employment* which would occur, should the indigenous sector contracts as a consequence of this labour loss, with the run-down of oil.

146

(Grieco, 1975). There was then a policy of discouraging local employment on the major construction sites in Shetland for some time. The extent to which such a policy was effective is another matter. (Grieco, 1977). The significant factor here is that from the Shetland perspective it was imperative that some form of control be exercised to protect the indigenous industries and the island economy from the impact of the alternative employment structure created by oil related development.

Oil as providing an alternative employment base, in an area which had previously experienced restricted employment opportunity from the local perspective, is rarely discussed under the general heading the *social impact* of oil. Consequently, this new situation of employment choice is rarely discussed *per se* and the expectations that such a situation created remain uninvestigated.

Even had Shetland favoured the use of local labour on the construction sites, the local labour market would not have been sufficiently large to cope with the demand for labour generated by construction activity on the island. (Grieco, 1975). Similarly, the level of construction skills present on the islands was not high, as in most peripheral areas the normal level of construction activity was low, with construction labour being imported when necessary. (Grieco, 1975). Thus labour for oil related construction activity would necessarily come from outside the area. As the long term employment potential of oil related developments in the area, i.e. operation of the reception facilities, was much lower than that of the short term, i.e. construction activity, this labour force would necessarily be composed of workers who could not look upon the area as a potential place of permanent residence and so could have no long term commitment to the area. The possibilities for the social integration of such a work force were correspondingly limited.

It is not in the long term interest of Shetland to have such a work force integrated into island life, for should it remain then problems of providing long term replacement must be necessarily intensified.

It is not surprising given these problems of a large transitory, alien labour force that Shetland's policy developed in terms of *containing* the impact. It is not then merely a case of containing the moral impact of such a labour force but also a case of attempting to preclude 'social integration', such integration creating long term problems. Shetland has already lost a considerable sector of its population as a consequence of such integration in the past; the Second War produced a situation in Shetland in which local girls had close contact with male outsiders, a situation which resulted in their departure from the islands all too frequently.

147

Thus integration may result, in the long term, in either the loss of females or the acquisition of males, both are problematic.

Even in terms of a mainland site with a balanced demographic structure, the integration of such a labour force would present problems but in the imbalanced demographic structure of Shetland the integration of such a work force was never a feasibility.

'Integrating' such a work force could only but be complicated by the cultural disparity between island and mainland life. Problems of adjustment on the part of the labour force were bound to be very real, the difficulties in journeying between the island and the mainland could only serve to alienate a disgruntled work force even further.

One can argue as to whether or not the *containment* of the impact of temporarily single males, was ever a realistic possibility, it is, however, in terms of such a policy direction that we must consider Shetland's desire to establish a central construction village and not solely in terms of physical planning considerations. The establishment of a construction village and council control of the standards within that village were seen as prerequisites to controlling labour force composition and behaviour. (Grieco, 1977).

b) *Oil related development as contributing to an ongoing process of industrialisation: the feasibility*

As an island site, Shetland could not conceive of North Sea Oil as part of a *process of industrialisation*, as could mainland sites such as Easter Ross or Peterhead. Oil related employment was to be a purely temporary phenomenon, the problem was one of reducing the industrial impact not one of extending it.

Thus for Shetland the benefits of North Sea Oil, if they were to be benefits at all, could not merely consist of the attraction of employment to the area. Benefits were required to be of a more tangible character, oil activities at the extractive end of the continuum could only be seen as *disruptive* of the island economy and as unlikely in themselves to contribute to a diversification of the island economy on any long term basis.

The probability of undirected private developers attempting to remedy such a situation by investing in such a peripheral area as Shetland was remote. Shetland's contact with the oil industry was not likely to result in any permanent industrial development whilst it was likely to result in considerable disruption of the island economy, which at the time of the initial negotiations between Shetland and the oil industry was in a boom situation; Shetland's power to influence the extent of such disruption by way of normal planning controls was minimal. Planning controls are primarily conceived of as instruments of *physical* and not *economic* planning.

Shetland had then a need for some form of control which would allow her to protect the economy against the inevitable disruption; to obtain financial benefits from the presence of oil activities which would contribute to the diversification of the economy in the long term was then the policy for which Shetland opted.

Thus Shetland's attempt to extend its planning controls, controls which move beyond the level of physical planning to that of the economic, must be understood in terms of the *unfeasibility* of the islands as a site of *manufacturing activity* present market considerations. It is this fact which primarily gives rise to the understanding of oil activity as essentially disruptive in the Shetland context.

c) *The need to prevent the proliferation of development sites*
Given the number of industrial agencies involved in oil production and the coastal character of Shetland, there was a very real likelihood of a proliferation of developments taking place. These developments all serving the same basic purpose, the reception of oil, may very well have been widely scattered had Shetland not attempted to gain control of the developments. Each individual developer may very well have considered the development of separate facilities for reception to be in his own best interest both in terms of cost and in terms of speed. It was in Shetland's interest however that joint user facilities be provided in terms of both onshore and offshore consideration.

At the level of onshore considerations, it was necessary that Shetland limit the cost of infrastructural provision to the local authority, central government being concerned to off-load the cost of oil related infrastructural provision on to the local authority where possible. To service more than one site in terms of road provision, etc., was not in the interest of Shetland. Joint user facilities would minimize both the physical impact of the developments and the cost of infrastructural provision to the local authority. There were obvious advantages to be gained by the local authority at the level of the processing of planning applications, an insistence on joint user facilities would restrict the volume of planning traffic considerably.

The need to protect fishing interests was a primary consideration underlying Shetland's attempts to gain control of the developments. By becoming Port and Harbour Authority for the area in which the oil reception facilities were to be based, Shetland would be able to exert a continuing control over the oil industry and so ensure that a sufficient degree of attention was paid to fishing interests.

As the potential for conflict between oil and fishing interests is not restricted to the construction phase alone i.e. spoiling of shell-fish beds, but will be present throughout the production phase i.e. oil spills, it was in Shetland's interest to develop powers of sanction which continued to operate after the construction phase was over.

## 2  The why and how of Shetland's success

The normal status of a local authority with regard to development is that of control over physical planning.   This normally takes the form of the granting or refusing of planning permission for developments on an individual application basis.   Shetland has been successful in extending these powers of control.  This extension of control was established by means of a private bill, advanced by the MP for Shetland and Orkney, which became the Zetland County Council Act of 1974.

Under this Act Shetland was empowered to purchase the land required for the development of the joint user facilities under compulsory purchase order, to play a developmental role with regard to the provision of such facilities and to exercise harbour jurisdiction in the areas affected by oil related development. (See Appendix A).

The structure of the council's developmental involvement is complicated and it is not our intention to examine it as such within the context of this paper, a list of the powers obtained by Shetland through the Act is attached (Appendix A) and a fuller analysis of the use to which these powers have been put it available.

When considering Shetland we are not merely considering an authority which has sought and gained wide powers of control over the developments taking place but are considering an authority which has gone beyond the bounds of normal practice.   It has involved itself commercially in the developments taking place within its area of jurisdiction and has thus become both an agency of development and an agency of control.

Although the commercial involvement of local authorities with developments within their own area of jurisdiction is to be found elsewhere in the UK, such local authority involvement takes the form of a 'sleeping partner' arrangement. Shetland is alone in terms of the extent to which the local authority has a directive and executive role to play in policy formulation with regard to the various commercial concerns.

The philosophy lying beyond such an unprecedented step on the part of a local authority is as we already indicated two-fold.

a) The continuous involvement of the local authority in the developments, as an agency of development, allows greater control over the direction of the developments than does the normal arrangement whereby the local authority's power, as an agency of control, is limited to the granting or refusing of planning permission, a necessarily 'one-off' mechanism of control.

b) To profit, in the economic sense of the word, from the presence of the oil industry on the islands. The strong position of the council with regard to the granting, with-holding or delaying of planning permission allowed it to contract arrangements and agreements of a most favourable, financial order to Shetland with the oil industry directly and those seeking to provide facilities necessary to the operation of the oil industry.

Shetland's power of control, and I would wish to stress, every bit as important, powers of delay, have been sufficient to ensure a fairly rapid compliance on the part of the oil industry with the demands made of it by the local authority. Not all of Shetland's demands have been met in full but Shetland seems on the whole to gain the better part of any compromise. The power of delay would seem to be a factor which initially enabled Shetland to take its power of control beyond those of the normal planning framework.

The power of delay is a power exercisable by any local authority, it is not unique to Shetland but a function of the individual developers obligation to obtain planning permission.

As planning permission is required on a project by project basis, Shetland was, given the nature of oil related developments, in a position to delay production by a significant amount of time. Thus the power to delay must be understood as part explanation of Shetland's obtention of further planning powers. These new powers themselves, however, place Shetland in, formally at least, an even stronger position to delay the developments. Actually, however, given Shetland's own commercial involvement in the developments such delays would be financially to her disadvantage. It is to this double situation of control and development that we will turn later in the paper. For the present purpose it is sufficient to say that within the normal planning framework Shetland had already three types of power, power to refuse, power to permit and power to delay. Shetland's original basis of power is best conceived of in terms of the latter.

Much of the negotiations between the local authority, the oil companies and the central government have not been conducted in public. The extent to which delays were threatened at any particular point in time must remain at the level of speculation. To threaten to delay the developments, whether at the pre-Act stage or after her powers had been extended, appears to have been sufficient reminder, both to the oil companies and to central government, as to how costly a business such a delay would be. It is not so much that Shetland has put her powers of delay into practice but that she has threatened to do so which underlines the importance of such a power. While in the last instance, Shetland would be unlikely to triumph over central government on any major issue, that is any issue likely to disrupt the rapid rate of extraction, it could effect a major upheaval by with-holding planning permission and thus forcing central government to undertake new legislation.

Such a delay would have been costly for the oil companies and central government had Shetland decided to resist development. Equally had central government and the oil companies strongly resisted Shetland's attempts to extend her powers of control, retaliation could easily have taken the form of with-holding of planning permission and extra-ordinary legislation would have been required on the part of central government for development to proceed.

It is to be noted that Shetland's involvement in oil related activities is mainly with the provision of facilities for receiving the oil, this involvement in the production phase of development, one could argue, has provided Shetland with the lee-way necessary to undertake such complicated bargaining and political procedure. Local authorities involved in the earlier phases of the development i.e. fabrication, exploration, have had little time or expertise available to initiate such bargaining procedures and there have been clear cut instances of central government interference with their policy decisions. (Hunter, 1976). The alignment of the oil industry with central government with regard to the rate of extraction has been a clear feature of North Sea Oil. Where it has been deemed necessary central govenrment has undertaken special legislation, of the most rapid character, in order to provide facilities for exploration and production activities, without recourse to local planning authority whatsoever. (Peterhead, 1975). This occurred, however, on a site with a peculiar legal status which in itself enabled such legislation. The more common situation is one in which local authorities are pressured into taking no action where the infringement of planning conditions take place.

Part of Shetland's success then is to be explained in terms of the phase of development with which she is involved. Shetland's involvement in oil related development was certain. One council had control over the total geographical area in which the oil from the Brent and Ninian fields cound be landed. By-passing Shetland was not possible. Yet Shetland's involvement was not to be immediate, there was time to plan institutional measures which would permit Shetland relative control of the developments.

Whereas on the mainland, the oil industry had been productive of situations of uncertainty, in Shetland, at least, there was some degree of certainty as to what North Sea Oil would bring. It is out of this situation of comparative certainty, comparative to that of local authorities coping with the fluctuations inherent in platform fabrication, etc, the ability of Shetland to formulate clear policy lines arose.

Shetland's strength has much to do with the extent to which it was prepared to initiate and undertake the development of the necessary facilities for oil related activities rather than adopting a policy of naked resistance to such developments, a policy which would have been doomed given the national interest in the exploitation of North Sea Oil.

It has also much to do with the fact that the Shetland Isles Council is an island authority, it is clear that the same powers to interfere with normal commercial practice would not have been granted to a mainland authority. Equally important mainland authorities are in competition for the developments i.e. consider the Shell/Esso application, and the bargaining power of any one authority is correspondingly weakened. Thus mainland authorities were not in the same position to construct strong policy directions.

I contend that even had any mainland authority presented central government with as tightly organised a development package as that of Shetland, it would not have been permitted the same powers. The island/mainland distinction is an important one when considering the policy framework within which decisions are taken.

Shetland's island status enters the equation of power/control in more than one form. The organisational structure of an island authority under regionalisation is substantially different to that of a mainland authority. An island authority is a single-tier, multi-purpose structure, whereas the regions are much more complex organisational structures with correspondingly different distributions of power.

I have argued elsewhere that affected communities have much less potential for directly affecting developmental decisions which concern them where they are part of a region, decision taking being more centralised (in terms of geography) as a consequence of regionalisation, than where they are part of an island authority. The relative weakness of the power of the District to the Region has been rendered apparent on a number of occasions. Gordon District in the Grampian Region issued a statement to the effect that the Region should not make its position on planning applications known before planning enquiries take place.

I would argue that the absence of conflicts between District and Region is a

153

clear advantage in the formulation of effective policy; the single tier authority is automatically at an advantage in this respect. Shetland has clearly
benefitted from such a situation, being able to establish clear policy lines and
to maintain them without any major alterations. One wonders what would
have happened had Shetland been subsumed under Highland Region as was
the original intention.

Within a single tier authority there can be no passing of the buck with regard
to the cost of infrastructural provision, no dumping grounds, thus to this extent at least there is a correspondence between the interest of the affected
communities and the local authority. In such a situation one would expect
tighter policies at the level of physical planning to be developed. Within the
Regional structure the potential for such conflict is greater, the interests of
Peterhead and the interests of Grampian Region providing perhaps the best
example of such a divergence of interests.

The single tier structure is not only important in terms of the extent to which
the interests of the affected communities are also the interests of the local
authority but also in terms of its internal decision taking structure. I would
argue that the single tier structure made possible a concentration of power in
the hands of senior officials, with a small supporting group of councillors,
which would not have been possible within the regional structure and that
this concentration of power is one of the major factors contributing to the
highly developed and tightly organised financial and physical planning policies of Shetland.

This concentration of power, in the hands of a few, was a necessary precondition for the success of the negotiations with the oil industry. It is my contention that policy in Shetland in the recent past has originated with the
Chief executive, that throughout he has sought or been provided with the
high powered technical advice from outside agencies, we have in mind here,
most particularly, Rothschilds the bankers.

Without wishing to make any claims of sinister dealings, I contend that the
extent of the Chief Executive's powers, both *de facto* and *de jure*, and the
extent of his personal contact *through office* facilitated the highly organised
strategies of Shetland.

It is easier to come to an arrangement through a central decision taken than
through a number of committees and individual office bearers. The need to
render public that which is commercially disadvantageous, in the case of the
oil companies, or that which is politically unwise, in the case of central
government, was much diminished as a consequence of the existence of a
central decision taker. The existence of such a central decision taker suited

the interests of all the affected agencies.

Shetland's negotiating strength was much increased by this situation of secrecy as to the nature of agreements made between the Council and the affected agencies. Secrecy has characterised much of Shetland's commercial negotiation. (Grieco, 1976; 1977).

These then are the factors which would seem to account for Shetland's success in obtaining control of the developments.

## 3  Agency of development and agency of control: the inherent problems

There would seem to be two sets of problems consequent upon Shetland's extended powers of control; the first is that of combining the need for secrecy with the demand of democracy, the second is that of resolving the conflicts of interest which result from the local authority being both an agency of development and an agency of control.

### Secrecy and democracy

An air of secrecy surrounds much of Shetland's commercial and financial operations.

There are good commercial reasons for the existence of such a situation, given Shetland's involvement as a developmental agency, but the inevitable outcome of such a situation is that the wider community is displaced from decision taking in any real sense. Not knowing the detail and contents of decision taken removes decisions taken as such from the province of voting as sanction. Voters are thus forced to vote on a trust basis or upon the basis of a secrecy/not secrecy issue, they are no longer in a position to vote on the basis of the effectiveness of policy as the full range of possible alternatives to any choice made is no longer known.

*The negotiating power of the council* has become a phrase much heard in Shetland, it is in the interest of the negotiating power of the council that much information is not released. But not released to the world at large means not released to Shetlanders either and often means not released to council members, policy decisions often being the province of the committees. Shetland in adopting a commercial posture has been forced to adopt commercial practice, thus profitability is consequent upon secrecy and secrecy in conflict with democratic participation.

However, even where a matter is free of commercial consideration as such, secrecy is often adhered to. Thus in May 1975 the Chief Executive talking of the commitment obtained by Shetland of the oil industry to the payment of disturbance money, a payment independent of commercial considerations stated that details of the agreement had not been released as it was felt that the negotiating power of the council was best safeguarded by secrecy. Similarly, commercial contracts awarded by Shetland have not been put out to competitive tender. Bargaining has taken place between the council and their prospective partners without any such formal hurdles to jump. While conducting the whole process of finding a suitable partner for developmental activity in secret is most certainly to the commercial advantages of Shetland, it also means that the community and a considerable sector must remain unaware of the state of the field. Thus the advantage of secrecy, that is the business community is in no position to agree terms within itself, must be balanced against the democratic cost of restricted access to information.

In the case of one of the partnerships contracted with an outside interest, the name of the outside partner was not known by the community at large at the time of the signing of the contract.

Secrecy has not only surrounded the dealings between the council and the various companies concerned but has also surrounded the use to which the profits of such encounters are to be put.

Much of the discussion which has taken place in Shetland around the issue of secrecy has focused on whether information has been provided around the undertakings of the council and council officials and not on whether such undertakings are themselves justified in terms of the wishes of the Shetland community.

Such an approach seems to me to avoid the issue of the desirability of particular policies formulated and the closed or open character of their formulation, replacing it with an analysis at a much lower level, that of the detail of that which has already been transacted.

Without secrecy, the general policy line of commercial involvement would have been endangered, with secrecy, policy formulation was necessarily restricted to a small group of political actors. Investment decisions, or for that matter the *decision to invest*, appear to have originated amongst such a group with very little real or effective discussion taking place around the issue at the level of the general council. Policy direction itself has been surrounded by an air of secrecy.

I would wish to argue that once Shetland had taken the initial decision to involve itself commercially in oil related developments a situation of linked decision making was established, the first decision implying and requiring a set of decisions to be taken consequent upon it.

Commercial involvement has set or fixed policy so that council decisions are determined by what is commercially viable and not what is socially desirable, thus the council is operating in an area of diminishing degrees of freedom in respect of the formulation and the execution of a new policy or changes in the existing policy. Council policy with regard to the use of the revenues and the rate of development is set by commercial and not social considerations.

As an agency of control and an agency of development, Shetland is bound to experience conflict between the satisfaction of social goals and the satisfaction of commercial and financial goals. There has already been considerable controversy over the issue of the use of the revenues obtained from oil, the official standpoint favouring a long term policy of financial investment against the short term social and economic policies articulated by other local interests i.e. indigenous industries.

The policy so far formulated by Shetland as an agency of development has been primarily financial in character, a policy appropriate to a commercial concern whose primary interest is in profitability.

Even had Shetland more explicitly attempted to operate as an agency of development with regard to social and economic goals, the conflict between its role as an agency of development and an agency of control would still have existed.

In the present situation of commercial involvement that which is in the community's financial interest may be detrimental to the community's social or cultural interest. Thus while for social reasons the expansion of the construction force beyond the size of the original estimates may be undesirable, it would be commercially impractical to resist such an expansion, resistence incurring significant financial costs to the council.

A council with the power to monitor the size of the work force and not *commercially* committed to keep pace with rapid rate of extraction policy of central government may have been better placed to pay attention to the community's immediate social interest.

REFERENCES

Grieco, Margaret, 1975. *Shetland preliminary report.* ISSPA unpublished paper.

Grieco, Margaret, 1976. *Towards a political sociology of oil related development: Shetland.* Robert Gordon's Institute of Technology, *Oil and the Council*, New Shetlander, 1977.

Grieco, Margaret, 1975 - 76. *Fieldwork Notes.*

Hunter, James, 1976. *Final Draft Report.* ISSPA, December, 1976.

*Peterhead preliminary reports*, 1975, ISSPA, unpublished paper.

\*   This paper was originally given as a conference paper at the International Conference of the Marginal Regions in July 1977. Due to lack of time the references were not augumented beyond the needs of a conference paper.

APPENDIX A

1    *Shetland Act*

    *Zetland County Council Act 1974*

    Compulsory Purchase powers (1) must be submitted to the Secretary of State for Scotland for Confirmation.

    18th June, 1974 — Compulsory purchase order Calback Ness 925 acres. Purchased from owners Nordport Company Ltd., Edinburgh (commercial enterprise which had intended providing facilities similar to those being developed by the council).

    *Powers government acquire under Offshore Petroleum Development (Scotland) Bill do not apply to Shetland*

    County Council Act gives power of
    a) exercising harbour jurisdiction.

2    (Draft) Provisional Order 1972: reference of compulsory purchase powers to Secretary of State only real change made in Act.

    — powers for improvement conservancy and development of the coastal area of the country for the exercise of harbour jurisdiction and for the acquisition of lands.

3    Zetland County Council Order 73.

    — Harbour authority — Baltasound and Sullom Voe.

    — Empowered to provide service facilities, warehousing.

    — Empowered to construct, place, maintain and operate works.

    — Power to sell works.

    — Power to lease — subject to Secretary of State's approval.

    — Power to dredge and blast.

    — Power to licence to dredge.

    — Power to appropriate lands and works.

    Power to hire out plant.

    Power to invest in securities of bodies corporate in order to facilitate provision of funds for (1) servicing, (2) carrying on of harbour undertaking, (3) transport or handling of goods, (4) carrying on of business beneficial directly or indirectly to council.

    Council can subscribe for, purchase, take up/hold/or dispose of stocks and shares, stock, mortgages. Period for compulsory purchase cease 31st December, 1982.

    Powers of compulsory purchase for purposes of harbour undertaking — power to dispose of land when no longer needed for the purpose.

    Compulsory acquisition of land belonging to local authorities not authorised, i.e. gas company (ref. St. Fergus). (Power to refuse entry/use of harbour facilities where goods considered as endangering persons or property.)

    Council may borrow such sums as necessary for the purpose of the order with consent of Secretary of State. Sums borrowed under section to be repaid in a period not exceeding 25 years.

Money received in respect of harbour undertaking shall be carried to and from part of the country fund as receipts for general county purposes and all payments and expenses made and incurred by the council in respect of the harbour undertaking or in carrying into execution the powers and provisions of this order shall be paid or transferred out of the county fund.

Reserve fund: any financial year where moneys received are in excess of moneys expended, the excess may be carried towards a reserve fund. Reserve fund may be used for (e) for any other purpose which in the opinion of the council is solely in the interests of the country and its inhabitants.

4    April 1974, Shetland County Council (Ports and Harbours) Bill becomes an act. Bill does not give wide purchase powers sought but allows acquisition of land for onshore development.

# 10  Oil and Shetland — A Comment

*Dan Shapiro*

Shetland has attracted much more than its fair share of research fiascos.  Despite my comments below, I do not think that Margaret Grieco's article falls into this category.  The questions that she raises in her first paragraph — why Shetland tried to gain control of oil related developments, why and how it succeeded in doing so, and the problems engendered by its very success — are important and interesting ones, and I know of no one else who is giving them serious attention.  Her investigative flair has been valuable not only for her own work but also for that of others researching 'the impact of oil', and I am glad to acknowledge the debt.

There are, however, aspects of this article with which I must disagree.  The first of these is the treatment of 'Shetland' as a single, undifferentiated entity, a 'community' whose interests, as against those of 'oil', are unitary and unproblematic.  Thus Grieco speaks of, 'the reasons why *Shetland* attempted to gain control of the oil related developments' (p.  146 ), '*Shetland* expressed some concern as to the social impact' (p. 146) 'from the *Shetland* perspective it was imperative that some form of control be exercised (p.147  emphases added).  On page147 she speaks of something called, 'the community's social or cultural interest'; and there are many other examples.  To identify interests with geographical location and with nothing else is theoretically suspect, empirically false, and vitates much of the argument.  Perhaps the clearest example of this is the conflict over the employment of Shetland labour in oil related construction, in which the Council attempted to operate, but was later forced to abandon, a policy of excluding Shetlanders.  I have myself argued that the policies of the Council (not of 'Shetland') largely reflect the interests of a very particular group.  They can only be understood within the context of an integrated local capitalist class whose interests are different from those of national or international capital and who enjoy a local hegemony.  Thus the profitability of indigenous enterprises is to be contrasted with the extremely low prevailing wage rates and the extensive use of female labour.  In this context the import of a policy of banning local labour from working in the 'oil' sector is clear.  To base an argument on the interests of 'the Shetland community', then, is directly misleading.

The second problem which seems to me to be important is the treatment in the article of the construction labour force.  Grieco has no hesitation in labelling this workforce as economically and culturally undesirable and in this she seems to be speaking for herself, not discussing the views of others.  She appears to be using a model of 'social integration' redolent of the worst 1950's race relations material, and in so doing she insults not only migrants but also Shetland labour, whose construction skills she characterises as 'not high' (p. 147). Our experience of oil related employers' opinions on this question tends to precisely the opposite conclusion: If they are excluded, it is not for this reason. Thus we learn that migrant labour, 'can have no long term commitment to the area' and that, 'possibilities for the social integration of such a workforce were correspondingly limited' (p.147). And that,

> 'it is not in the long term interest of Shetland to have such a workforce integrated into island life, for should it remain then problems of providing long term replacement must be necessarily intensified. It is not surprising given these problems of a large, transitory alien labour force that Shetland's policy developed in terms of *containing* the impact. It is not then merely a case of containing the moral impact of such a labour force but also a case of attempting to preclude "social integration", such integration creating long term problems' (p.147).

We need only cubstitute 'Pakastani' for 'labour force' throughout to see how objectionable, and how stale, this argument is.

The example of this 'social undesirability' that is given is that,

> 'Shetland had already lost a considerable sector of its population as a consequence of such integration in the past: the Second World War produced a situation in Shetland in which local girls had close contact with male outsiders, a situation which resulted in their departure from the islands all too frequently' (p.147).

So, the vituperative pattern is complete: they have different habits, they take our jobs and they rape our women. One hardly expects this 'analysis' from a sociologist. For it is surely to reproduce local myth at the crudest and most uncritical level. It is primarily systems of land tenure and land ownership, changing terms of trade for primary commodities and consequent changes in patterns of occupation that produce peripheral depopulation. Who 'seduced' all the womenfolk away from the peripheral West of Ireland? If so suspect an argument is to be put it should be meticulously backed with evidence, but we are offered none. There is, indeed, a cavalier disregard for evidence throughout the article, and the idiosyncratic references offer us little help.

The third area of the paper about which I have misgivings is the organisational-cum-political discussion of the relation between the Shetland Council and the oil companies, and its manner of arriving at decisions. The sole discernable tenets of Grieco's theory of organisations would seem to be that decision-taking is easier where it is centralised and restricted to few people, and that secrecy is in the interests of all affected agencies when operating commercially. This would be inadequate at the best of times since, if it were so, it would be hard to see why bureau-

162

cracies ever develop complex decision-taking procedures. But it must be particularly suspect in the context of local political decisions, where an important part of the task is to engineer consent among the affected parties. Nor do I see why secrecy necessarily serves the ends of all agencies concerned, even where all are operating in 'commercial' mode, or necessarily strengthens the negotiating position of the Council. It cannot be argued that the commercial interests are identical, since it is hardly in the oil companies' interests to have the Shetland Islands Council at all, and one can envisage a number of commercial issues — e.g. the central one of the level of 'disturbance' payments — where the mobilisation of public support might have strengthened the Council's bargaining position considerably. There is also a danger of exaggerating the difference between the present ('commercial' therefore secret, undemocratic) and previous ('social', therefore open, democratic) situations, which is proposed as the paper's main finding. To stress that, 'the wider community is displaced from decision taking in any real sense' (p.155), implying a prior situation of genuine 'democratic participation' (ibid.), seems naive, and would probably not be recognisable to many Sheltanders. We may, again, get further in analysing the activities of the Council, including its secrecy, through looking at conflicts of interest within Shetland rather than at a single conflict between a mythical Shetland community and a commercially co-opted Council.

It may seem disingenuous to finish by repeating my welcome for Margaret Grieco's article. But it is largely thanks to her work that there is even a basis on which to disagree.

# 11 Oil and the Cultural Account: Reflections on a Shetland Community

*Anthony P. Cohen*

I

I do not propose a thesis here. My intention is to suggest that discussion about the effects of oil-related developments on indigenous cultures must recognise (a) the diffuse character of such consequences; (b) the pervasiveness and empirical ramifications of a culture; and (c) that oil-related development or any other similar exercise in sudden industrialisation cannot properly be separated out from the host of other pressures and influences on a culture. I have reluctantly been led by considerations of time to depart from my usual and preferred practice of building specific arguments out of ethnographic cases. My title may be taken literally: the reflections which follow are mine, although they concern the ways in which the Shetland community of Whalsay may be seen to reflect upon itself.

I will not be concerned here with the magnitude of structural changes in the Shetland economy, nor with such indeces of putative social transformation as burgeoning crime rates, population increase, labour mobility, land-price inflation, council revenues, structure plans, planning consultants, vagrants, vandals, technological miracles, immigrant ghettoes, pipelines, platforms or pollution. I mention these only to emphasise that I shall henceforth ignore them – and thereby distinguish my own views of the consequences of oil-related developments in Shetland from those of the numerous proposals for 'impact' studies which have proliferated over the last five years. It was, perhaps, as much by luck as by good judgement that most of these studies have sunk without trace; they would not have achieved the ubiquitous objective of diagnosing the likely consequences of oil-related developments on what is inaccurately and ineptly called 'The Shetland Way of Life". The great splurge of sociologists' research proposals, consultants 'impact' prognoses economists' statistical extrapolations have exhibited two kinds of basic incompetence: first, the inappropriateness and inadequacy of their investigative techniques; and, secondly, their consequent failure to apprehend the most fundamental effects of sudden industrialisation. With two important exceptions the proposals known to me have ignored intensive longterm ethnographic fieldwork, which, of all sociological methodologies, is uniquely suited to the description of cultural process. They have thus failed to reveal the fact that the oil developments in Shetland do nothing so simple as alter the Shetland way of Life – for no such simple mode exists. There are *ways* of life, and even these are fraught with ambiguity: practices which appear to the observer to be ostensibly similar may well mean quite different things to their various practitioners. To give an example: the fashioning of a wheelbarrow may be, to one Whalsayman, quite unremarkable. It is simply a chore which he, like his brothers and their father and grandfathers before them, had to do. Since it has to be done it should be done well, to serve the purpose and because *everything* should be done well. But to another man it is a skill and a self-sufficiency which clearly marks him out as a Whalsayman from the 'handless' and dependent outsider.[1] That, I will contend, is the cultural impact of oil. By forcibly making people aware of others, they are made aware of themselves. The great terminal at Sullom Voe, the service bases and all the other paraphernalia might physically and structurally change Shetland. But the most fundamental impact of oil occurred before the first lay-barge or helicopter pilot appeared on the scene. It occurred when the possibility of those structural changes was first mooted for it was at that moment – that instant in which the spectre of radical and possibly cataclysmic change was presented – that cultural accounting began to take place. It is at such historical junctures that people become conscious of their values. It is the traumatic and irrevocable induction into the realisation that the familiar may not, after all, be permanent; it is a reminder that the security of the familiar cannot be taken for granted but must be thought about. As such it is the beginning (though the most important phase) of the process which will continue into the future. Adaptation to the structural changes is the mere surface expression of these processes of cultural transformation which underpin everything else.


II


I am not comfortable with the kind of generalisation in which the present paper indulges. I succumb with reluctance but console myself with the thought that at least I have not fallen quite so low as the person responsible for the title of this conference which expresses a gross, unempiric and unsociological generality, 'Scottish Society'. Collective identities are tactical: a collectivity is either subsumed as such by *alter*, or subsumes itself as such for the limited purposes of its interaction with *alter*. The collective identity can never be faithful to the variety which it subsumes. The richness of difference is only abdicated for collective identity either when the collectivity has no choice in the matter – as when we glibly designate the social mass between Berwick and Muckle Flugga 'Scottish Society' – or when it is expedient for it to do so. I am not concerned here to make the gratuitous point that Scottish culture is a fiction, but to raise the issue of how one group of people regards itself in relation to some other – for that is at the heart of cultural accounting. A simple model of this process is the individual contemplating his navel and asking himself, 'who an I?' If he is ever able to answer that question, he might proceed to another, 'how should I present myself?' In those circumstances when he moves only in entirely familiar surroundings, going through the customery routines of life and meeting the same folk day after day, the first question would probably rarely be asked and would usually be easily answered, and the second would hardly ever arise. Difficulties occur usually in circumstances of unfamiliarity, when the unknown — an unexpected event, a stranger — intrudes. Then one has to summon up a consciousness of oneself to face the situation.

Something like this, I would suggest, is what happens in deeply-rooted social milieux faced with imminent unheaval and crisis. In Shetland the process was rather more complex for perennial crisis there had made a consciousness of cultural identity a permanent and prominent feature of social life. With a history which included invasion, clearances, alien and exploitative Scottish lairds, the harshness of the *Haaf* fishery, morale-sapping depopulation, remoteness from markets and centres of power and decision, and of climatic conditions which combine the worst of the northern North Atlantic with those of the northern North Sea, it would hardly be surprising to encounter an imperative rationale for Shetlanders. But the very achievement of enduring, of surviving and routinising crisis itself helped to establish the popularity propagated collective self-identity of Shetland. It was equal to most challenges, properly respectful of them but determined, and intensely — if quietly — proud of its achievement and character. The rest of the world (the source of much of the crisis) was an odd place, populated by folk who did not cope well with their own circumstances and led by people arrogant enough to impose their own ineptitude on others. Remoteness, cultural as well as geographic, served to render Shetlanders more wholly competent in their own eyes than *Sooth* folk.[2] This confident distinctiveness was bolstered by the widely promulgated myths of Shetlander's Norse ethnicity, by the tradition of dialect literature, and by the supreme skills of the traditional industries. It was vindicated as Shetland, without much external assistance, climbed out of its endemic economic slough in the late 1960's through the increasingly profitable and modernising fishing fleet and the growing demand for Shetland knitwear. But the confidence of this collective identity was based largely on the island's remoteness. The islanders' cultural destinies lay to a great extent in their own hands. Oil, with other contemporary pressures, breached that remoteness and, in so doing, created the need for a renewed cultural account.

That such a process did indeed take place is indicated by the intensity with which the possible implications of oil-exploration were debated throughout the islands. The discussion was not confined to the Lerwick intelligentsia (as reflected on the executive boards of *The New Shetlander* and the Shetland Council of Social Service) but was conducted in the rural townships and villages, on fishing boats, indeed the subject seemed to arise wherever people gathered. My own experience from Burra Isle and, much more extensively, from Whalsay is that oil was generally regarded as a discovery which they would rather had not been made, but which would be exploited in Shetland regardless of the wishes of Shetlanders. Its development was regarded as inevitable and, that being so, one might as well buckle down and make the best of it. The frenetic and, in the event, rather ludicrous speculations about the scale of the developments in Shetland which filled the headlines in the early 1970's seemed to preoccupy social scientists much more than Shetlanders who also were rather less amazed than outsiders at the accomplishments of the County Council in establishing a substantial degree of control over the activities of the oil companies. Outside the areas which were to be physically involved,[3] the practical concern was mostly about the likely effects of oil on the traditional industries. In Whalsay, the possibility that oil-related development might radically affect culture (our old friend, The Way of Life) was largely and properly discounted. But the fact that Whalsay people did not agonise over the susceptibility of their culture to oil was a manifestation of their confidence in its durability, and that confidence was a product of the process of accounting which had been renewed by the imminence of oil.

The specific debate about oil and the cultural account are distinct though related processes. Here I must resist generalisations for Whalsay is not typical of the Shetland Islands; indeed, the circumstances of each of the islands are so different that an aggregate picture is necessarily misleading. Whalsay, with a population in 1970 of approximately 1,000, already enjoyed full-employment. Its fishery was thriving; many of the crews were placing orders for new vessels as, indeed, they still are. The herring purse-seining fleet was growing. The island had a recently established fish processing plant and a knitwear business which was divided among home knitters and a small mechanical unit. In addition, the one hundred and thirty odd crofts provided a stable, if minimal subsistence base and the possibility of acquiring advantageous financial conditions for the erection of new houses. The island had never suffered from the high rates of depopulation which debilitated other parts of Shetland, and in the early 1970's people found little reason to suppose that it would remain stable. The primary external threat was not the oil industry, but the proposed introduction of a continuous car-ferry service[4] which might jeopardise the local shops, make it feasible for Whalsay people to work outside the island and, above all, breach the boundaries of 'conceptual' remoteness which kept the isle distinct in its own eyes and which enhanced the integrity of its discrete culture.

In Whalsay, then, the debate about oil could be conducted with rather less personal involvement than in other parts of Shetland. Moreover, the cultural account could disregard the infrastructural consequences of oil-related development for the local community. There *was* an occupational interest since some fishing grounds would be closed, harbour facilities on Mainland would be affected, pollution would be an obvious danger, and processing plants might find themselves short of labour. But these were presented as 'fishy' problems rather than as affecting Whalsay itself. Some of the other parts of Shetland could not be so dispassionate. The traditionally depressed areas like Northmavine and Yell desperately needed employment. Places with under-exploited harbour potential like Sandwick and Baltasound, were obvious candidates for service bases of one kind or another. Lerwick itself was clearly going to be transformed by the influx of a substantial transient population, by the redevelopment of the Greenhead to provide the principal off-shore service base, and by the need to provide central services to the onshore developments.


### III


What, then, did the process of cultural accounting look like? Certainly, I do not want to suggest a picture of people gathered round their hearths with brows furrowed in introspective reflection on their spiritual condition. Nor was there a *deliberate* attempt to construct a comprehensive ideology of 'being a Whalsayman'. Rather, this consciousness of distinctive identity emerges coherently but piecemeal, related to particular events and specific situations. I remarked earlier that such a consciousness of Shetland identity seems to have long been a prominent feature of Shetland culture. One may assume that the same is true of Whalsay. My earlier experience in other parts of Shetland had been of people impressing me with Shetland's putative distinctiveness by pointing to the Norse derivations of local dialect and of family and place names. But in Whalsay it was, and remains, primarily a consciousness of the isle's distinctiveness from the rest of Shetland; sometimes Whalsay people identify with other rural areas of Shetland, only occasionally — and generally in relation to 'da Sooth' — would they identify with Lerwick or with Shetland as a whole. (Far, then, from accepting the integrity of the category 'Scottish society', I find the notion of 'Shetland society' insensitive. Apart from the important structural differences I have already mentioned, it fails to capture the celebration of distinctiveness which is central to social life in Whalsay and, I would guess, in other Shetland communities as well.)

Whalsay people articulate the distinctiveness of their own culture in a variety of idiomatic forms which are far too rich to be encapsulated here. But a frequent means is the implicit contrast with values and behavioural practices from elsewhere. Thus, people would not say, 'this is what we do here, and isn't it good . . .' Rather, the behaviour of, say, a Burra man would be recounted as if it was somehow puzzling, or people might shake their heads quizzically and conclude, 'that's a strange thing, isn't it?' There is less reserve in the discussion of non-Shetlanders for their behaviour can be more explicitly treated as odd, and their performance in tasks in which Whalsaymen have an expertise can be ridiculed. A typical example which might convey some sense of this attitude is as follows. Tied up one night at Balti, at the end of a long day's fishing, the Whalsay crew had just finished gutting the catch from the last two hauls. An old Fraserburgh boat was berthed alongside and her crew seemed to be slower in cleaning its catch. The Whalsaymen commented to each other about this, one of them remarking:

"One aald bugger does twartree sneuklings at it afore he gets his knife in. They'll still be there da morn's morning.'

Another similarly mundane instance: an oil service boat took the wrong passage through the Whalsay Sound. In apparent disregard of the treacherous rocks near rhe surface, her skipper blithely turned the vessel about and went around the other side of an island in the Sound. Three Whalsaymen, whose 'foureen' might well have been struck in the process, watched aghast at such manifest incompetence. One of them remarked after the manoeuvre, 'ye'd har tocht he'd hae looked at his cherts. I dinna ken what the aald men (i.e. the Whalsaymen of previous generations) would hae mad' o' that.' Note that the eccentricity of the manoeuvre is given particular emphasis by the explicit contrast with putative indigenous and traditional standards.

Of course the distinctiveness of a culture is not exhibited only by means of evaluation contrast. Aspects of Whalsay life are celebrated for their own sake. Like all indigenous humour, Whalsay's is extremely complex. One of its features is an invocation of the intimate knowledge which islanders have of each other. Thus, the narration of some quirk in x's behaviour is also a celebration of the fact that each knows the other so well: it is an expression of the coherence and closeness of the community. By the same token the communal allocation of identity to individuals may be seen as a manifestation of the normative holism of the community — in contrast with the individualism which is contrived and constrained in local social interaction.[5]

The expression of cultural distinctiveness takes many forms. We have seen as examples, explicit differentiation from non-Whalsay folk, and the assertion of the reality and integrity of culture through the emphasis on communality and shared knowledge. It may also take the form of the suggestion of orthodoxy for every routine task in the conduct of life, adding an evaluative dimension to all public performance.[6] It may underpin the endless debunking of outside officialdom and interference. It may inform the conduct of the Saturday night spree, or the fishermen's investment plans, what one does in the event of a motor accident or how you greet someone in a Lerwick street. Cultural distinctiveness is to be found in all manifestations of idiomatic behaviour. And cultural accounting consists quite simply in *a consciousness* of that distinctiveness. Thus, it is not when one behaves distinctively, but when one is conscious of so doing. It is the moment at which one says to oneself, 'I am a Whalsayman, and there are therefore particular ways in which I do things.' A culture is only perceived by its members when they reach its boundaries — that is, when they encounter a different culture. By the same token, cultural accounting is renewed when the intrusion of extraordinary events — a manifestation of the boundaries — creates a renewed consciousness of the culture.

Whalsaymen were somewhat removed from the immediacy of oil; but it was, nevertheless, an extraordinary intrusion into what previously had been an idiomatically secure world. It would produce a lot of outsiders. It would focus massive public attention on Shetland and inevitably result in massive misinterpretation of the situation, at least as perceived by Whalsay people. It would mean more political interference. It would mean a subordination in the minds of the politicians and the bureaucrats of the problems of the traditional communities and industries to the problems of oil. Everybody would be talking oil, thinking oil, and would ignore the customary heart of Shetland. It would mean unknowing, incompetent outsiders, inexperienced in the profound accomplishment of Whalsay people in coping with their own circumstances, telling us what to do. It might mean that we will be trampled.

If one adds these fears and suspicions to the island's residual assertion of its cultural integrity, prompted by its remoteness and encapsulation, one would find, not surprisingly, a recognition of the urgent need to proclaim local interests and the axiomatic values of the collectivity. One therefore finds the oil-related developments and, I would suggest, the associated cultural account, being accompanied by a newly energetic engagement in a number of aspects of social life. Some Whalsay fishermen, for example, have recently shown a willingness to participate actively in national fishery politics which they would not have contemplated a few years ago. The 1977 elections to the community council were contested in every ward whilst previously there was difficulty in finding a sufficient number of candidates to fill the available places. The local fish-processing company has just opened a large new factory, having raised a substantial amount of capital from among the local fishermen — again, a co-operation which would have been unattainable until recently. Year after year, the local landscape is changed by newly-erected houses. The island is shortly to get a substantial improvement to its harbour. A new local partnership is manufacturing trawl nets. The owners of one of the local shops, having invested considerably in reconstructing their premises, are now fuelling fishing vessels. The more active crofters have recently formed a co-operative purchasing organisation and have acquired permanent sale facilities. The local sports associations are building and buying improves facilities: a slipway for the Regatta club, a catwalk for the Model Yacht Club, dinghys for the anglers' association, a nine-hole course for the golfers, an enlarged football pitch. The community council is negotiating for the establishment of an old people's home, for improved water supply and sewerage facilities. The crew of a new purse-netter will soon take delivery of Shetland's first

£1 million fishing vessel, and other crews are continuously investing enormous sums of money in improvements to their vessels.

Now, I do not suggest anything so simple-minded as the proposition that, without oil none of this would have happened. One really can not know. But I do argue that this renewed dynamism *is* an expression of the cultural account. It is a community's declaration that, having taken stock of events and circumstances, it has sufficient faith in itself to justify massive investment and substantial involvement in the negotiation and management of its own destiny. The response to the fearful possibility of being kicked in the teeth by strangers has been to show that the community is more than equal to the challenge, and is well able to look after itself.

## IV

Whether or not all this might have happened without oil must, then, be a matter for speculation, but the speculation is not without interest and could run along several persuasive lines. (1) The mind-boggling finances of oil-related development, and the ineptitude of those present in Shetland because of oil — viz. the proliferating stories of technical incompetence, of alien criminality, and so forth — serve to emphasise that Shetlanders were and still are left to cope with their *customary* circumstances and means of subsistence with relative pittances in a way of government aid and without any political support. Similarly, the attention which Shetland now receives because of an exogenous and inanimate resource contrasts with a history of callous neglect by government and the media of its indigenous and human resources. People might well reason as follows: such neglect might become even more deleterious, for the government could consider Shetland's economy to be secure because of oil, and thus fail to recognise the pressing need for political and financial attention to the fishery and agriculture and the oil-provoked urgency of stabilising the rural communities. Therefore *we* must become more active in the determination of our own fate. We cannot trust government (at central or local authority levels) to have correct priorities or to understand local requirements. (2) Oil brings work. It also coincides with improved transportation (the car-ferries) and received aspirations (from immigrant workers, television, etc). The fish-stocks are badly depleted and nobody can agree how they should be managed. The stability of the population may become a cause for anxiety. A declaration of faith in the future is required. (3) The degree to which the Shetland council managed to control oil-related developments (or to which it has so presented itself) encouraged a belief among Shetlanders in their own capacity to stand up for themselves against the outside world and to declare resourcefulness.

171

Another dimension of this speculation, and the most difficult to deal with, is that the cultural account, provoked by extraordinary events or by suspicion of their imminence, actually leaves a culture changed. Once one has become conscious of culture, it must be perceived and handled in a different way than previously. Hence, the recounting of what life was previously like must always be, to some extent, a *reconstruction* rather than a mere recall. Similarly, consciousness of present circumstances must intrude upon remembrance of the past. If the contemporary situation is one of the power of outsiders and external agencies to affect one's own life, then a similar construction may well be placed upon the past. (Equally, such a mediated construction of the past may well produce an account in which the outside world is unreally absent). The past, in cultural accounting, becomes a powerful guide to the interpretation of the present. Certainly, the contemporary indigenous diagnoses of Whalsay's past misfortunes tend to place a burden of responsibility on external agencies. Historically, the model is the exploitative Scottish laird with his callous disregard for local sentiment and sensibility. Many Whalsay 'yarns' recount the cunning expropriation of land by the laird from unsuspecting Whalsaymen, often resulting in the permanent exile of the latter. Another recurrent alien enemy was the press gang, still remembered in stories of desparate retreat into 'da hill' where remants of these hiding places are still to be found. Stories of the Far Haff fishery also contain the implicit contradition of the incredible skills and endurance of the fishermen put entirely to the service of the laird's profit. Surprisingly, commercial antagonisms seem to have made little impact on the collective memory. During the 1975 inshore fishermen's blockade, I told my Whalsay companions that in 1892, Whalsay fishermen had struck successfully against Hay's, the Lerwick outfitting merchant, an action which resulted in the despatch of the gunboat *Watchful* to restore order locally, which was raised in the House of Commons and was reported in the national press.[7] No one to whom I mentioned the incident knew anything of it. Current resentment of the enormous catches in Shetland waters by foreign fleets seem to refer to recent years and does not extend into the past. Competitors are, perhaps, different creatures than exploiters. Contemporary accounts of the misfortunes of Whalsay refer extensively to the intrusion of exploitative, partonising or incompetent external agencies. Most 'expert' opinions, especially if it also emanates from Authority, is suspect. Whalsay is thus felt to suffer from the failure of successive governments to have a sympathetic fisheries policy; from the governments' neglect of the isle which is the repository of precisely those values — hard work, enterprise, community — which are always being invoked 'in the national interest'; from bad planning; from excessive bureaucratisation, a highly prejudicial transport policy, insufficient foresight by the water, electricity and telecommunications authorities, VAT, the CAA, the Northern Joint Fire Committee, the Inland Revenue, the Herring Industry Board (which fails to properly administer the quota arrangements); from politicians of all parties; from the Church of Scotland (which repeatedly sends ministers who are unsympa-

172

thetic to local life); from the fish merchants (not processors), who manipulate the market; from the Aberdeen 'lumpers' (shore porters) who similarly abuse their monoply rights to unload vessels for market, and so on, and so on.

In the past, Whalsay's insularity was so clear, despite the mobility of her own men through fishing and deep-see sailing, that the fact of her juxtaposition with the rest of the world required little symbolisation. But in contemporary circumstances, epitomised by oil, the world intrudes remorselessly and cannot be pushed back. With geographical boundaries thus breached, the need of her members to assert their cultural distinctiveness has become much more pressing. It is important to remember that oil cannot be isolated from the galaxy of other contemporary pressures and events. It is one among many and, hence, we *cannot* do more than speculate about its consequences.


V


I have suggested various ways in which Whalsay people might be seen to have affirmed their self-confidence and self sufficiency in the face of oil. I move on briefly and finally now to some events which suggests a similar affirmation by other Shetlanders, and which might also be regarded as the products of cultural accounting.

The apparent reluctance of the previous Shetland Islands Council to commit the county to compliance with a Scottish Assembly was often presented in the press as an expression of Shetland's new-found financial strength. I would argue that it was, rather, the latest chapter in an historic quest for some form of dissociation from Scotland. It is simple-minded in the extreme to deny any affinity between Shetland and Scotland. As has often been pointed out, a careful analysis of Shetland dialects and of historical demography would reveal influences as obviously Scottish as Norse.[8] That is not at all surprising, for not only did the Viking penetration of Scotland reach far beyond Orkney and Shetland, but the cession of Shetland to the Scottish crown began a substantial immigration of Scots to Shetland. But is was precisely by virtue of their displacement of traditional social organisation and udal law that the need for an emphatic expression of difference from Scotland became an imperative element in the Shetland cultural tradition. The argument is not confined to the romantic Victorian literary genre of the Nordic origin myth; it is very much alive today. Indeed, the idea of some degree of autonomy seems to have been continuously discussed since the War.[9] I suggest, then, that it would be quite erroneous to explain present developments by simple reference to financial resources. Rather oil — the encroachment of the outside world — has provoked an urgent need for the renewal of symbolic distinctiveness.

Scottish devolution and the feared subsumption of Shetland in a Scottish Assembly exacerbates that need still further. Contemporary economic circumstances mean that the practicalities of some measure of dissociation are not so lightly dismissed by Shetlanders as they were previously. Moreover, the successful passage of the Zetland Act 1974, and of the recent 'Grimond' amendment to the Scotland Bill, both against formidable opposition, conjures an image of native skill and informed principle confronting metropolitan bungling and cynical ignorance, a picture which is entirely congruent with the indigenous cognitive juxtaposition of Shetland and 'da Sooth'. Less David against Goliath, then Diogenes against the world.

Time alone will show the extent to which the Council's reservations about the devolution legislation are representative of Shetlanders. But I would have thought a general judgement of Shetland's special circumstances and interests may be inferred from her majority 'No' vote in the EEC referendum.[10]

A further development which might profitably be regarded as a product of the cultural account is the increased activism of Shetland fishermen in the Scottish fishermen's organisations. It would be simplistic to interpret the militancy of recent years to a sudden burgeoning of solidarity among Scottish inshore fishermen in the face of dwindling stocks, exploding costs, and the issues of fisheries limits and quotas. The interests of fishermen from different areas of the coast are markedly dissimilar as, indeed, are those of men from the same areas who prosecute different kinds of fishery. Moreover, there was a strong feeling among some of the Whalsay herring men that the Shetland boats were specially disadvantaged in the imposition of herring quotas in 1976 and, indeed, that they alone among the Scottish herring fleet did not attempt to subvert the restrictions. There are good grounds for supposing that the active participation by Whalsay men in fishery politics is an assertion of Shetland and Whalsay interests, rather than of the interests of the north-east coast fishermen as a whole.

The origins of this activity may be traced to the fishermen's blockade of oil-related ports in 1975. In recent years sociologists have properly come to recognise the explanation of collective behaviour to be very much more complex than the ostensible purposes of any collective action might suggest.[11] This is certainly the case with the Whalsaymen's participation in the blockade. Whilst the six issues to which the blockade explicitly drew attention were all keenly felt (and, again, related to external agencies) they do not account either for the decision of the Whalsaymen to join the protest, nor the process of the blockade once it came into being. Tilly suggests that a social movement materialises as an expression of the highly varied and differing circumstances of its members, and should be understood by a careful consideration of these social and historical specificities. My own analysis of the situations of the blockaders has led me to the view (which present readers will

174

have to take on trust for the moment) that their participation in the protest was partly an expression of a pent-up frustration at the intrustion of external forces which they seemed powerless to resist. Moreover, the experience of the blockade made tangible the juxtaposition of alien power and local interests. My contention is that without a consciousness of themselves as belonging to a discrete and valued socio-cultural entity — Whalsay — the Whalsay fishermen would not have participated as they did. That consciousness is the product of a process of cultural accounting. My *speculation* is that without oil (the epitome of the world's intrusion) the cultural account might well have eventuated in a rather different consciousness in which the fishermen might have been endowed with a more ambiguous evaluative identity.[12] The commander of the Shetland blockade, who is skipper of Whalsay's (and Shetland's) largest fishing vessel, later became Chairman of the Shetland Fishermen's Association. Both he and another Whalsay skipper (who superintended the blockade of the North Mouth of Lerwick harbour) are directors of the Scottish Fishermen's Organisation.

*Conclusion*

The process of sudden economic change in Shetland are misunderstood if it is assumed that their qualitative effects are separately identifiable. The effects are diffuse and pervasive, but they cannot be distinguished from the mass of forces which are exerted on a peripheral community at any point in time. They cannot be set aside to evoke an indigenous account of what life may have been like previously, for they must intrude upon such a reconstruction of the past. The individual who moves through a variety of idiomatic millieux in the course of his everyday life does not simply play a different role appropriate to each one. He is, at any time and in any one milieu, the accumulation of his experience in *all* his social interaction.[13] The same must be true of collectivities. Oil is intrustion of many kinds and its perception by Shetlanders must be regarded as informed by their previous experience of other forms of intrusion into their cultural world. By the same token, experience of oil, even of its imminence or only of its possibility, must colour their perceptions of the past, of themselves as individuals and as collectivities, and of their relations with others. Members become conscious of their culture when they reach its boundaries — such as when intrusion occurs or is threatened — and in that consciousness they become aware of its values. Having once done such cultural accounting, neither they as individuals, nor their culture can be quite the same again. The implications of this view for sociologists and social anthropologists is that if we are concerned with the consideration of the influences of oil-related development on a discrete community, we are bound to an intensive view, through comprehensive and detailed ethnography of the holistic interrelations of community and culture. People are not simply made by culture. They also make and remake it through their everyday interaction. It is only when we achieve a substantive understanding of these processes that we can properly approach the question of the cultural influences which might be imputed to drastic structural change.

NOTES

1 In other circumstances it serves similarly to distinguish him from his neighbour.
2 The process was like the overcommunication of stigma which I describe in my article, 'The Definition of Public Identity: Managing Marginality in Outport Newfoundland following Confederation', *Sociological Review*, 23 (1), 1975.
3 The Brae-Voe-Sullom area, Sandwick and Lerwick and, to a lesser extent, Scalloway and Sunburgh.
4 This was finally initiated in 1975.
5 See my article, 'The Same — But Different!' The Allocation of identity in Whalsay Shetland', *Sociological Review*, 26, (3), 1978. (Presented to the Fourth International Seminar on Marginal Regiona, ISSPA, July, 1977).
6 See my article, 'Ethnographic Method in the Real Community', *Sociologia Ruralis*, 18, (1), 1978.
7 I am indebted for this information to Bronwen J. Cohen.
8 C.F. J. Peterson, 'The Shetlands — Do They Exist?' *The New Shetlander*, 50 April-June, 1959.
9 See, for example, the frequent contributions on the issue by 'Sheltie' and others to *The New Shetlander* in the early 1950's, an extremely bleak economic period in Shetland. The Shetland Development Council and its later incarnation, The Shetland Council of Social Service, investigated Faroes government as a model for Shetland in 1962.
10 Shetland and the Western Isles were the only two regions of the UK to vote against EEC membership.
11 I refer here especially to the enlightening work of Charles Tilly and his school.
12 That, indeed, was the prediction I made at the Second International Seminar on Marginal Regions at this university in 1974, (see my article, 'Social Identity and the Management of Marginality', *The Changing Fortunes of Marginal Regions*, (P. F. Sadler and G. A. Mackay, eds) Aberdeen: ISSPA, 1977) and which last year I acknowledged (at the Fourth Seminar) not to have materialised.
13 c.f. T. H. Turner, 'Role-Taking: Process versus Conformity', *Human Behaviour and Social Processes*, (A. M. Rose, ed) London: Routledge, 1962, 20 - 40.